TS CRAFTS CRAFTS CRA
AFTS CRAFTS CR
TS CRAFTS CRAFTS CRAI
AFTS CRAFTS CRAFTS CR
TS CRAFTS CRAFTS CRAI
AFTS CRAFTS CRAFTS CR
TS CRAFTS CRAFTS CRAI
AFTS CRAFTS CRAFTS CR
TS CRAFTS CRAFTS CRAI
AFTS CRAFTS CRAFTS CR
TS CRAFTS CRAFTS CRAI
AFTS CRAFTS CRAFTS CR
TS CRAFTS CRAFTS CRAI
AFTS CRAFTS CRAFTS CR
TS CRAFTS CRAFTS CRAI
AFTS CRAFTS CRAFTS CR
TS CRAFTS CRAFTS CRAI
AFTS CRAFTS CRAFTS CR

Volume 8

THE COMPLETE ENCYCLOPEDIA OF CRAFTS

Distributed by Columbia House, 51 West 52nd Street, New York, New York 10019
Printed in U. S. A.

COLUMBIA HOUSE/New York

Contents

Front Cover Photograph: Melvin Grey
Back Cover Photograph: Peter Dorp

Design Know-how

Paper

Plastics

Cloth / Sewing

Yarn / Weaving

Metal

Yarn / Needlepoint

Cloth / Toys

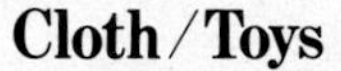

Cloth / Quilting

*** Not suitable for children without adult supervision**

ADDRESSES OF MAIL ORDER SUPPLIERS

ARTS & CRAFTS, GENERAL

California
General Craft Supply
1570 East Edinger St./Suite I
Santa Ana, California 92705

Florida
National Handicraft Co., Inc.
337 Lincoln Road
Miami Beach, Florida 33139

Illinois
Leewards Creative Crafts, Inc.
1200 St. Charles Street
Elgin, Illinois 60120

Triarco Arts & Crafts
7330 N. Clark Street
Chicago, Illinois 60626

Massachusetts
M. Siegel Co., Inc.
186 South Street
Boston, Massachusetts 02111

Missouri
Skil-Crafts Div. of Brown Leather Co.
305 Virginia Avenue
Joplin, Missouri 64801

New York
Arthur Brown & Bros. Inc.
2 West 46th Street
New York, New York 10036

Albert Constantine & Son Inc.
2050 Eastchester Road
Bronx, New York 10461

Craft Service
337-345 University Avenue
Rochester, New York 14607

North Carolina
Earth Guild Inc.
Hot Springs, North Carolina 28743

Oregon
Novelcraft Manufacturing Co., Inc.
5309 Rogue River Highway
Rogue River, Oregon 97537

Texas
American Handicrafts Co.
2617 West 7th Street
Ft. Worth, Texas 76107

Wisconsin
Sax Arts & Crafts
Box 2002
Milwaukee, Wisconsin 53201

BASKETRY

California
Kit Kraft Inc.
12109 Ventura Place
Studio City, California 91604

Connecticut
H. H. Perkins
10 S. Bradley Road
Woodbridge, Connecticut 06525

Illinois
Dick Blick Co.
Box 1267
Galesburg, Illinois 61401

New York
Ace Rattan Products
60-19 54th Place
Maspeth, New York 11378

BATIK

Michigan
Polyproducts Corp.
28510 Hayes Avenue, Box 42
Roseville, Michigan 48066

New York
Vanguard Crafts
2915 Avenue J
Brooklyn, New York 11210

Utah
Intertwine
101 Trolley Square
Salt Lake City, Utah 84102

BEADS

California
The Bead Game
8071 Beverly Boulevard
Los Angeles, California 90048

New York
Grey Owl Indian Mfg. Co., Inc.
150-02 Beaver Road
Jamaica, New York 11433

BOTTLE-CUTTING

Michigan
Delphi Supply Center
2224 East Michigan Avenue
Lansing, Michigan 48912

CANDLE-MAKING

California
General Craft Supply
1570 East Edinger St./Suite I
Santa Ana, California 92705

Illinois
Triarco Arts & Crafts
7330 N. Clark Street
Chicago, Illinois 60626

Missouri
Skil-Crafts Div. of Brown Leather Co.
305 Virginia Avenue
Joplin, Missouri 64801

ADDRESSES OF MAIL ORDER SUPPLIERS

New Jersey
The Candle Farm
625 S. Church Street
Mt. Laurel, New Jersey 08054

Pennsylvania
Wax Kettle
7 E. Main Street
Schuylkill Haven, Pennsylvania 17972

Texas
American Handicrafts Co.
2617 West 7th Street
Ft. Worth, Texas 76107

Vermont
The Candle Mill
Old Mill Road
E. Arlington, Vermont 05252

Washington
Barker Enterprises
15106 10th Avenue, S.W.
Seattle, Washington 98166

Wisconsin
Sax Arts & Crafts
Box 2002
Milwaukee, Wisconsin 53201

CANING AND RUSHING

California
Naturalcraft
2199 Bancroft Way
Berkeley, California 94704

Connecticut
H. H. Perkins
10 S. Bradley Road
Woodbridge, Connecticut 06525

Illinois
Dick Blick Co
Box 1267
Galesburg, Illinois 61401

New York
Craft Service
337-345 University Avenue
Rochester, New York 14607

CERAMICS MATERIAL AND CLAY

California
Marshall Craft
1240 North 13th Street
San Jose, California 95112

Minnesota
Paramount Ceramic Inc.
220 N. State Street
Fairmont, Minnesota 56031

New York
Buffalo Ceramic & Art Supply
Center Inc.
437 Franklin Street
Buffalo, New York 14202

DECOUPAGE

Illinois
Dick Blick Co.
Box 1267
Galesburg, Illinois 61401

Missouri
Skil-Crafts Div. of Brown
Leather Co.
305 Virginia Avenue
Joplin, Missouri 64801

New York
Craft Service
337-345 University Avenue
Rochester, New York 14607

Texas
American Handicrafts Co.
2617 West 7th Street
Ft. Worth, Texas 76107

DYES

California
Naturalcraft Inc.
2199 Bancroft Way
Berkeley, California 94704

Illinois
Leewards Creative Crafts Inc.
1200 St. Charles Street
Elgin, Illinois 60120

New York
Vanguard Crafts
2915 Avenue J
Brooklyn, New York 11210

Oregon
Wildflowers Fibers
205 NW Second Avenue
Portland, Oregon 97209

Utah
Intertwine
101 Trolley Square
Salt Lake City, Utah 84102

ENAMELS AND ENAMELLING MATERIALS

Illinois
Thomas C. Thompson Co.
1539 Old Deerfield Road
Highland Park, Illinois 60035

Missouri
Skil-Crafts Div. of Brown
Leather Co.
305 Virginia Avenue
Joplin, Missouri 64801

New York
Allcraft Tool & Supply Co., Inc.
100 Frank Road
Hicksville, New York 11801

ADDRESSES OF MAIL ORDER SUPPLIERS

Texas
American Handicrafts Co.
2617 West 7th Street
Ft. Worth, Texas 76107

FLOWER-MAKING MATERIALS

New York
S. Beckenstein, Inc.
125 Orchard Street
New York, New York 10022

GLASS (STAINED)

California
The New Renaissance Glass Works
5151 Broadway
Oakland, California 94611

Nervo Distributors
650 University Avenue
Berkeley, California 94710

Michigan
Delphi Supply Center
2224 East Michigan Avenue
Lansing, Michigan 48912

New Jersey
The Stained Glass Club
Box 244
Norwood, New Jersey 07648

New York
S. A. Bendheim Co., Inc.
122 Hudson Street
New York, New York 10013

Glass Masters Guild
621 Avenue of the Americas
New York, New York 10011

Texas
American Handicrafts Co.
2617 West 7th Street
Ft. Worth, Texas 76107

JEWELRY FINDINGS AND MATERIALS

California
California Crafts Supply
1096 Main Street
Orange, California 92667

Florida
Rosenthal Jewelers Supply Corp.
117 NE First Avenue
Miami, Florida 33132

Illinois
Dick Blick Co.
Box 1267
Galesburg, Illinois 61401

Maryland
Macmillan Arts & Crafts Inc.
9645 Gerwig Lane
Columbia, Maryland 21046

New York
Allcraft Tool & Supply Co., Inc.
100 Frank Road
Hicksville, New York 11801

Vanguard Crafts Inc.
2915 Avenue J
Brooklyn, New York 11210

KNOTTING AND WEAVING

California
Spin It, Weave It Studio
840 Leland Place
El Cajon, California 92020

Maryland
Macmillan Arts & Crafts Inc.
9645 Gerwig Lane
Columbia, Maryland 21046

LEATHERCRAFT

California
Drake Leather Co.
3500 W. Beverly Blvd.
Montebello, California 90640

Illinois
Triarco Arts & Crafts
7330 N. Clark Street
Chicago, Illinois 60626

Massachusetts
M. Siegel Co., Inc.
186 South Street
Boston, Massachusetts 02111

Missouri
Bona Venture Supply Co.
17 Village Square
Hazlewood, Missouri 63042

New York
Leathercrafters Supply Co.
25 Great Jones Street
New York, New York 10012

METALCRAFTING

New York
Allcraft Tool & Supply Co., Inc.
100 Frank Road
Hicksville, New York 11801

Oregon
Montana Assay Office
610 SW Second Avenue
Portland, Oregon 97204

Wisconsin
Sax Arts & Crafts
Box 2002
Milwaukee, Wisconsin 53201

MOSAICS

New York
Vanguard Crafts, Inc.
2915 Avenue J
Brooklyn, New York 11210

ADDRESSES OF MAIL ORDER SUPPLIERS

Wisconsin
Sax Arts & Crafts
Box 2002
Milwaukee, Wisconsin 53201

NEEDLECRAFTS

California
Naturalcraft Inc.
2199 Bancroft Way
Berkeley, California 94704

Illinois
Leewards Creative Crafts Inc.
1200 St. Charles Street
Elgin, Illinois 60120

New York
Bell Yarn
75 Essex Street
New York, New York 10002

Texas
Meribee Needle Arts & Crafts
Box 791
Ft. Worth, Texas 76101

PAPERCRAFTS AND PAPIER-MÂCHÉ

Illinois
Dick Blick Co.
Box 1267
Galesburg, Illinois 61401

Missouri
Skil-Crafts Div. of Brown Leather Co.
305 Virginia Avenue
Joplin, Missouri 64801

PLASTICS

Illinois
Pyramid Paper Co., Inc.
Box 27
Urbana, Illinois 61801

Michigan
Cadillac Plastic & Chemical Co.
15841 Second Avenue, Box 810
Detroit, Michigan 48232

New York
The Plastics Factory
18 East 12 th Street
New York, New York 10003

Pennsylvania
Plastic Center Inc.
1215-1221 Wood Street
Philadelphia, Pennsylvania 19107

ROCK POLISHING

Wisconsin
Sax Arts & Crafts
207 North Milwaukee Street
Milwaukee, Wisconsin 53202

SILKSCREEN

New York
Arthur Brown & Bros., Inc.
2 West 46th Street
New York, New York 10036

WIRECRAFTING

California
California Crafts Supply
1096 N. Main Street
Orange, California 92667

Illinois
Dick Blick Co.
Box 1267
Galesburg, Illinois 61401

Missouri
Skil-Crafts Div. of Brown Leather Co.
305 Virginia Avenue
Joplin, Missouri 64801

New York
Allcraft Tool & Supply Co., Inc.
100 Frank Road
Hicksville, New York 11801

WOOD

California
Robert M. Albrecht
18701 Parthenia Street
Northridge, California 91324

Illinois
Craftsman Wood Service Co.
2727 S. Mary Street
Chicago, Illinois 60608

New York
Albert Constantine & Son Inc.
2050 Eastchester Road
Bronx, New York 10461

YARN

California
Spin It, Weave It Studio
840 Leland Place
El Cajon, California 92020

New York
School Products Co., Inc.
1201 Broadway
New York, New York 10001

Ohio
Colonial Woollen Mills, Inc.
56 Lebhough Street
Cleveland, Ohio 44103

Oregon
Oregon Worsted Co.
8300 SE McLoughlin Blvd.
Portland, Oregon 97202

Pennsylvania
The Mannings
RD #2
East Berlin, Pennsylvania 17316

Peter Heinz

Creative ideas 28

Ladybug checkers

This ladybug checkers set shows you that you can make board games even more fun to play.

You will need:

1 piece of thick white cardboard, 30cm x 30cm (12¾" x 12¾").

1 tube each of peacock blue, red, yellow, black and white designer's gouache.

Transparent adhesive film for covering board.

2 small paintbrushes (one fine sable).

Ruler with beveled edge (to simplify marking a straight edge).

24cm (9½") of dowel 25mm (1") in diameter.

Saw, sandpaper, clear varnish.

Rule the board into a 1cm (⅜") border and 3.5cm (1½") squares, eight on each side. Mix some blue and white paint to make pale blue and paint in every other square with this color and leave to dry. Then with the sable brush and ruler carefully paint the darker blue squares. Put the ruler edge up against the line to be painted and over the light square. Paint along the edge of the ruler. Remove the ruler by lifting it straight up. Do not drag it away or the line will smear. Wipe the ruler's edge before doing the next line. Leave to dry.

Prettily painted checkers game by Kay Cunliffe.

Copy these motifs or design your own playing pieces.

Iain Reid

Clear a work surface and try to keep it as dust free as possible. Cut a square of transparent adhesive film larger than the board. Place on surface, sticky side up, peel off protective cover. Lay the right side of the checkerboard onto the film. Turn over and start pressing firmly from the center to the edges to get rid of any air bubbles. Trim away excess film.

To make the checkers mark and saw the dowel into 24 1cm (⅜") pieces and sand each one down. Trace the designs or make your own, and transfer them to one side of each piece of dowel. Paint on the designs and varnish each one.

Stick pots and decorative oxides

Stick pots or plunge pots are made by pushing one end of a stick or blunt-ended rolling pin into a block of clay. It is a very simple, direct way of working and lively, attractive pots can be made this way.
It is not at all a sophisticated technique, and the effects will always be weighty, rough and vigorous. With this in mind, keep the shape of the pots crisp and angular.
Round pots need a more precise shape and finish to look attractive, and are better made by other methods.

To make a stick pot

Small, fired stick pots make excellent plant pots without needing to be glazed.

Stick pots are often large and heavy, and adapt well to use as solid lamp bases or vases. The stick pots here, designed by Lesley Pearson, are glazed in natural colors. The next chapter deals with some glazing techniques.

Nelson Hargreaves

For a pot about 15cm (6″) high, 15cm (6″) wide

You will need:

A square or oblong block of clay weighing about 1Kg (2lb). Sharp sand, coarse grog or builders' sand.

Rounded stick or rolling pin.

The finished pot will have an attractive textured look if, when you knead the clay in preparation, you knead in 10 to 15% sharp sand or coarse grog. Builder's sand will do if these are not readily available.

☐ Take the block of clay and push the stick into the center (fig.1).

☐ Gradually ease it downward, rotating it slightly if necessary.

☐ Push until the bottom end of the stick is about 6mm (¼″) from the bottom of the block of clay.

☐ Then smooth the clay up the rolling pin with the fingers to thin it out (fig.2). Use a stroking motion, pressing upward firmly but gently.

This will have the effect of giving the pot more height, as well as thinning the walls. You could also thin down the side walls by slicing away the surplus with a cutting wire.

☐ Hold the wire taut and place it about 6mm (¼″) away from the inside of the clay wall.

☐ Slice downward to the bottom of the block to remove the side (fig.3).

☐ Do this on all four sides.

☐ Rub away rough edges with fingers.

☐ Leave the clay to stiffen slightly, then cut a small hole in the bottom for drainage for a flower pot (fig.4).

Texturing the surface of the clay. Sand or grog in the clay will give a rough appearance to the surface of the pot, but if you would like a more definite coarse finish, tap the surface of the clay with a rough stone while it is still soft (fig.5). A piece of wood pressed onto the surface will also give a deeper texture to the pot.

To make a larger vase

You will need:

For a vase about 30cm (12″) high, 15cm (6″) wide.

A block of clay weighing about 2Kg (4lb). Sand or grog if desired.

Rolling pin or rounded stick.

Piece of wood for texturing.

☐ Open up the block of clay in the same way as the smaller piece—the finished walls should be about 6mm (¼″) thick.

☐ Give the sides a 'faceted' finish by pressing into the clay with the side of the piece of wood.

☐ You can achieve a 'stepped' effect in this way which will add a sculptural quality to the piece (fig.6).

☐ Experiment by pressing into the clay at different angles, so that the faceted surface of the completed piece creates an effect of light and shade.

1. *Push the stick down into the block.*

2. *Press the clay up against the stick.*

3. *Slice away the sides of the block.*

4. *Cut out a small hole for drainage.*

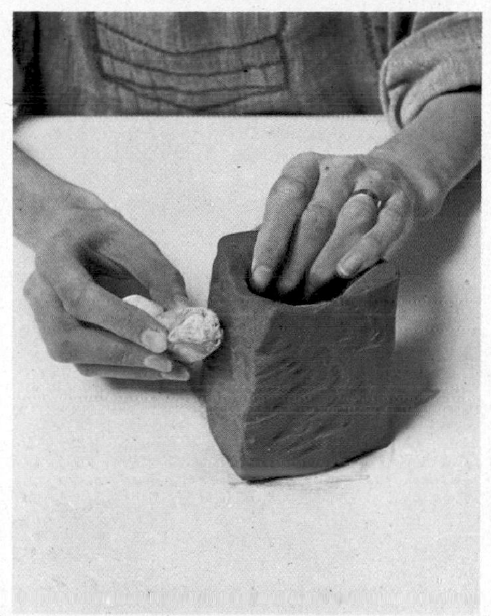

5. *A rough stone can add some texturing.*

6. *Or give the sides a 'faceted' finish.*

Nelson Hargreaves

To make a lamp base

You will need:
A block of clay weighing 2Kg (4lb).
Rolling pin or rounded stick.
Light fitting and electric cord. Fittings can usually be bought with adjustable fixtures and these are ideal for pottery lamp bases.

□ Hollow out the block of clay as described above. The lamp base can be oblong or square, but try to keep the shape angular, with simple lines.

□ When you have hollowed out the clay and thinned the sides of the pot, remove the stick from the center.

□ Leave the clay to stiffen to the leather hard stage.

□ When the pot is stiff, turn it upside down so that the hole is underneath and the top surface is closed in.

□ Cut a small hole in the 'top' to accommodate the lamp fitting (fig.7). Remember that clay shrinks as it dries, so have the fitting beside you when you cut the hole and make the hole 10% larger to allow for shrinkage.

□ Push a small hole in the bottom side of the pot to take the cord, allowing for shrinkage in the same way (fig.8).

7. *A hole accommodates the fitting.*

Nelson Hargreaves

8. *Cut another small hole for the cord.*

Oxides

A suitable decorative medium for these pots and those which have been made in preceding chapters is the metallic oxide.

Oxides are metallic compounds, occurring naturally in the earth, which can be used as coloring pigments for both clays and glazes. In their natural state oxides color rocks, stones and some clays—red earthenware, for example, is given its characteristic color by iron oxide.

The most common metal oxides are iron, copper, manganese, cobalt, nickel and chrome. These are mined, then chemically refined, purified and ground into fine powders which disperse in water to form a suspension. Metal oxides can be bought from potters' suppliers in this ready-to-use powdered form. Many are identically black in powder form, so keep jars clearly labeled (fig.9).

Oxides as a decorative medium

Pots can be colored with oxides in several ways. Oxide can be mixed into the basic clay, or applied directly to the pot. Slip can be colored with oxides, or the oxide can be used as part of the composition of the glaze. Some oxides, used in combination with a glaze, undergo a dramatic color change although they only look black or brown before firing.

If the oxides are used without a glaze—as discussed in this chapter—colors do not change dramatically. Shades of rust, ochre, black and brown will appear, giving pots a soft, earthy finish.

The following is a simple guide to the colors that can be achieved by applying oxide directly to a finished pot, without the use of glaze.

Iron gives a rust or ochre color.
Copper gives a toast to black color.
Manganese gives brown.
Cobalt gives black when used directly onto the pot if the pot is left unglazed.

Try using individual oxides at first, and then experiment by combining two or more oxides to give varied tones. The oxides will break up the sandy textured surface and accentuate the tones.

Applying oxides directly

If the oxide is to be applied directly to the pot, first mix the oxide with a little water.

For a small pot take about half a level teaspoon of oxide and mix it with water until it is about the same consistency as water-color paint.

Make sure that the mixture is well stirred—metal oxides are heavy and will sediment quickly.

9. *Powdered oxides all look very alike.*

10. *Paint on a thin coat of the oxide.*

11. *Rotate the wheel to make a stripe.*

Brushing on. Use a large, soft brush. Apply in a thin wash—if the oxide is too thick it will look very black and will flake off (fig.10).

A banding wheel is useful for the painting process if you are working on a small pot without sharp angles. This is a small wheel that can be spun by hand, and it is a basic item of the studio potter's equipment.

Place the pot in the center of the banding wheel, load the brush with oxide, and begin to apply it. Hold the brush at the top of the pot, spin the

12. *Move the brush further down the pot.*

13. *Use a toothbrush to spray it on.*

14. *A sponge can give a stippled effect.*

wheel and gradually move the brush downward toward the bottom.
This technique combined with the use of the large brush helps to avoid brush marks.
You could also apply even bands of color by holding the brush in one place. Spin the wheel and then move the brush to another position to give another band of color (figs.11,12).
Spraying. This gives a mottled, 'thrushes' breast' effect. A small plastic spray container can be used for this purpose, or an old toothbrush or nail brush. Load the brush with oxide, then pull the bristles back with the fingers. Direct the resulting spray so that it splashes gently onto the pot (fig.13).
Sponging. You could also use a small piece of natural sponge to apply the oxide. Dampen the sponge first, and dip it into the oxide. Press the sponge onto the pot to give a stippled effect (fig.14).

Firing

Pots decorated in this way need to be fired only once. If you have facilities for firing your pots you now have a good range of building and decorating techniques on which to test the kiln and the effects that can be achieved.

Quiet, natural tones are characteristic of oxides. The cylinder pot has a bold incised decoration in which a deeper shading of oxide has gathered. Designed by Bob Dawe. The smaller pot has a rough texture that is ideally complimented by the brownish red color of iron oxide. Designed byJoanna Constantinidis.

Peter Heinz

Pictures from fabric and glue

Fabric collage is similar to appliqué in so far as shapes are cut from one fabric and attached to another. In a collage, however, instead of being stitched to the background, the shapes are glued into place using a fabric adhesive for interfaced, or small, shapes. If, on the other hand, you are using large, uninterfaced pieces of fabric for your collage, a contact adhesive (see below) is a good choice.

Which fabrics?

A strong, firmly woven cotton is a good choice for background fabric and this can be incorporated into the picture or covered completely by the various shapes.

As collage is a purely decorative technique, it is not necessary to use fabrics of a similar type and weight to make up the picture—in fact it is a good idea to collect as varied a selection of scraps as possible. Small pieces of leather, felt, PVC (cloth-backed vinyl), velvet, brocade, satin, cotton, lurex or lamé, and tweed, as well as braid and ribbon, are well worth saving to provide a variety of textures.

A country landscape in winter could be made almost entirely from tweed scraps in various tones of brown; whereas, for an interior, like the one shown here, you would need a wide range of textures and colors.

It is not essential to match the grain on the shapes to that of the background, just cut fabric to make the best use of its pattern or weave.

Note: The various parts of the picture can be cut from fabric which has been mounted on iron-on, non-woven interfacing, which adds stiffness and prevents the pieces from fraying. You may find, however, that you wish to drape, gather or perhaps pleat fabric to obtain an effect, in which case you should not use interfacing.

Found objects, such as buttons, beads, artificial flowers, feathers and even twigs can be most useful extras when picture making.

Mounting a picture

Before starting work on your picture you will need to decide how it is to be finished.

If it is to be mounted into a frame, the background fabric should first be glued to a sheet of fiberboard or Masonite of the intended size using contact adhesive. This type of adhesive is spread on both surfaces and the two stuck together when the glue is nearly dry, which means it is unlikely to seep through the fabric.

The completed picture can be attached to a piece of particleboard, in which case the background fabric should be cut large enough to turn over to the back of the board, where it can be secured with adhesive or by using a staple gun. It is best to fix the fabric to the board before you begin to work the picture.

With either of the above methods the picture can be enclosed in a braid border. Choose your braid before cutting out the background fabric and allow enough space around the edge to glue this in place.

Alternatively neaten the edges of the background fabric and make a small hem at the top and bottom. Insert doweling rods, which are slightly longer than the width of the collage, through each hem. Attach cord to the top rod and hang it from this (fig.1).

Victoria Drew

1. *Collage hung from doweling rod.*

If using this method, it is a good idea to pin the work flat onto a large piece of Masonite or cardboard while you work.

This collage designed by Sue Murdoch is a replica of a wall of her bedroom.

Steve Bicknell

791

Making collage pictures

You will need:
Adhesive.
Background fabric(s).
Scraps of fabric in a variety of weights and textures.
Iron-on, non-woven interfacing (optional).
Braid (optional).
Masonite, particleboard, doweling (depending on the chosen finish).
Large sheet of construction paper (optional).
Tracing paper (optional).

Working techniques depend on individual methods of approach, two of which are given here.

Method 1. Take a piece of Masonite or some particleboard and then divide the background into two or three main areas. Cover each area with a different piece of fabric, as in the still life collage shown here. You will find that just by this simple device you will begin to get ideas as to the picture you wish to create.

Cut out other shapes and move them around on the background until you are happy with the arrangement, then glue them in position.

As you get used to the medium you will find that you get more and more ideas for pictures.

Method 2. You may find, however, that you prefer to work from a detailed sketch and to plan the complete picture before you begin to work, as with a realistic collage like the interior featured in this chapter.

It is best to start with a simple picture and work up to something more ambitious and detailed.

Make an actual-size sketch of your picture, noting where shapes overlap, and mark in the outlines of the design on the background fabric lightly in pencil.

Trace the principal shapes from the sketch onto tracing paper and cut them out to use as patterns. Then cut out each shape in the appropriate fabric and glue it to the background.

Finally, add finishing touches, such as bits of ribbon, beads, feathers and any additional fabric shapes.

Note: The principal shapes which make up the picture can be overlapped (fig.2) or can be fitted together rather like a jigsaw (fig.3), according to choice, the nature of the fabric and the dictates of your design.

Still life made using the technique described in method 1. The shapes in this collage overlap as in fig.2. Designer of both collages on this page Laura Balston.

2. *Top: collage shapes overlapping.*
3. *Bottom: shapes fitted together rather like pieces of a jigsaw puzzle.*

Landscape made from various bits and pieces including a yellow duster.

Roger Philips

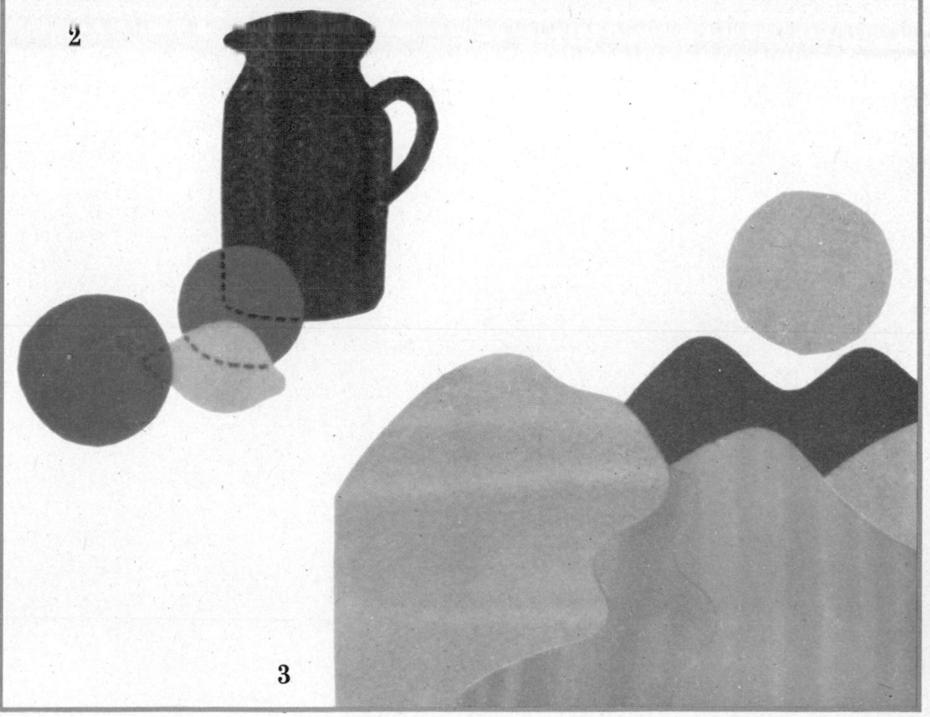

Victoria Drew

Making a monoprint

Of all the traditional forms of print making the monoprint (or monotype) is the simplest, easiest and cheapest. It requires very little in the way of equipment yet its sense of spontaneity and range of styles make it widely appealing.

Monoprinting involves making an image or pattern on a flat surface such as glass, usually with printing inks, and then pressing paper or cloth against it to print the image. But unlike other forms of printing, it is only possible to make one print from the master image.

William Blake used monoprinting in combination with etching and Degas, Toulouse Lautrec, Gauguin and Matisse have all explored its possibilities. Yet it is equally popular with young children because it is easy to do and invites complete freedom of expression.

Materials

There are no strict rules about what you do and don't need in monoprinting and the more you improvise the better. The main thing is to find the best way to get the effect you want and basically to do this you will need color, a printing surface on which to make the image and some paper or cloth on which to print it.

You should also bear in mind that your finished print will be a mirror image of the design on the printing surface and in some cases this may make a difference.

Printing surface. This is the surface on which the inky image is made. Normally a sheet of glass is used but any smooth, flat surface such as Formica is suitable. If the printing surface is somewhat larger than the material to be printed you can use one end as a palette for mixing inks.

Colors. Oil or water based printing inks, available from artists' suppliers, are the best colors to use for paper (with oil based inks you will also need some turpentine for diluting color). For printing onto textiles use special fabric printing inks or dyes.

Material for printing the image. Paper is the traditional monoprinting surface and any fairly absorbent paper may be used from the cheaper construction papers to the good quality, mold-made, handmade and Japanese papers. Working with textiles can be more difficult than with paper and beginners are advised to become used to the technique of printing on paper first. When you are ready to print on textiles you can either use a thinnish cloth such as muslin or a heavier canvas of

Jerry Tubby

The designs and textures that can be made by monoprinting are numerous. Drawings and portfolios, Ann Marshall.

To make a monoprint roll out color onto a glass slab. The design above was drawn in the paint with a matchstick, then paper was lowered on top to make a print.

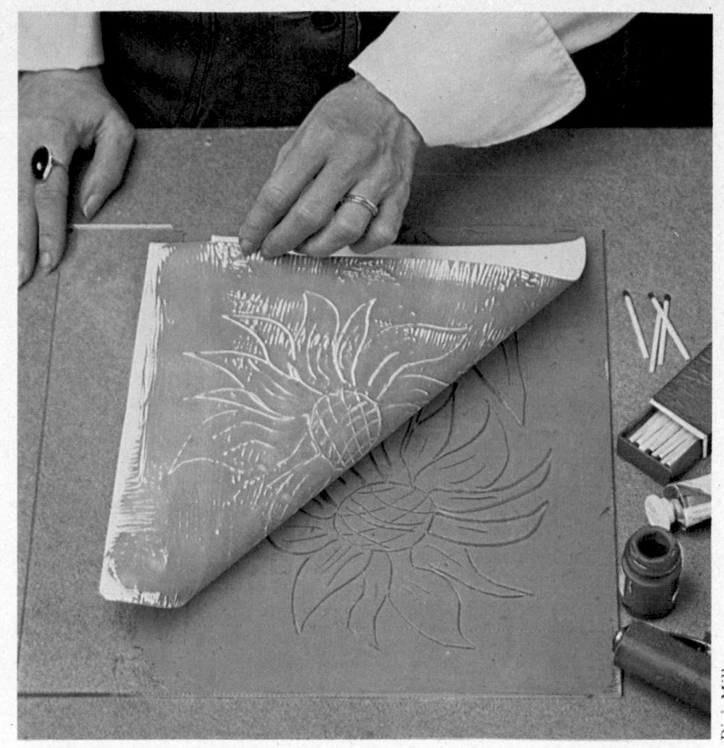

Dick Miller

As the paper is lifted, it shows the image transferred onto it. This is the monoprint. The textured effect was made by not diluting the color.

the type used in bookbinding. Always use a natural fiber (cotton, linen, silk) or viscose rayon with cold water fabric dyes.

Tools for applying color and making images depend entirely on your own imagination and on the type of image you want to produce. If it is to be a multi-colored picture you can apply ink to the printing surface with a paint brush just as you would apply color to canvas or you can use a palette knife (also useful for mixing inks).

A roller for rolling ink onto the printing surface is invaluable and a small 10cm (4″) wide artists' roller is sufficient. Large heavy printer's rollers are excellent but also expensive.

Pencils, combs, or knitting needles can all be employed successfully to scratch images into the rolled out inks and if you use your fingers, sponges or paper towels you will get effective blotted looks and textures.

Making a monoprint

This is the basic method for making a monoprint:

☐ Apply ink or fabric dye to the printing surface either by rolling it on with a roller or using a paintbrush, palette knife or other tool.

☐ When the design is ready lay paper or cloth gently on top of the inked surface and rub the back of it carefully by hand. Printmakers often use the back of their closed fingers to do this; inky hands are unavoidable.

You can raise one corner of the sheet very carefully to see how the paper or cloth is receiving the ink. More rubbing may be necessary.

☐ Lift the paper off when the image has been transferred onto it; this is the monoprint.

☐ Turn the print face upward on a table top or pin it to a clothesline to dry. You can make further use of the residual ink on the glass or Formica and develop it into another image by reshaping or adding more ink.

A patchwork of different monoprinting techniques. Designed by Ann Marshall.

Chris Holland

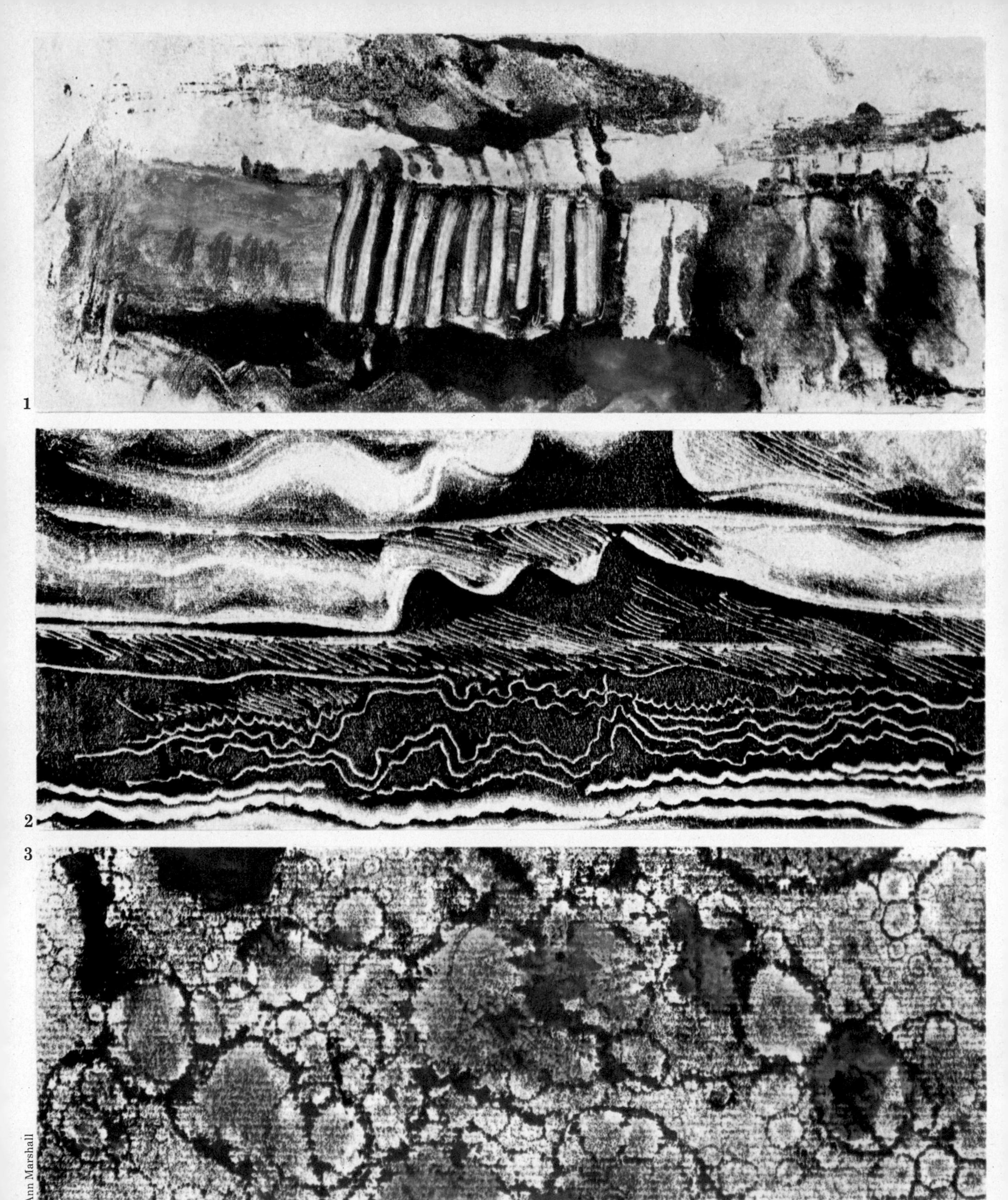
1
2
3
Ann Marshall

Monoprint techniques

Painting directly onto the glass with a paint brush, palette knife, fingers or anything that will make texture is a way of making a multi-colored design or of painting a picture as you would on canvas (fig.1). If you want to paint an image but are uncertain of your ability to draw free-hand, you can make a preliminary pencil sketch and then slip it underneath the glass printing surface. It will be visible through the glass and you can ink in the glass accordingly. Ink can be applied thickly, in the

style known as impasto, or it can be thinned (if oil based, use turpentine, if water based use water) to create watercolor type washes.

Incised drawing is a remarkably easy way to work. Using a roller, cover the printing surface with an even film of ink (or, if you want a multi-colored background, use a paint brush). The design can be drawn in with a pointed tool. Very little pressure is needed to slide the point over the glass and a free flowing line can be made fairly simply. The point removes a small trough of ink from the glass, resulting in a white line on the finished monoprint (fig.2).

Splashing. Exciting abstract images can be created by spreading oil based ink freely and arbitrarily over the printing surface and then splashing it with turpentine (fig.3). Introducing an element of chance, even in a carefully drawn design, often produces the most rewarding results. In fact, the happy accident is almost the essence of monoprinting and designs where the fall of the paper and the spread and absorption of the ink have not been completely controlled are some of the most successful.

Resist techniques refer to methods whereby color is prevented from marking certain areas of the finished surface, thus shaping a design.

Paper stencils or torn papers placed over parts of the ink spread will make blank shapes on the finished print (fig.4). When dry the first stages can be over printed with the stencils and the addition of another color. Masking tape also makes it possible to get different effects such as hard edges on different parts of the print as seen in the notebook cover illustrated.

Transfer drawing. Delicate and exciting interpretations of line drawings can be made by this simple method. Place paper or cloth over the inked printing surface and then draw with a pencil or ball point pen on the back of the material while it is gently resting on the thin coat of ink. Do not apply pressure to any other area, the ink will prevent the print from sliding. Fig.5 shows a print made in this way. Similarly, you can press a leaf or other familiar object against the back of the material and this will print on the other side. The same film of ink if smoothed over will probably be sufficient for several monoprints made in this manner.

Experimenting with different tools and consistencies of ink is part of the enjoyment of monoprinting. Different techniques can often be combined and new ones discovered by taking advantage of initial mistakes.

1-5. *Different techniques of monoprinting result in a fascinating variety of styles.* **1.** *is made by painting on glass and pressing printing paper to it;* **2.** *uses incised lines;* **3.** *involves splashing the printing surface;* **4.** *using stencils and* **5.** *drawing on the back of the print. By Ann Marshall.*

Colored glass window hangings

Once you have started to use lead came to hold together pieces of glass, you will find that the scope of your glass work expands enormously.
When using lead for the first time it is a good idea to practice on a few odd bits of glass. This way you will get the feel of the leading and you will avoid spoiling large sheets of glass which are sometimes expensive.

After practicing on a little scrap glass you will be able to make some decorative glass hangings like the ones illustrated here. They are made of small pieces of glass surrounded by lead came and solderered at the joints. They look attractive hung in front of a window or other light source.

The window hanging

Instructions are given here for making the green, blue and red hanging, although the same techniques apply equally well to the coral colored version and the tulip hanging (p.801).
You will need to buy (or sometimes improvise) a number of tools which you may not have used before. Once you have acquired them you will be able to use them for all glass and leading work.

You will need:

Tools

Glass wheel cutter.
Lead cutting knife or a utility knife such as a Stanley knife. This knife can also be made from a palette knife. Cut it down to size with a hacksaw (fig.1).

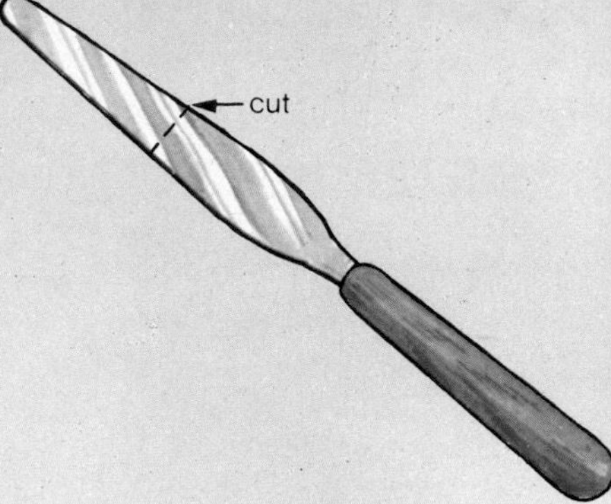

1. *A cut-off palette knife.*

Oyster knife for opening the leaves of the lead cames. This is a thick-handled knife with a short, blunt blade but any similar knife will do.
Grozers (glazier's pliers). Ordinary blunt-ended pliers are satisfactory.
Lathekin or a flat piece of wood about hand size used for smoothing the lead over the glass.
Soldering iron, either a 75-100 watt electric one, or an old-fashioned copper one requiring a gas flame for heating.
Gas stove or bunsen burner if using an old-fashioned soldering iron.
Asbestos mat, about 15cm (6″) square.
Goggles.
Pencil.
Coin, about 2.5cm (1″) in diameter.

Materials

Antique glass such as Pot glass or Reamy glass:
23cm x 15cm (9″x6″) of red.
10cm x 10cm (4″x4″) of blue.
15cm x 7.5cm (6″x3″) of green. These quantities of glass are generous to allow for mistakes.
Flat double channeled lead came, 1.5m (5′) in length, 0.6cm ($\frac{1}{4}$″) in height and 0.6cm ($\frac{1}{4}$″) in width of leaf. (See Glass chapter 6, page 702.)
Solder, 55cm (22″) long, 1.5mm ($\frac{1}{16}$) thick. This comes in a long stick and joins two cut pieces of lead together.
Flux or tallow candle to assist the flow of the solder.
Wire steel wool or wire brush for cleaning lead joints.

Steve Bicknell

Lampblack for polishing lead when finished (optional).
Felt, or thick cloth, for padding the glass while cutting it.
Nails easily pulled out of wood, such as finishing nails or lasting pins as used by shoemakers, for holding the glass and lead in place while working on it.
Masonite or smooth piece of wood at least 30cm x 30cm (1′x 1′).
Piece of white paper about 30cm x 30cm (1′ x 1′).
Wire, about 0.8mm (20-21 gauge) thick or strong jewelry chain for the hanging.

☐ Place the white paper on a table and put the coin in the middle of the paper.
☐ Draw around the coin.
☐ Following the diagram of the hanging (fig.2) move the coin to another position about 1.27cm (½″) away and draw around it again.
☐ Repeat again to make six circles around a central circle. At this stage ignore the spaces allowed in the diagram for the leading.
☐ The remaining two pieces are pear-shaped and a little larger than the circles. Practice on a scrap of paper to get the right shape then transfer to the sheet of paper positioning them as in fig. 2.

The opacity of the lead clearly defines the brilliance of the glass. Hangings designed by Pixie Dorchy.

Cutting the glass

☐ Put the felt or cloth on a flat surface and place the sheet of paper on it.
☐ Place the red glass over the paper.
☐ Cut the six red circles (the circle in the middle is blue). To do this hold the glass firmly with one hand and with the other draw the cutter toward you in a smooth curve, following the line of the circle on the paper. The glass need only be lightly scored (see

lead came
overlap lead
lead joint
glass
nails

2. This working drawing will enable you to cut the glass and set it out with the lead ready for soldering.

Paul Williams

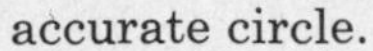

Glass chapter 4, page 450 for instructions on cutting glass). The circles are much easier to cut if the cutter is drawn along in several long curves (fig.3). Three or four strokes of the cutter should be enough to cut an accurate circle.

☐ Hold the glass continuously while cutting each circle. Move bodily around the circle if this makes cutting any easier.

☐ When you have completed all six circles pick up the glass and, with the handle of the glass cutter, firmly tap along the score lines. The glass should start cracking along the lines.

☐ Small pieces of glass surrounding the circle can sometimes be stubborn. If this happens put on the goggles and use the pliers or grozers to snap off the glass. Hold the glass between the pliers and firmly jerk down, away from your face.

Do not worry if the circles are still a little ragged. The leading will cover minor deficiencies.

☐ Place the blue glass over the remaining central circle and cut in the same way.

☐ Cut the green pear-shaped pieces so that the tapering point touches an edge of the glass (otherwise you will never manage to extricate the piece from its surrounding glass). Follow the cutting line as shown in fig.4.

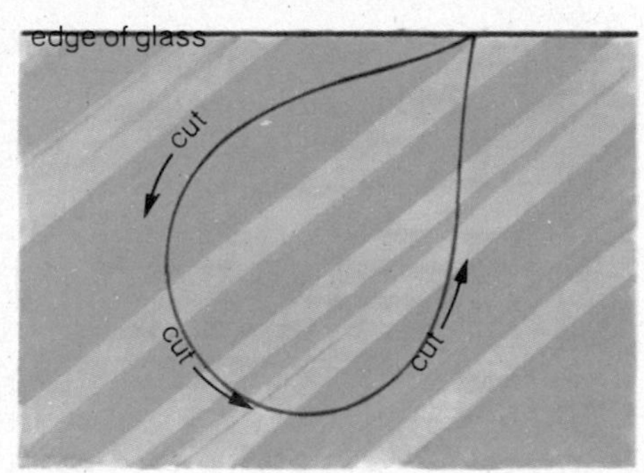

4. *Cut the green pieces up to an edge.*

When cutting any glass be careful not to brush the work surface with your bare hand. Use a dustpan and brush to sweep up glass particles. If any glass particles should get in your eye seek

Trim the glass with the grozers.

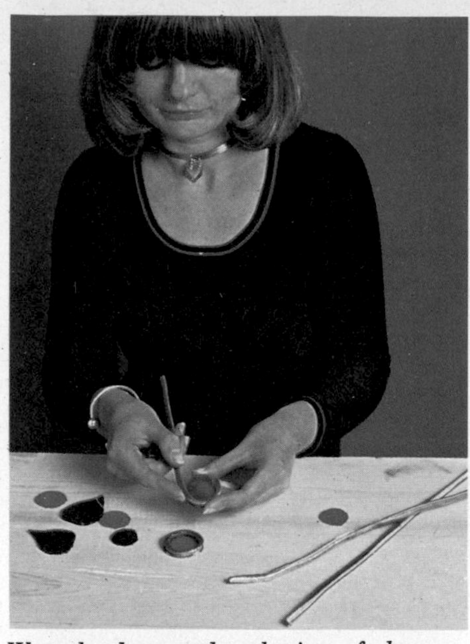

Wrap lead around each piece of glass.

Dick Miller

Rub the lead with a tallow candle.

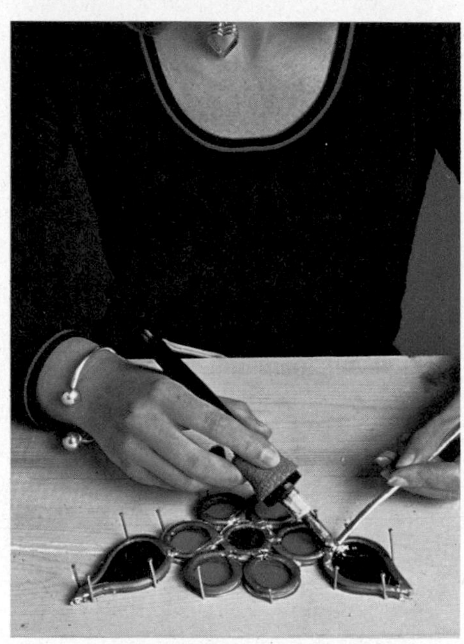

Touch the solder with a hot iron.

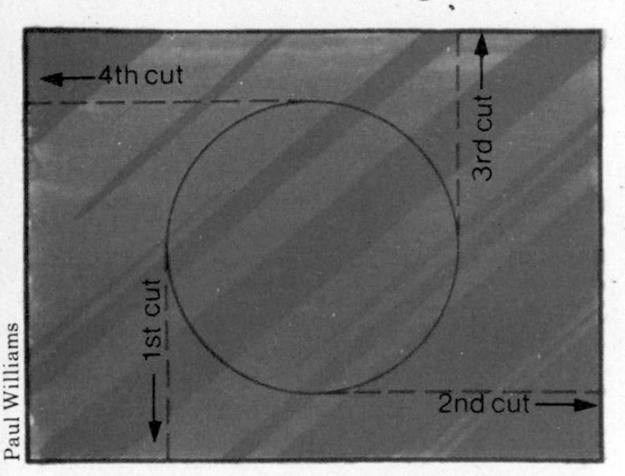

Paul Williams

3. *Cut the glass with several strokes.*

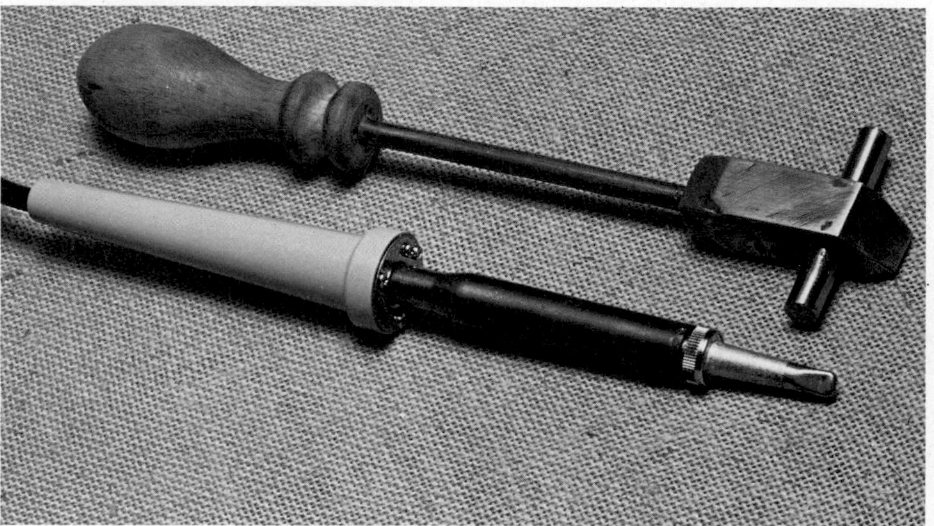

Dick Miller

Top: an old-fashioned soldering iron. Bottom: a modern electric iron.

medical advice immediately. Otherwise, wash small cuts under a running faucet and bandage lightly.

Leading

☐ Untwist the lead, then stretch and straighten it.
☐ To do this place one end of the lead under the heel of your foot and grip the other end with the pliers. Pull the lead up and over your shoulder. If you do it in this way you won't hit yourself with the pliers should the lead slip.
☐ Place the lead on a working surface and separate the leaves of the lead with the oyster knife or other similar knife. As you will be working with small pieces of glass you may find it easier to cut the lead came into 30cm (1′) lengths.
☐ Take any one of the seven circles and bend the lead around it.
☐ Where the lead meets around the glass make a small mark with the cutting knife. Ease away from the glass and cut.
☐ Making sure that the glass fits snugly in the lead leaves replace the lead so that the two ends meet around the glass. As lead is fairly pliable it is quite easy to squeeze and ease the lead to fit the glass.
☐ Hold the lead up to the light and check that there are no gaps between lead and glass. If there are cut off a tiny piece of lead and try again. It does not matter if the glass rattles slightly so long as the glass is safely inside the leaves of the lead.
☐ Using the lathekin smooth down the edges of the lead onto the glass.
☐ Repeat for the remaining six circles.
☐ When all the circles are complete arrange together as in fig.2 with the blue circle in the middle and the other six around it and touching the blue circle. If the circles are overcrowded it is possible that one circle has been cut too large or the lead has not been pushed closely enough into the glass. Check the leading first and, if the circles are still jostling each other, you may have to unlead a circle and nibble at the glass with the pliers until you get it slightly smaller.
☐ Now lead up the green pieces. The procedure is the same except that the top tip of lead runs a little further than the glass (fig.2). Cut this lead at an angle, making sure that the lower lead fits against the top lead.
☐ Arrange all the pieces of leaded glass on the Masonite (fig.2) and turn the lead cuts of the circles to the center. Line the lead cut of the blue circle to one of the cuts on a red circle.

Another simple but effective hanging. Tulips designed by John Burford.

Steve Bicknell

☐ Arrange the two green pieces so that their lead slightly overlaps the lead on two of the red circles.
☐ Hammer in nails to hold the pieces steady when soldering. (See fig.2 for positions of nails.)

Soldering

☐ Clean the ends of the lead joints with wire steel wool. This is important since solder will not adhere well to a dirty surface. Also clean the end of the soldering iron with steel wool.
☐ Heat up the soldering iron. An old-fashioned iron can be heated over a bunsen burner or the flame of a gas stove; an electric iron can be plugged into the household electricity supply. Always lay a hot soldering iron on an asbestos mat, never directly onto the unprotected working surface. Achieving and maintaining the right temperature of iron takes a little practice. Test for the proper temperature by melting a little solder in a metal lid and letting it cool. Rub the end of the iron on the solder and when it starts to flow you will know you have reached the right temperature. Turn off the electric iron occasionally to stop it overheating.
Once the iron is tinned—a smooth 'puddle' of tin should adhere evenly to the end—you are ready to start soldering.
☐ Rub the joints of the individual pieces of leaded glass with flux or a tallow candle to aid the flow of solder.
☐ Place the stick of solder close over the joint and touch with the soldering iron so that a small drop of solder falls on the joint. Spread smoothly over the joint with the tip of the iron. Be careful not to let the solder fall on the glass as the heat may crack it. Do this to all the joints.
☐ Once all the individual pieces of leaded glass have been soldered the pieces can be joined together.
☐ Clean down the soldered joints with wire steel wool and rub with flux.
☐ Solder the six red circles onto the blue circle and the two green pieces onto two red circles as in fig.2. Solder in the same way as for the individual pieces of glass.
☐ When the soldering is completed on one side, remove the supporting nails, lift piece up and turn over. Solder the back in the same way.
☐ When finished the leading can be rubbed with lampblack to give a good polish.
To support the hanging you can either solder a wire or chain to the tips of the leading around the green pieces or, alternatively, thread the wire along the lead channel at the bottom of the hanging, twist the two ends of the wire together, and support it in this way.

French knots and other stitches

For picture making choose a theme with bold and simple shapes. Break down the composition into stitch areas, fitting an appropriate stitch to the type of texture which will best express each part. As you gain experience, more detailed subjects may be attempted with the texture provided by a greater variety of stitches, and probably with some invented by yourself.

Background. To start with, choose a finely woven, natural-colored fabric. When you have become more confident you can use backgrounds which will play a part in the composition of the design with textures of the fabric as well as the stitching becoming an integral part of the picture.

Borders. If you wish to embroider a frame around a picture, choose one that is in keeping with the subject—a rose-festooned one as shown here—or a geometric border for a more modern picture. Of course, many pictures look their best when set in a plain picture frame.

Yarn quantities. For a small picture, such as the one shown, one skein of each color is usually more than enough. However, if one color predominates or if the stitches are very closely or thickly worked, two skeins may be needed.

Transferring a picture design. Trace the design onto tissue paper, being careful not to tear it. Lay the tissue paper over the fabric. Using sewing or basting thread and a fine needle, sew through the tissue paper and fabric with back or small running stitches around the outline or indicate the position of the areas to be embroidered. Tear the tissue paper away. The stitches not hidden by the embroidery are removed when the embroidery is complete.

Apple blossom picture

The apple blossom on the tree in the picture is superbly suggested by the use of French knots. These are also used on the girl's dress and hair band and this holds the picture together. Bold straight stitches which lie flat are used for the trellis in front of the bushes. These add a little perspective and contrast in texture.

The colors used are light to medium tones and give the whole picture a pretty, country air.

You will need:

Piece of fabric 38cm (15″) x 30cm (12″).

1 skein each of stranded floss in each of the following colors: brown, pale pink, rose pink, light green, mid green, sage green, golden brown, white.

1 ball pearl cotton No.5 in two shades of brown and pale blue.

Small amount of gold lurex yarn for trellis.

□ Working from the photograph enlarge the picture to measure 33cm (13″) x 25cm (10″)—see Design Know-how, chapter 4, page 112.

□ Using pearl cotton, work as follows:
The girl's dress, chain stitch and stem stitch.
Bark of tree and branches, stem stitch.

□ Using all strands of 6-stranded floss, work as follows:
apple blossom, flowers under tree, girl's hairband and part of girl's dress; closely worked, loose French knots. Place some knots over the branches of the tree.
Grass and flower leaves, random straight stitches.
Background bush, feather stitch.
Foreground bush, herringbone stitch outlined with stem stitch.
Girl's hair and feet, stem stitch.
Girl's hairband, French knots.
Girl's arms, backstitch.

The trellis. Use all strands of floss and work a lattice, couching it with the gold lurex yarn. In front of the trellis work the flowers in French knots and leaves in detached chain stitch.

The border. The border consists of herringbone in stranded floss with stem stitch in pearl cotton on each side.

Work the rosettes in stem stitch from the outside toward the center, and add one or two French knots at the center. Work leaves in detached chain stitch.

To press the picture, lay it right side downward on a well-padded ironing board, cover with a damp cloth and press it lightly. When dry mount the picture as described in Needlepoint chapter 7 page 120.

Basic stitches

French knots (fig.1). Bring the thread out at the required position, hold the thread down with the left thumb and encircle it twice with the needle as in A. Still holding the thread firmly, twist the needle back to the starting point and insert it as close as possible to where the thread first emerged. Pull the thread through to the wrong side and secure if you are working a single knot or pass to the next.

Couched lattice (fig.2). Lay threads along the lines of the design and, with another thread, secure the intersections down by taking a small stitch into the fabric.

Feather stitch (fig.3). Work in a vertical line.. Bring the needle through to the right of the center line of the design and take a small vertical stitch to the right as shown, catching the thread under the point of the needle. Continue making a series of stitches to the left and right of the design line, catching the thread under the needle.

Herringbone stitch (fig.4). Work from left to right. Bring the needle through above the center line of the design and insert it below this line to the right, taking a small stitch to the left, keeping the thread above the needle. Then insert the needle on the upper line a little to the right, taking a small stitch to the left with the thread below the needle. Continue working these two movements alternately.

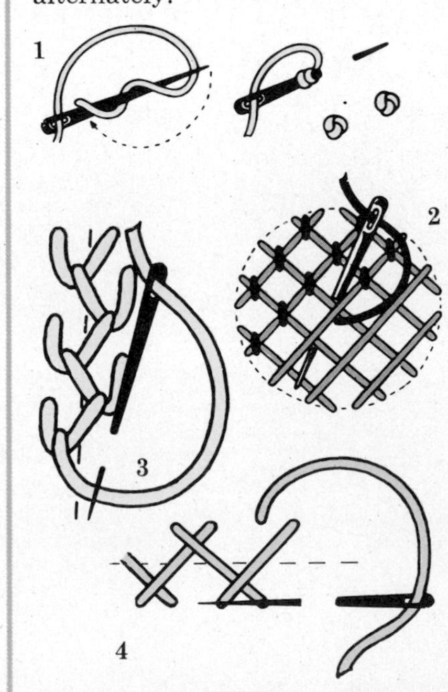

Texture is created in this pretty picture by the use of French knots for blossom and couching for the trellis.

Padded panels and shallow buttoning

The techniques for upholstering a solid wood surface which were used for a padded bedhead can be adapted to make a back rest for banquette (pronounced 'bawnkette') seating or for a divan.

Whenever you upholster a solid surface with foam padding for seating, it is essential to edge the foam with muslin strips which are tacked to the foundation. This helps you to position the foam on the foundation accurately and also prevents it from moving around inside the cover during use. The method described in Upholstery chapter 5, page 748 can be used for back rests if the panel is elaborately shaped. Where they are simple rectangles however, the foam can be glued directly onto the foundation.

Size and position of panels

Length. Start by deciding the size of the wall panel. If it is to run behind a bench seat in your kitchen, for example, you should make it the same length as the bench or slightly longer. If it is to run along the length of a bed, you could make two or three small panels and have spaces between them.

The height. When choosing the height of the panels, you must establish the most comfortable position for your back and possibly your head when you are sitting down. If you are unsure, ask someone to sit on the bench or bed while you measure the wall behind.

Flush mounts are used for fixing the panels to the wall. The mounts consist of two plates (fig.1), one of which is screwed to the wall and the other

Striped butcher's cloth makes a sturdy covering for padded back rests.

Jerry Tubby

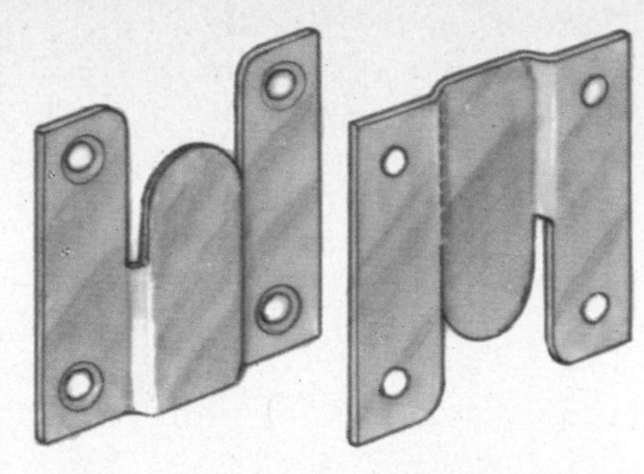

Paul Williams

1. *Flush mounts give a hidden fixing.*

to the back of the panel. At least two mounts should be used for each panel. When the panel mounts are hooked onto the wall mounts, the fixings are hidden and the panel is firmly held.

The fabric

Most kinds of fabric which are sold as suitable for slip covers and upholster can be used for wall panels, although if you are making the panels for a kitchen you might prefer to use a leathercloth which can be wiped clean.

Leathercloth is made from expanded PVC and has a knitted backing. It is easy to use for upholstery because it is strong and pliable. It is sold in widths between 130cm-137cm (50″-54″) and in a wide range of plain colors. Do not be tempted to use the unexpanded PVC fabrics which are sold for raincoats and so on because they do not stretch or mold satisfactorily. If you are intending to shallow button the wall panel, you should buy a small piece of matching unbacked leathercloth sold specially for covering buttons. This is thinner than the regular fabric and is easier to press over the button molds.

To make a wall panel:

You will need:

Foundation panel of the desired size in 15mm (½″) particleboard or plywood.
Cover fabric and muslin lining, 15cm (6″) larger all around than the foundation board.
Foam pad, 5cm (2″) thick and 1.5cm (½″) larger each way than the foundation panel.
Clear adhesive.
Several 1cm (⅜″) fine tacks.
Tack hammer.
Staple gun.
Two flush mounts.
Eight No.8 screws 4cm (1½″) long and appropriate wall plugs.
Eight No.8 screws 1cm (⅜″) long.
Screwdriver, awl.
Drill and No.8 masonry drill bit.
Equipment for buttoning see next page.

Preparing the foundation board

□ Start by drilling holes through the board about 15cm (6″) intervals to ventilate the foam when it compresses. However, if you are going to button the board, drill the holes in the positions for the buttons (fig.2).

□ Mark the position for the panel on the wall lightly in pencil. Measure down 7.5cm (3″) from the top corners and draw a line across. Measure the same amount from the sides and draw lines at right angles to the first one. Repeat on the board. Mark the positions for the flush mounts by placing the top outside corner of each mount exactly on the intersection of the marks (fig.3). Check all your measurements carefully as it is essential that they correspond on the wall and panel exactly if the mounts are to lock together.

□ Place one half of each mount with the flange facing down in position on the board. Start the holes for the screws with the awl and then screw on the mounts using the 1cm (⅜)″ screws.

□ Mark the holes for the other half of the mounts, with the flange facing up, on the wall and drill and plug them. Use the 4cm (1½″) screws to screw the mounts in position.

□ Try the board in position. If you need to make any correction to make the halves of the mounts fit, it is generally easier to alter the sections screwed to the wood.

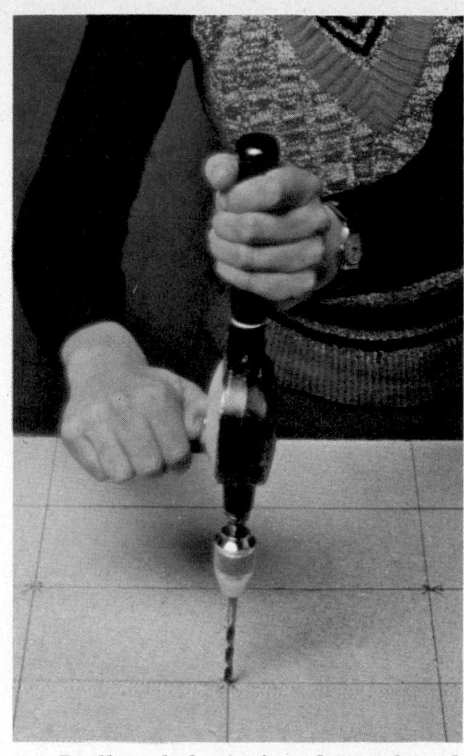

2. *Drilling holes in foundation board. The grid shows the button positions.*

Dick Miller

3. *Screwing the flush mount, flange down, to top corner of the foundation.*

Attaching the foam

☐ Mark the center of each edge of the foam and the foundation board.
☐ Mark a border in pencil 5cm (5″) wide all around the perimeter of the front of the board (the opposite side from the mounts). Mark a border of the same size around the perimeter of the foam.
☐ Spread adhesive along both borders

4. *Spreading adhesive along the border.*

and allow it to become sticky (fig.4). Place the foam, adhesive side down, centrally onto the front of the board and press firmly. There should be a margin of foam 6mm ($\frac{1}{4}$″) wide overlapping the board. Leave to dry.

Attaching the lining

☐ Mark the center of each edge of the muslin and place it onto the foam so that the center marks correspond. Take the muslin over to the back of the board and tack and staple it down following the method used in Upholstery chapter 5, page 748.

Attaching the main cover

☐ Attach the main cover in the same way.
The corners are finished in a square pleat (fig.5). Cut away the surplus fabric before tacking down.
Slip stitch the folds at the pleat using strong thread and a curved needle.

Dick Miller

5. *Forming a square pleat at the corner.*

Shallow buttoning

Shallow buttoning adds extra interest to a plain padded surface and is not difficult to do. It can be used for a wall panel, for padded bedheads and on chairs and stool tops.
Basically the buttons are placed onto the surface of the board in a regular pattern and pulled down into the padding with twine which is taken through the padding to the back of the board, through a drilled hole, and fastened off securely.
Unlike deep buttoning where the buttons are sunk into the padding by some 5cm-7.5cm (2″-3″), the buttons in shallow buttoning merely compress the padding by about 15mm ($\frac{1}{2}$″). The fabric is not distorted much beyond forming a few wrinkles (in deep buttoning the fabric is distorted so much that it is generally formed into pleats between the buttons), so the buttons can be added when the front cover has been completely attached.
Buttons. Use metal buttons, of about 2cm ($\frac{3}{4}$″) diameter, which can be covered in fabric to match the main cover. The buttons should have a metal shank on the back so that the twine used to secure them can be slotted through. The shank sinks into the padding and is completely hidden when the buttoning is complete.
The buttons can be made professionally by a soft furnishing supplier or you

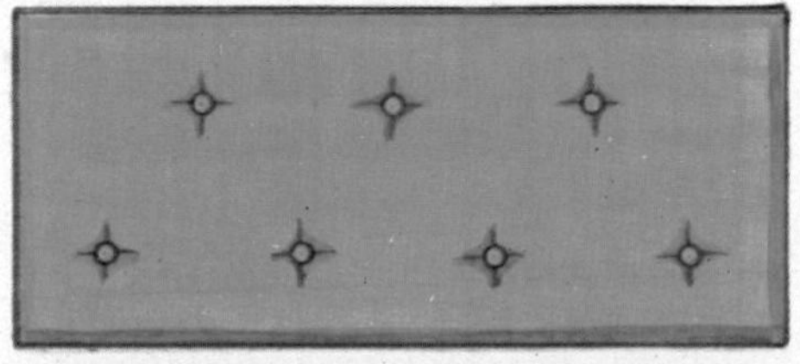

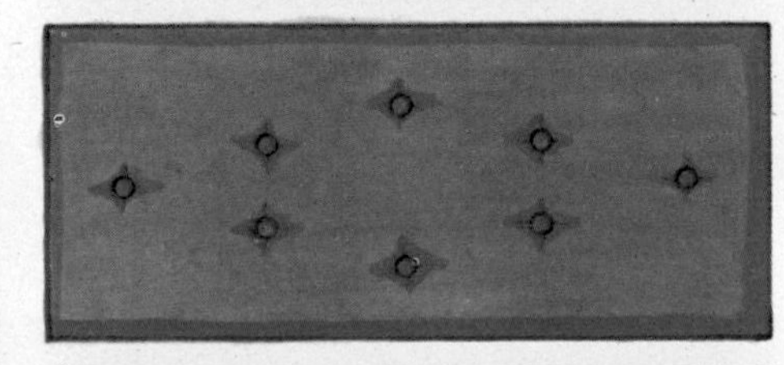

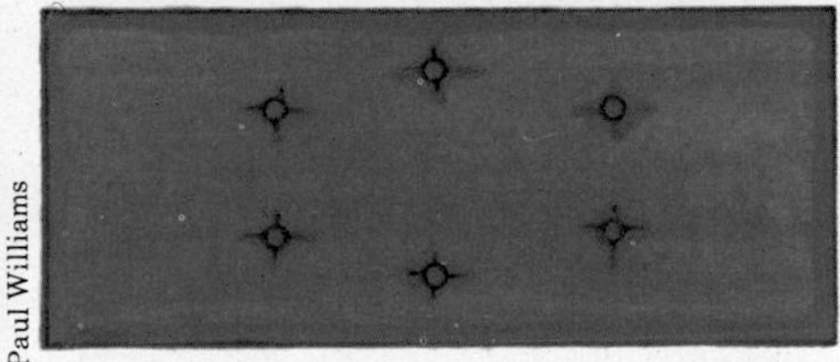

Paul Williams

6. *Some designs for shallow buttoning. The buttons compress padding slightly.*

could make them yourself using a button kit.
The buttoning design. With shallow buttoning the buttons can be placed exactly as you want them and you can have as many or as few as you like. You could place them in a rectangle, in a large diamond, a triangle or even a circle (fig.6).

To make a buttoned surface:

You will need:
Buttons.
Upholstery twine and long upholstery needle.
Two 12mm ($\frac{1}{2}$″) improved tacks for each button.
Drill and wood drill bit (No.8 size).

Buttoning onto firm foundations

Preparing the board. The foundation board should be prepared for the buttoning before the padding and cover are attached.
Start by marking your board with the positions of the buttons (fig.6 gives some ideas for designs). Mark each position with an X and then drill a hole for each one with the wood drill.
Attaching the buttons. When the padding and cover are complete, place the board, padded side down, onto your work surface. Place two improved tacks on opposite sides of each hole and hammer them halfway down.
Thread the needle with a length of twine and tie one end around one of the tacks. Hammer the tack completely home (fig.7). Pass the needle through

7. *Passing the needle through the hole.*

the hole and padding to the front of the board, checking that you are keeping the needle straight. Pull the needle completely out on the padded side and thread it through the button shank. Push it back into the padding and hole, making a small stitch on the surface of the cover (fig.8).
On the back of the board pull the twine as tightly as possible so that the button compresses the padding, and wrap it around the second tack (it

often helps to have an assistant at this stage).
Hammer the tack home, keeping the twine wound around the tack as tight as possible. Cut off the excess twine, leaving a tail of about 2.5cm (1″).

8. *Making a small stitch on the front.*

Buttoning onto webbed foundations

Shallow buttoning is normally worked onto padding with a firm foundation but, with care, it can also be worked onto padding with a webbing foundation, such as a dining chair.
Marking the design. Mark the design for the buttoning lightly in pencil or tailor's chalk onto the cover of the padding.
Attaching the buttons. Thread the needle with a long length of twine. Pass the needle through the padding from the top on the marked position and bring it out on the underside, passing it through a strand of webbing. Leave a long tail of twine on the top side of the padding.
Return to this length and thread the needle with it. Pass the needle through the button and pass the needle through the padding again, making a small stitch on the surface of the padding. Pull the twine right through and remove the needle.
Roll up a small piece of spare webbing or canvas and place it between the two lengths of twine on the underside of the webbing. Tie the ends in a slip knot (fig.9) and tighten knot around the little roll. The roll helps to prevent the knot from pulling through the webbing. Secure the knot firmly to prevent it from slipping and then cut off the excess length.

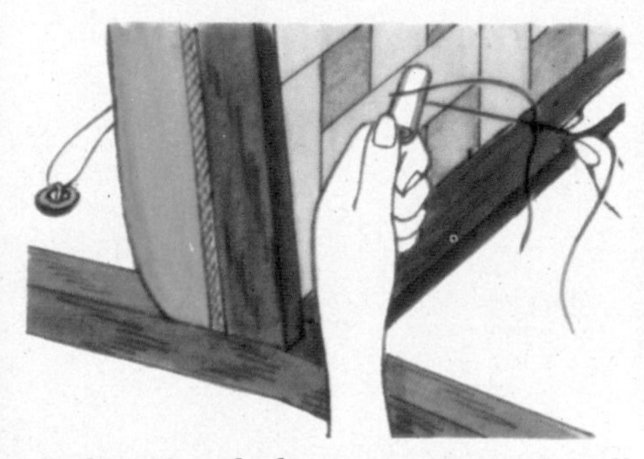

9. *Securing the knot around canvas roll.*

Graham Henderson

Shallow buttoning adds interest to this bedhead which is hung with flush mounts.

Decorative feather objects

2. *Feathers attached with a cross stitch.*

Feathers are by no means as fragile as they appear and the number of feather objects still around from earlier eras are proof of this. Besides their durability, their brilliant colors and unique textures make them an appealing material for a variety of purposes.

Attaching feathers

Feathers are attached to other surfaces by gluing and by sewing and the most suitable method depends on both the surfaces being decorated and the type of feathers used. On hard materials such as wood, for instance, it is always necessary to use a glue while on cloth you can use glue in some cases but sewing is generally preferable unless the feathers are extremely fine.

Gluing. Glue can be applied to the central shaft of each feather before it is pressed against a surface and this method is especially suitable for wing and tail feathers because they have sizable central shafts. Finer plumage can be attached by making a line of glue or spreading a coat of it onto a surface and pressing or dropping the feathers onto it. (The drop technique is used primarily for special effects in picture making.) Both techniques are quite simple.

Use a clear adhesive; for most items a general purpose type is suitable. Cloth, however, requires special milliner's glue available from milliner suppliers and some notions shops. This is a rubber based glue that dries clear.

1. *Feathers can be attached to fabric by stitching through central shaft.*

Sewing. Feathers can be stitched onto cloth by either piercing the central shaft with the needle and thread (fig.1) or with cross stitch at points near base of each feather (fig.2). When working a straight line, feathers can often be machine stitched if the plumage is not too fine to escape the needle's path.

Headdress

The most popular use of feathers has, of course, been in head-dresses and whether floating from the headband of a warrior or the hatband of a cavalier they have nearly always suggested an air of flamboyant self-importance. We even refer to a person's success as a 'feather in his cap'.

The most elaborate headdresses of all were produced by American Indians and making a headdress for a child's birthday or Christmas is bound to bring whoops of joy.

Traditional Indian head-dresses were made of eagle or turkey feathers, and turkey feathers could be used for this pattern although the fanciful variation shown would doubtless thrill an Indian chieftain or a child.

You will need:

1 black and white hornbill feather.
4 striped black turkey wing feathers.
4 speckled peacock wing feathers (or a selection of 9 other wing or tail feathers).
9 peacock tail feathers.
60 goose wing feathers.
46 turkey body feathers.
100cm (40″) curtain tape with draw-

string for gathering and pockets for pleats.
Hot water dye in blue and green.
Large scissors for trimming.
Needle and thread.
Sewing machine.

Begin by dyeing blue and green feathers according to instructions in Featherwork chapter 1, page 772, and on the dye packet. To get paler shades of blue you can leave some feathers in the dye bath for a shorter time or you can dye them separately in a prepared paler shade.

To make the headdress band pull out 30cm (12″) of drawstring from

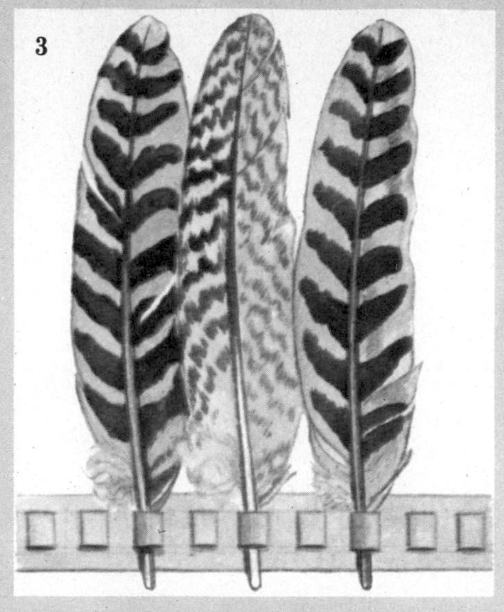

3. Feathers are secured in curtain tape.

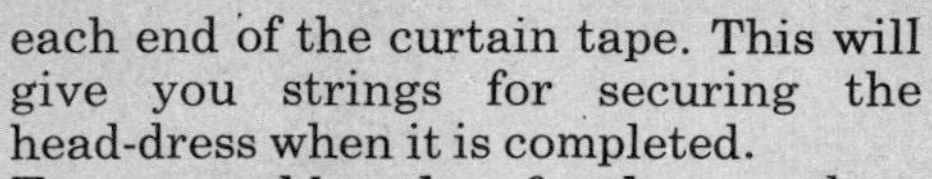
each end of the curtain tape. This will give you strings for securing the head-dress when it is completed.

To assemble the feathers, place the upright ones into the pockets of the tape (fig.3) in the following order: put the hornbill feather in the center of the tape. Next add the turkey and speckled peacock wing feathers on each side of the center so that they alternate and overlap slightly.

With the scissors trim the peacock

Alasdair Ogilvie

The headdress was made on a base of curtain tape. Design by Pamela Woods.

Steve Bicknell

Fanciful Indian head-dress would please a child or a chieftain.

The shimmering colors of a butterfly reproduced in feathers by Pamela Woods.

4. Tracing pattern for butterfly motif. The size shown opposite measures 25.5cm (10″) across and 19.5cm (7¾″) high.

Paul Williams

tail feathers almost down to the 'eyes' but leaving a little for sticking into the tape. Push a peacock feather into the pocket of the tape with each of the large upright feathers.

Then fill all the remaining pockets with pale blue and pale green goose wing feathers, arranged alternately. If any of these feathers are smaller than others then place them at the ends of the curtain tape.

When all the vertical feathers are in place, secure them firmly to the tape by machine stitching along the length of the tape. Keep the stitch small so that the needle will penetrate the central shafts of all the feathers.

The turkey body feathers are arranged horizontally along the face of the tape to cover it. Again the blue and green colors are alternated and in this case the feathers also overlap one another. These feathers are sewn in place by hand (fig.2).

Butterfly motif for lampshade

Feathers are not only beautiful when light is shining on them, but equally so when they are lit from behind for they take on a skeletal look which gives an interesting variation to their appearance.

The motif shown is made entirely by gluing. Peacock feathers are used but other types and colors will do as well.

You will need:

About 50 feathers for outline (blue body feathers).

About 24 feathers for inner line (green back feathers).

About 55 speckled feathers for main wing area (body feathers).

3 dark, flat feathers for butterfly back.

1 tail feather for antennae and eyes.

An all purpose clear adhesive.

Lightweight canvas or other material for backing.

Large scissors for trimming.

Feathers are applied in an overlapping fashion and they are glued down by applying a dab of glue to the central shaft only but before you begin to glue the butterfly remove any fluff from the feathers. You will be working only with the flat tips of the feathers.

☐ Trace the motif outline (fig.3) on the fabric backing and cut it out. The finished motif will be larger than the tracing pattern since the feathers should overhang the edges of the backing for the length of their fringe about 2.5cm (1″).

☐ Fill in the outline as illustrated with blue body feathers pointing outward over the edge of the backing.

☐ Next, make a row of green back feathers down the side of the wings, overlapping the base of the blue ones.

☐ Fill in the wings with speckled body feathers following the contours of the pattern.

☐ Trim three dark flat feathers and overlap them down the center spine to make the body.

☐ The antennae and the eyes are single bracts taken from a tail feather. The natural curve is sufficient for the antennae but the eyes must be curled by hand (according to the method described in Featherwork 1, page 772).

☐ Glue or sew the finished motif to a lampshade or, if you prefer, stick it to a windowpane or a piece of Plexiglas where the light can shine through it.

Steve Bicknell

Abstract pattern

Abstract means to 'draw from' or to 'select'. In an abstract pattern the intention is to convey the essence of something, and its significance, rather than what it looks like in real life or how it can be broken down geometrically.

There are no rules on how to draw abstract designs. It is more a question of looking at patterns around you: oil on water, light on soap bubbles, patterns made by hair, cloud formations or stone which has been weathered by wind and water.

Look at the illustrations here and, without reading the captions, see if you know what the photographs represent. Now read the captions and have another look at the photographs. Can you pick out which are the most important features of each one? Which pattern shows the stress lines of a hard impact? Which one is compact, solid and coiled around itself? Which one radiates in loops from the center? What effect does the painting have on you? Now try making a few abstract patterns yourself.

Experiment 1

You will need:
Newspaper, large sheet of white paper, water-based paints, inks or dyes, a paintbrush and a drinking straw.

☐ Spread the newspaper on the ground, put the white paper on top and mix up the paints or dyes.
☐ Drop the paint onto the paper to make splashes of color.
☐ Tilt the paper to make the paint run.
☐ The paint can be spread about by blowing through a straw across the surface of the paper.

Try again with another piece of paper and see what happens.

Experiment 2

You will need:
Piece of white cardboard with peephole cut out of the middle. Color magazines, white paper, pencil, crayons, felt-tipped pens.

☐ Move the cardboard over a page in the magazine, keeping your attention on the peephole. See what shapes and rhythms you can isolate through the peephole.
☐ Copy or enlarge what you see onto the sheet of paper and color in the pattern.

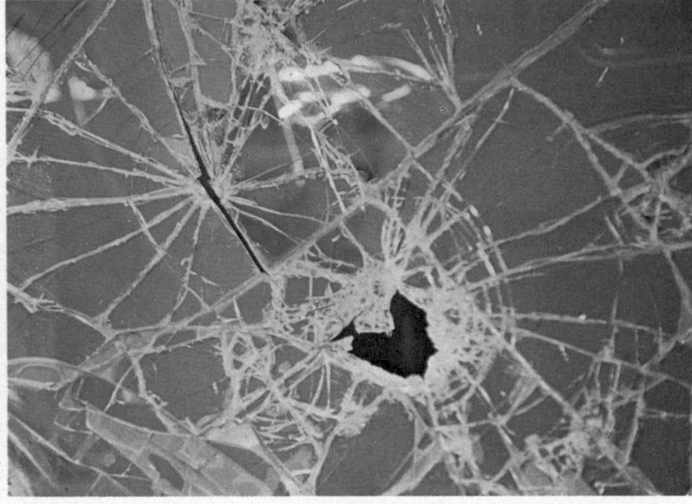

Mary Seyd

The windshield has been shattered by several hard blows.

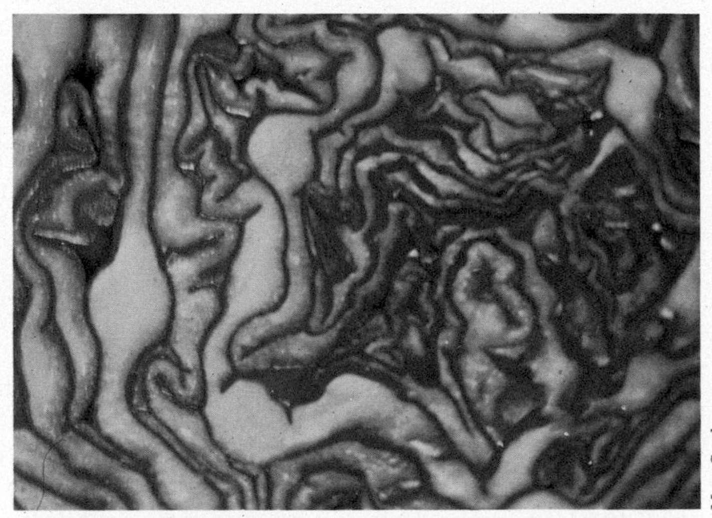

Mary Seyd

The closely-packed intricate layers of a cabbage.

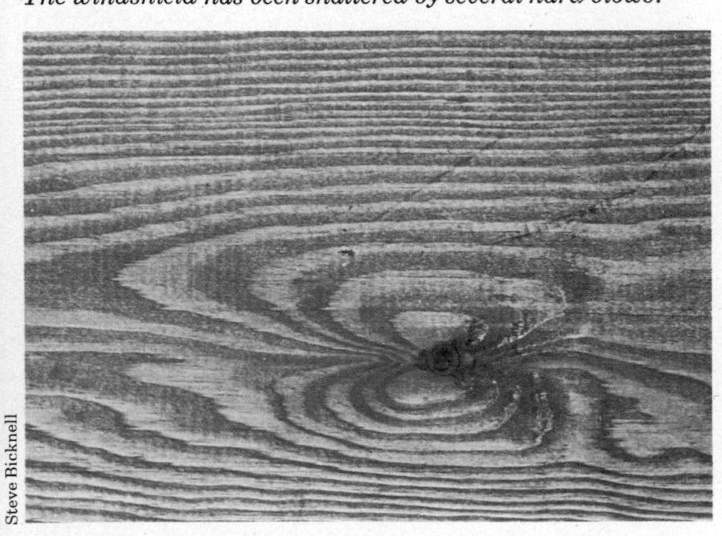

Steve Bicknell

Irregular growth lines surrounding a knot of wood.

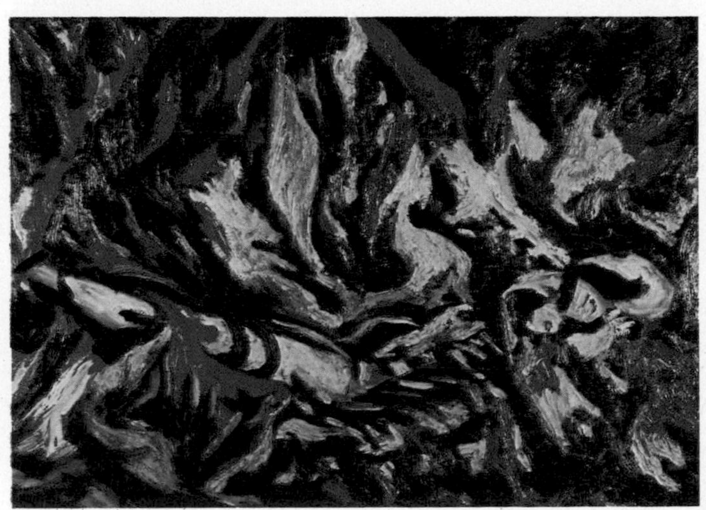

Snark

'The Flame' by Jackson Pollock.

Creative ideas 29

Ribbon violets

Here is a refreshing way to use gift-wrapping ribbon—make tiny 'violets' which can be used to decorate gifts or enhance a centerpiece of candles.

You will need:
16mm (⅝″) wide self-adhesive ribbon in mauve and yellow.
Pair of scissors.

Cut a 15cm (6″) length of mauve ribbon. Cut each end diagonally. Cut the same length of yellow ribbon and snip the ends into a fringe. Gently tear the ribbon along the snips into thin strips.

Fold the mauve ribbon into an S-shape and tie in the middle with a strip of yellow ribbon trimming ends close to the knot.

Repeat for second set of petals.

Kate Simiak

Criss-cross the two sets of petals and tie together in the center with yellow ribbon. Holding center of violet between forefinger and thumb, open out each petal-loop by inserting and opening scissors.

Attach to gift boxes with a small piece of double-sided adhesive tape.

For candle base obtain a square of floral foam and cover it with strips of ribbon held in place on the bottom with straight pins. Leave a space in the center and cut a hole into it for standing the candle.

Cover with violets stuck on with pins. Fill in any gaps with loops of ribbon secured in place with pins. Spray with flame proofing solution before using.

Roger Phillips

'Honeycomb' paper garlands

Cut and stuck with care, a little tissue paper will go a long way, so paper garlands are inexpensive and, in spite of their complicated appearance, surprisingly easy to make.
You could use slightly thicker paper, but the finished garlands would not be so elastic and would be difficult to pack flat again once used.
These very simply cut paper shapes can look quite spectacular with imaginative use of color when glued together on the 'honeycomb' principle.
Tissue paper is a fragile material, so don't cut too finely or the garland will quickly tear under its own weight. Too many cuts will also make the tissue paper difficult to unfold, and the garland may look spindly and thin when you have managed to unfurl it.
A few simple cuts are easier to do and, as you can see from the photographs, will produce very effective looking garlands with plenty of 'body'—which means they will stand up to wear and tear better than intricately cut designs.
Tissue paper is available in a truly splendid choice of shades, and there is no need to use only one or two colors. You could produce a gorgeous rainbow effect by using papers of four or more different hues. But do remember to plan you color sequence before gluing the cut out shapes together, and take care to follow the order you have decided on — a random assembly of mixed colors could look messy!
A simpler way to get a multi-colored effect would be to use one paper only — a toned tissue paper. Toned tissue papers are usually a graduation of shades of one color (from icy pale blue, through hyacinth to royal blue, for example) and can produce subtly exciting garlands.
Use the tracing pattern and follow the instructions for making the two illustrated examples. Use them as they are, or have fun adapting them for your own color schemes and shapes.

Orange and red garland

You will need:
Red and orange tissue paper.
Paper glue.
Small piece of cardboard.
Fine string or button twist, needle.
Paperwork scissors.

☐ Cut a pile of tissue paper shapes (fig.1) in orange and red.
☐ Stick them together in pairs, one orange to one red, with a very small dot of paper glue at points A B C D (fig.1). Let the glue dry thoroughly.
☐ Now stick each orange and red pair to another orange and red pair, this time placing the little dots of paper glue at the corners E F G H (fig.2).

White garlands make a delicate window frame without blocking out the light.

1
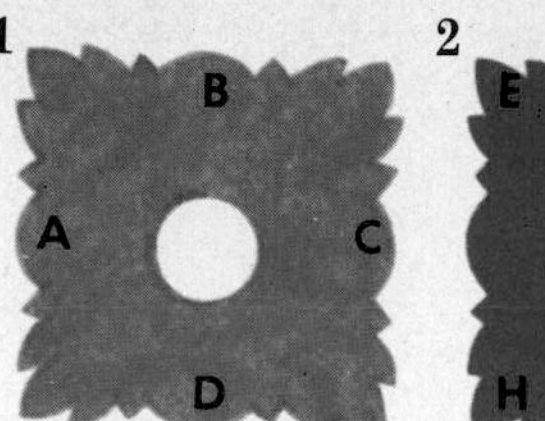

2
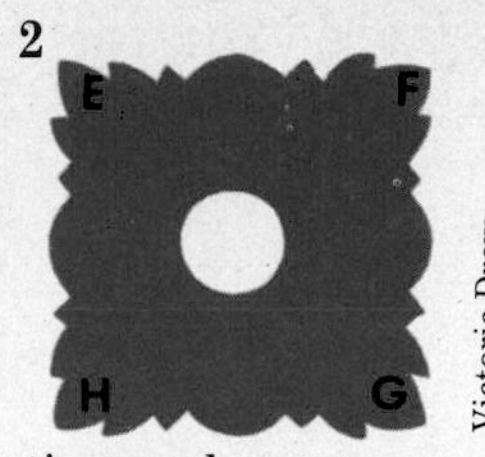

Victoria Drew

1. *Glue each red tissue shape to an orange one at points A B C D.* **2.** *Then glue each pair to the next at E, F, G, H. Below: tracing pattern shows only half of cut-out garland shape.*

☐ When all the shapes have been glued together and the garland has dried, reinforce it by gluing a small piece of cardboard to each end covering holes.
☐ Then strengthen the whole garland by threading a length of fine string or button twist through one cardboard end piece, down the center of the tissue garland, and out through the cardboard at the other end. Open your garland to its full extent to see how long your thread needs to be, then cut the thread accordingly. Knot it and make a loop from which the garland can be hung.

White curtain garlands

You will need:
White tissue paper.
Paper glue.
Cardboard.
Fine string or button twist, needle.
Paperwork scissors.

The more garlands you make for this, the more generous your curtain will look, but the use of a single color and a very simple repeated shape are the secrets of its charm.
☐ Cut a pile of tissue paper shapes as shown in fig.3.
☐ Stick them together in pairs, with a small dot of paper glue at points A B C D (fig.3). Let the glue dry thoroughly.
☐ Now stick one pair to another, this time running a small line of paper glue down the center E (fig. 4).
☐ Then proceed to reinforce the garland as described in the instructions for the orange and red garland.

3 4
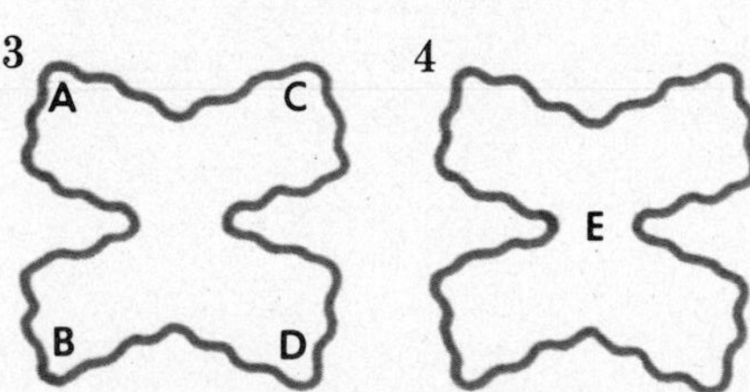

3. *Glue tissue paper shapes of the same color in pairs at points A B C D.*
4. *Then glue pairs to each other at E. Right: gay garland alternating red and orange tissue shapes. Multi-colored effects can be achieved by including more colored papers in the 'sandwich', or by using toned tissue paper.*

Dick Miller

Low-temperature enameling

There are two plastic enameling techniques available for craft work: cold enameling (Plastics chapter 4, page 230) and low-temperature enameling.
In low-temperature enameling plastic powders are fused to any number of surfaces such as metal, glass, wood, china, pottery and cardboard, either over a candle-heated hot-plate, under the broiler of a stove or in the oven itself.

Dick Miller

This method is an ideal way of enameling if you do not have a kiln. It is also safe, easy to use and, provided they are supervised, suitable for children. While it produces very attractive results it is not as hard or durable as traditional enameling so do not expect it to stand up to a vast amount of wear. You should avoid touching the surface of the enamel with a lighted cigarette or exposing the enameled object to high temperatures.

In its true setting: a sinuous dragon curls along a bamboo wall in front of a bonsai tree. Stencil from Japan; plaque designed by Kenneth Hammond.

You can buy kits containing low-temperature enameling tools and materials and this is probably the best introduction to this technique. Once you have had a little experience you can buy the plastic powders separately (which works out a lot cheaper in the long run). You will also be able to make your own blanks (surfaces to be enameled) from a variety of materials as this type of enameling sticks to most surfaces.

Peter Heinz

Another dragon stencil; this type of stencil is ideal for plastic enamels, or you can make your own stencils.

To enamel

You will need:

Enamel colors suitable for low-temperature enameling; these will be plastic powders.

A tube shaker or fine strainer for sprinkling the enamel.

A source of heat such as a candle-heated hot-plate (which comes in a kit) or a domestic oven. An oven will accommodate larger objects and is useful for blanks which may be damaged under a direct flame. It is easier, however, to work on the molten enamel while firing on the candle hot-plate. The broiler of a stove can also be used.

Blanks for enameling. These can be made of metal, wood, pottery, glass, cardboard or metal foil. The blank can be flat or it can be gently curved.

Small metal spatula or palette knife.

Tools for decorating the enamel. These are not at all specialized and can be improvised from objects found around the house such as a knitting needle, darning needle, small screwdriver or penknife, as well as thin copper wire and a small artist's brush. For stenciling either buy stencils, make them from cardboard or use a paper doily or piece of netting.

Asbestos square about 30cm x 30cm (1′ x 1′). Pot holders.

Liquid detergent, medium grade sandpaper and several sheets of white paper.

If you are making jewelry from metal blanks you will need a hand drill to make suitable holes and thin metal chain to thread through the holes. Alternatively, use an epoxy adhesive to stick jewelry findings to the back of the

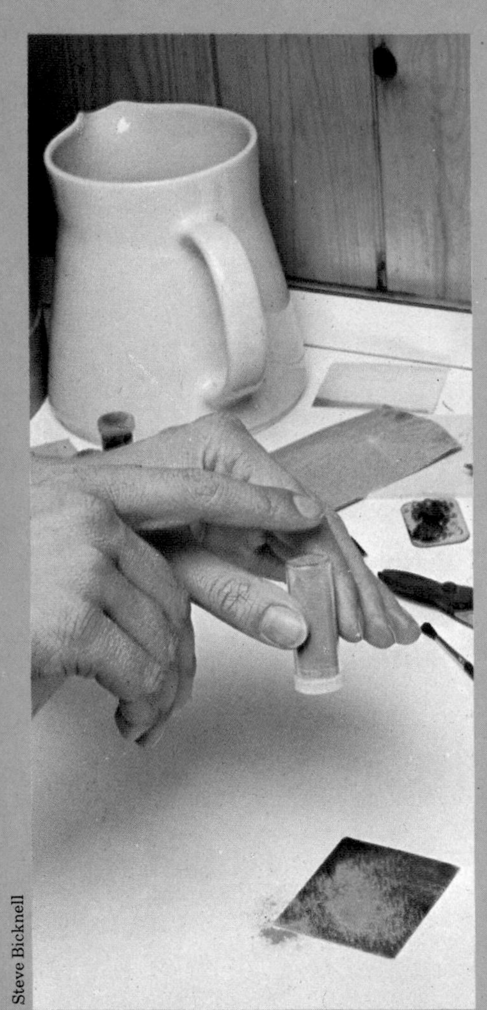

Steve Bicknell

The enamel powder is dusted over the blank with a shaker (above) or a strainer. The intention is to completely cover the surface of the blank with a thin, but even, coating of powder.

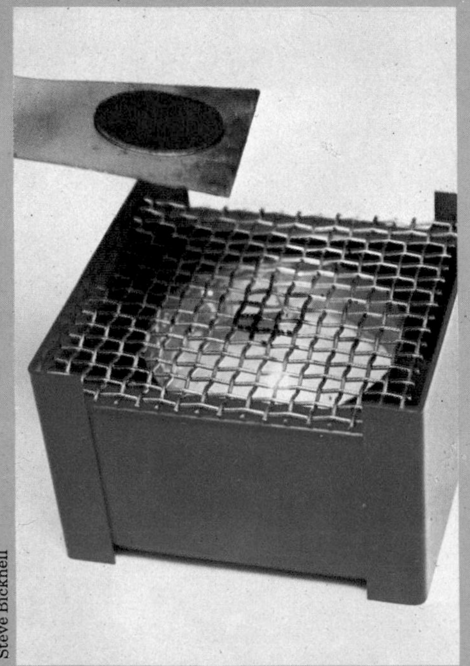

Steve Bicknell

A candle-heated hot-plate is especially intended for this type of low-temperature enameling.

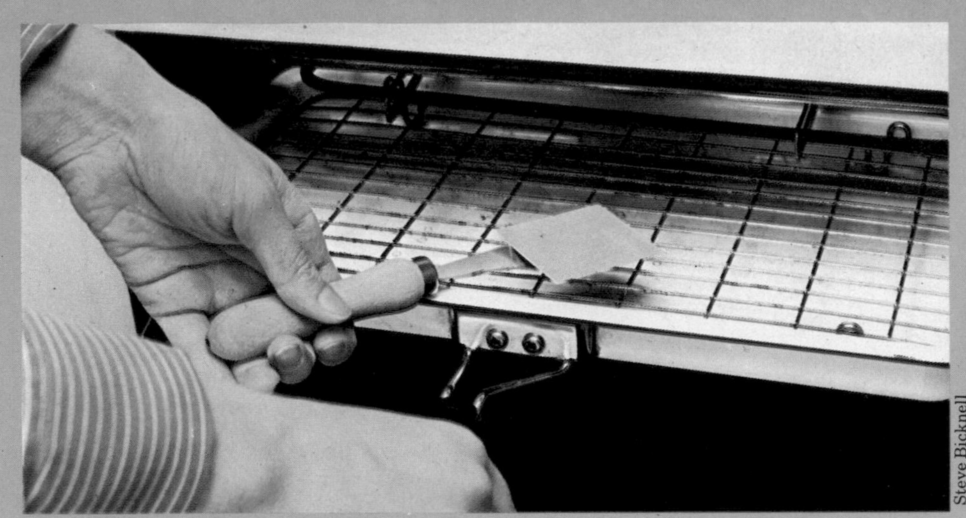

Steve Bicknell

Firing under the broiler: remove the blank when the enamel becomes shiny.

Peter Heinz

Larger designs or three-dimensional objects are best fired in an oven.

blanks for making such things as rings or pendants.

☐ Lay out all the tools and materials onto a clean, flat working surface.

The secret of success with all enameling is to ensure that the blank is perfectly clean and slightly roughened.

☐ Clean the blank with liquid detergent and rub the upper surface with sandpaper. Do not touch the blank with your fingers afterward as this will leave slightly greasy marks.

☐ Any holes needed for jewelry should be drilled at this stage.

☐ Light the candle if you are using a candle-heated hot-plate or turn on the oven if you are using this as a source of heat. Set the oven at 350°F or Mark 4 or set the broiler to Low. By the time you come to fire the blank the temperature will be correct.

☐ Lift the blank by its edges onto a sheet of white paper. The paper will catch any excess enamel powder which can then be poured back into its container.

☐ Dust the surface of the blank with a coat of enamel powder. This will form the base color. To do this shake the powder through a strainer or shaker onto the blank making sure that no metal is showing through and that the surface is evenly covered with powder.

☐ Using a spatula put the blank into the oven, under a broiler or on top of the hot-plate.

☐ Watch the blank continuously as it will fire in a few minutes or less than a minute if put under the broiler. Correct firing is very much a matter of observation as the time needed will depend on the size of the blank and the exact temperature of the oven or hot-plate.

It is important on the first firing to remove the blank from the heat as soon as the enamel takes on a shiny, 'orange peel' texture.

☐ Use the spatula or palette knife to transfer the blank to the asbestos square. Take care not to touch the surface of the enamel until it has cooled. Pottery and glass take longer to cool than metal.

☐ When the blank is cool enough to pick up place it on a clean sheet of paper and dust with a second coat of powder enamel. If you wish you may decorate the blank with a number of traditional enameling techniques.

☐ Fire again.

☐ You can dust the blank with a third, or even fourth, coat of powder but the last firing takes longer and the enamel should be left in the oven until it becomes smooth and glassy in appearance.

☐ Remove from the heat with the spatula and place on the asbestos mat. Once the enamel has fully set it cannot be refired again.

☐ Rub over any rough edges of the blank with sandpaper.

Dick Miller

Plastic enamels can be used to decorate the surface of a variety of objects such as small bowls, key-rings and pendants. The examples shown here demonstrate a number of techniques such as scrolling, stenciling, sgraffito, inlay and painting. Designed by Kenneth Hammond.

Decorating techniques

Sgraffito. A background color is first fired onto the blank. When cooled a contrasting color is dusted over and a design scratched into the dry powder using a needle or knitting needle. The blank is fired again.

Stencils. Fire a base color, cool and place a stencil over the blank. Sprinkle on a contrasting color. Carefully remove the stencil without disturbing the design. Alternatively, make a simple shape from cardboard and lay that on the pre-enameled blank. Sprinkle a second color over the surface and remove the cardboard. The shape will be reproduced in the base color. Fire the blank.

Scrolling. After firing the base color place some small piles of various colors on the blank with the end of a small screwdriver or penknife. Fire again and, while firing, draw the end of a knitting needle through the powder to intermingle the colors.

Inlay. Clean and degrease some copper wire with liquid detergent and bend into a design. Sprinkle the blank with the base color and lower the wire to the blank taking care not to disturb the powder. Fire. When the powder melts the wire becomes embedded in the enamel. You can also fire a second or third color into the compartments made by the wire.

Experiment by embedding other objects in the enamel. You will find that the object must be very clean, not too heavy and must have a reasonably large surface against the blank.

Painting. Make a mixture of enamel powder, water and liquid detergent (about four drops of detergent to a tablespoon of water) to a consistency resembling thick cream. Paint onto the blank with a small paintbrush. Wait until the 'paint' hardens before firing. This technique is particularly useful when coating a curved surface where the powder would otherwise run off.

A smock from head scarves

Headscarves can be used to make a lightweight smock top. You could take one color scheme for the yoke and sleeves and another for the 'body' or make it wholely from identical scarves. The pattern, which is drafted from your own measurements, would be just as effective if each piece was cut from different remnants of fabric to give a patchwork effect.

Taking your measurements

To do this successfully you will need a tape measure, a length of tape and the help of a friend. Use figs. 1a and 1b as a guide. You will need these measurements when making your patterns.
The first and one of the most important

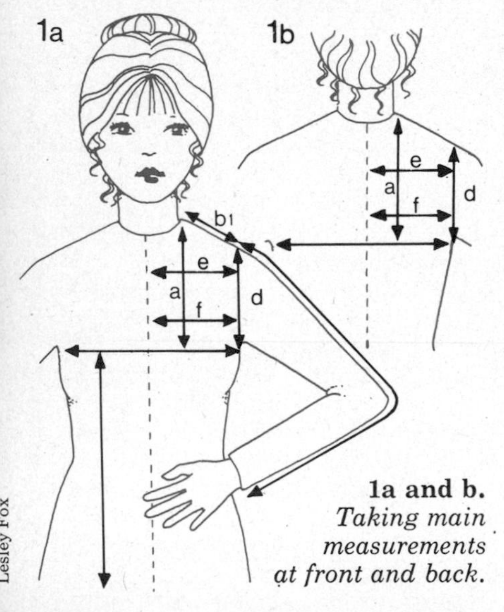

Lesley Fox

1a and b. *Taking main measurements at front and back.*

measurements to take is that around the body 5cm (2") above the bust point. Pin a length of tape around the body at this level and measure on the line of the tape. Leave the tape in position as a guide when taking other measurements.
At front take measurements at: base of neck at shoulder to the tape; shoulder at top of arm to tape; measurements for armhole from center front to armhole position 7.5cm (3") and 15cm (6") from base of neck at shoulder. Do the same for the back.
Measure shoulders from base of neck to top of arm and, with arm bent, measure from top of arm at shoulder to wrist.
Measure from tape to length of body required.

Making the pattern

Note: It is not necessary to make a pattern for the body piece as no shaping is necessary.
You will need:
Graph or other paper.
Pencil.
Ruler.
Make patterns for the front and back yokes and the sleeves following figs. 2-4. In each case start by drawing a horizontal line and then the center front, center back or shoulder to wrist line as shown.
Add on 1.5cm ($\frac{5}{8}$") seam allowance all

2. Front yoke pattern—*cut two in fabric.*
a, b_1, d, e and f correspond with measurements in fig.1a.
b = 7.5cm (3").
c = one quarter body measurement at tape, plus 1cm ($\frac{3}{8}$") ease.
g is 1.3cm ($\frac{1}{2}$") from center front.
x is 14cm ($5\frac{1}{2}$") from center front (position mark for skirt gathers).
y is 5cm (2") up from line c (position mark for sleeve ease).

3. Pattern for yoke back—*cut one in fabric with center back on fold. a, b_1, d, e and f correspond with measurements in figs.1a and b.*
b = 9cm ($3\frac{1}{2}$").
c = c on front yoke.
h = 2.5cm (1").
x is 14cm ($5\frac{1}{2}$") from center back (position mark for skirt gathers).
z is 7.8cm ($3\frac{1}{8}$") up from line c (position mark for sleeve ease).

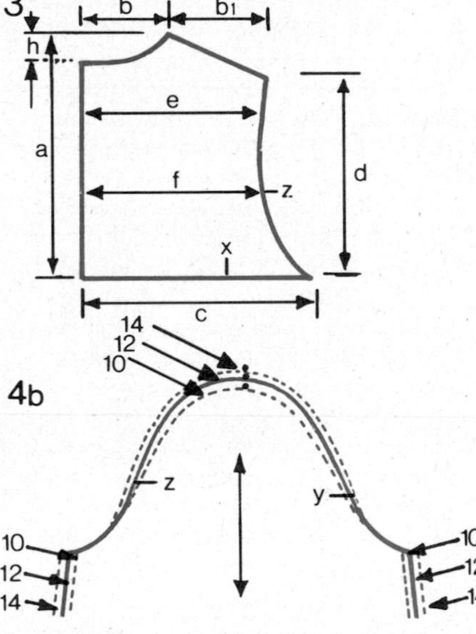

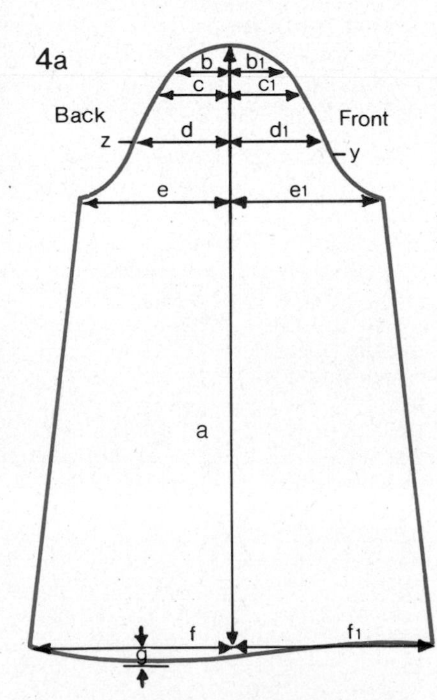

4a. Pattern for size 10 sleeve.
a = top of arm at shoulder to wrist (see fig.1a), plus 5cm (2").

b, c, d and e are 2.5cm (1"), 5cm (2"), 10cm (4") and 16.5cm ($6\frac{1}{2}$") below top of sleeve.
b = 6.5cm ($2\frac{1}{2}$"), b_1 = 5cm (2").
c = 7.8cm ($3\frac{1}{8}$"), c_1 = 7cm ($2\frac{3}{4}$").
d = 10.5cm ($4\frac{1}{8}$"), d_1 = 10cm (4").
e = 16.5cm ($6\frac{1}{2}$"), e_1 = 16.5cm ($6\frac{1}{2}$").
f = 21.5cm ($8\frac{1}{2}$"), f_1 = 21.5cm ($8\frac{1}{2}$").
y and z are 5cm (2") and 7.5cm (3") respectively above line e (position marks for ease).
g is 2cm ($\frac{3}{4}$") below line f.
Curve the lower edge of the sleeve as shown.

4b. Grading for sleeve head. *On successive sizes the shoulder point is 6mm ($\frac{1}{4}$") higher and line e is extended by 6mm ($\frac{1}{4}$") at each end.*

Trevor Lawrence

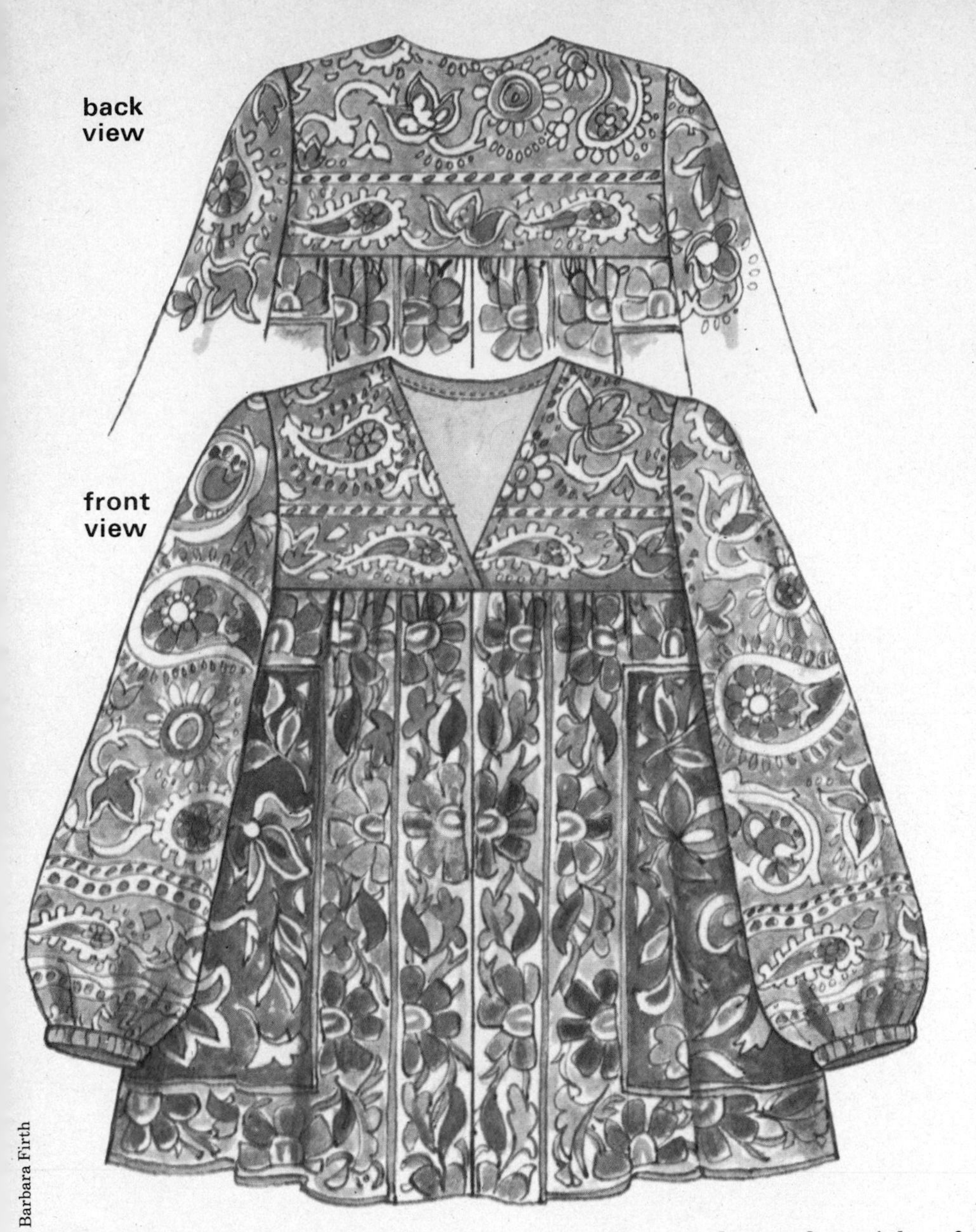

around each yoke piece except for the center back which is placed on the fold when cutting out in fabric. On the sleeve allow 1.9cm ($\frac{3}{4}$") on lower edge and 1.5cm ($\frac{5}{8}$") on other edges.

To make the smock

Finished length can be to your own requirements up to a maximum of about 86cm (34").
Remember that the seam allowance is 1.5cm ($\frac{5}{8}$").

You will need:
5 scarves 68.5cm (27") square.
1.3cm ($\frac{1}{2}$") wide matching bias binding for neck edge.
6mm ($\frac{1}{4}$") wide elastic tape for wrist edge.
Matching thread.

Preparing the pieces

☐ With right sides together, fold one scarf in half along the lengthwise grain. Pin back yoke pattern with center back on the fold and the front yoke pattern on the straight of grain. Cut out.

☐ Place two unfolded scarves with right sides together and straight of grain matching. Pin sleeve pattern pieces centrally onto them on the lengthwise grain. Cut out.

☐ Mark positions for gathers, position for ease on armholes and sleeves, top point on sleeve, center back of yoke and center front on each front yoke piece with tailor's tacks.

☐ The last two scarves make up the front and back body of the smock. Use the whole width, but cut each scarf to the length required, plus 3cm ($1\frac{1}{4}$") for seaming and hem.

☐ Fold each scarf in half lengthwise and on top edge of each mark fold with a single tailor's tack (sides of smock).

☐ Make a single tailor's tack at a point the same distance from each side as that of x from the side edge of the front and back yoke (gathering positions).

Yoke

☐ To prevent stretching, work a line of machine stitching along the front neck edges.

☐ With right sides together, pin, baste and machine stitch shoulder seams and sides.
Smooth and press seams open (fig.5).

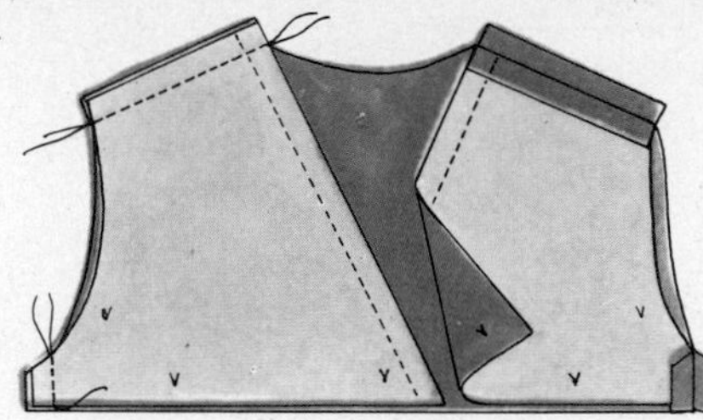

5. *Shoulder and side seams stitched.*

☐ Unfold one edge of bias binding and, with right sides together, pin, baste and machine stitch to the neck edge of yoke, matching fold line of binding to stitching line of yoke (fig.6).

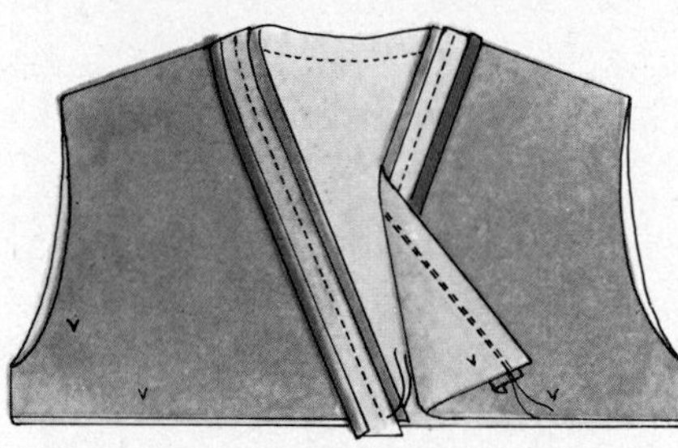

6. *Edge of binding stitched to neck.*

☐ Trim turning on neck edge level with the edge of the binding. Clip neck curves.

☐ Turn bias binding to the inside of neck edge, baste (fig.7a) and press.

☐ Topstitch 1cm ($\frac{3}{8}$") in from the edge all around neck, to secure the binding (fig.7b).

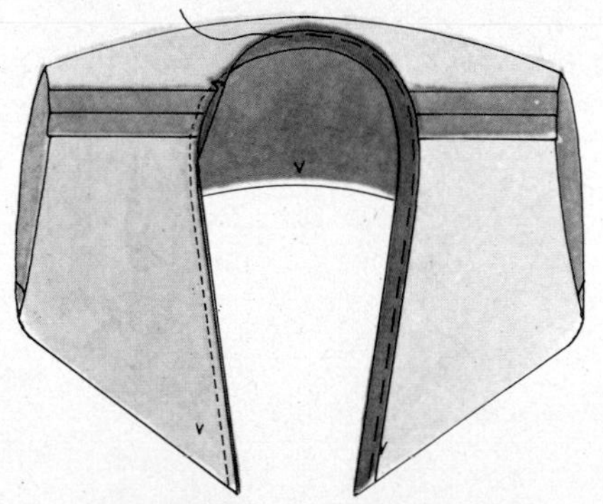

7a. *Basting binding in position.*

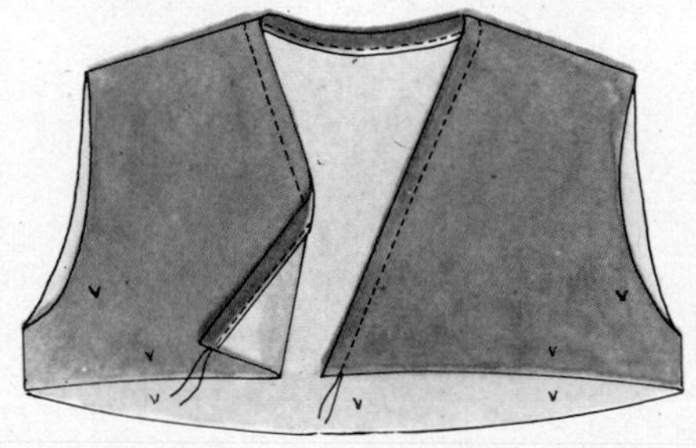

7b. *Binding secured with topstitching.*

Body

☐ With right sides together, pin, baste and machine stitch the center front and center back seams from hemline upward. Press seams open.

☐ Work two rows of gathering across front and two rows across back between marks indicated on front and back of body.

Joining the two parts

☐ With right sides together and matching sides, center front, center back and gathering positions, pin body to yoke. Pull up gathers to fit between the marks. Baste body to yoke (fig.8).

8. *Body pinned to yoke, with gathers pulled up to fit. Then body and yoke basted together.*

☐ Try on smock and check that back skirt does not droop. If it does correct as described in Sewing chapter 9, page 716.

☐ Machine stitch along line of basting, trim seam and smooth turnings together. Press upward.

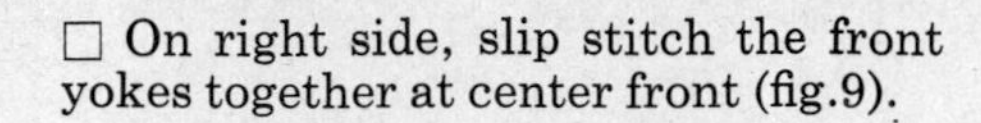

☐ On right side, slip stitch the front yokes together at center front (fig.9).

9. *Slip stitching front yokes together.*

Sleeves (make two)

☐ Work two rows of gathering stitches around the sleeve head on stitching line, between marks indicated.

☐ With right sides together, pin, baste and machine stitch the sleeve seam. Smooth seam and press open (fig.10).

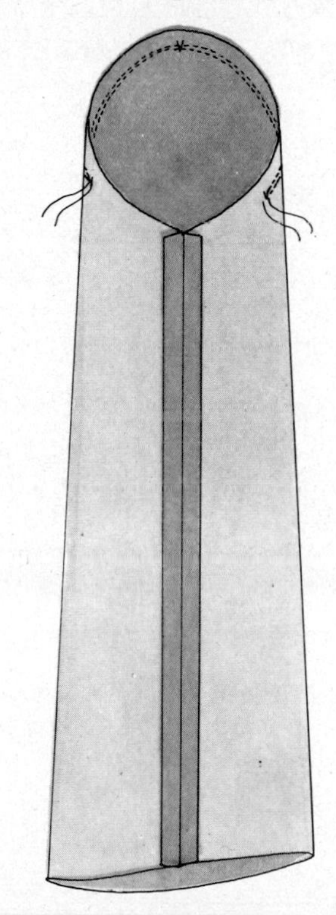

10. *Sleeve seam stitched and pressed.*

☐ For the sleeve hem, turn in 6mm (¼") and then 1.3cm (½"). Pin, baste and machine stitch close to the inner edge leaving a small opening at the underarm seam for inserting elastic tape.

☐ With right sides together, matching ease positions, underarm seams and shoulder point on sleeve to shoulder seam, pin the sleeve into the armhole, easing in fullness to fit. Baste and stitch with sleeve uppermost (fig.11).

11. *Sleeves stitched into armhole, with sleeve uppermost.*

Smooth turnings together and press toward the sleeve.

Finishing off

☐ Cut a piece of elastic tape for each wrist, long enough to fit the wrist comfortably, plus 2.5cm (1") for joining. Thread tape through each sleeve hem and stitch the ends together by hand. Slip stitch the opening in the hem.

☐ Make a rolled hem to finish the smock.

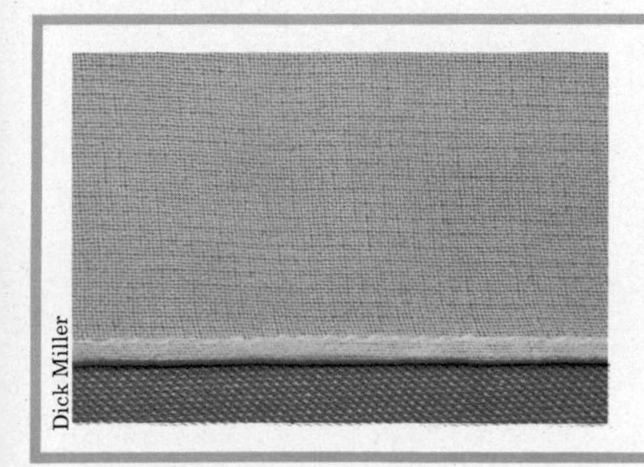

Rolled hem

This is used on handkerchiefs and scarves and on any very light fabric when an 'invisible' hem is required.

Work a line of machine stitching 6mm-1.3cm (¼"-½") from the raw edge. Trim close to stitching. Roll fabric between thumb and forefinger, several inches at a time, and then stitch in position with tiny, neat slip stitches. Do not baste or press.

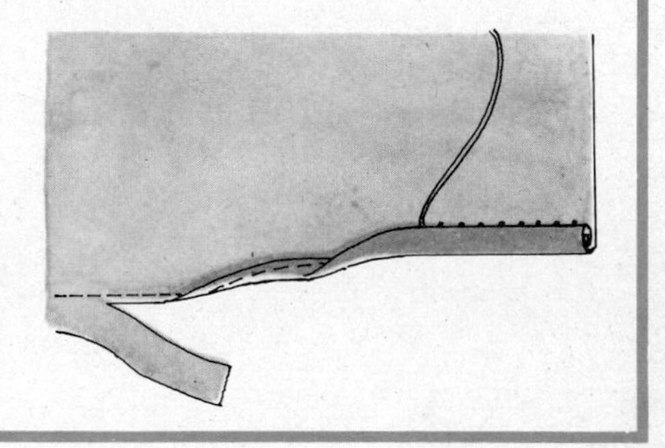

Create your own tapestry designs

By this stage you should be sufficiently familiar with all the basic tapestry shapes (Weaving chapters 8 page 632 and 9 page 652), to enable you to work on your own designs. This can be done by modifying and combining one or more of the techniques already learned. You will find that your own designs, whether pictorial or abstract, can be broken down into straight lines, diagonals or curves in one way or another. You can draw a cartoon before you start as shown for the totebag (fig.3, page 827), or you may find it more exciting to create the design on the loom itself. Before you start weaving your own designs, you will need to have some guidelines in the selection and spacing of your yarns.

The warp

The warp should be made of a strong thread, relative to the size and heaviness of the weaving to withstand the tension and support the weight. It should also be reasonably smooth to allow the weft to be beaten down easily. The warp yarn must have some elasticity so that it can recover from the stretch imposed when making a shed. The yarn should also have a good twist as this increases strength and soft yarns with little spin are liable to fray and break during the weaving process. Two of the most suitable yarns are cotton twine and linen warp yarn.

Cotton twine is strong, elastic and easy to dye.

Linen warp yarn must have a good twist otherwise it will fray, but it is strong and its natural color is very pleasing. It is a little more difficult to handle having little elasticity and should be avoided until some experience is gained.

Warp color

The warp color is unimportant where the warp is to be completely covered by the weft. With more experimental kinds of weaving such as weaving with unusual materials or objects, the warp may not be completely covered and would therefore need to be chosen with this in mind.

Warp spacing or set

The closeness of the warp threads to each other determines the thickness of the tapestry to be woven. For a fine weaving with detailed and precise shapes a closely set warp is necessary. This could contain as many as twenty warp ends per 2.5cm (1″) or more. However, to weave something so fine is very time-consuming and generally results in the loss of texture and yarn qualities. In tapestry, the average spacing of the warp ends is between four and twelve ends per 2.5cm (1″).

With the frame loom made in Weaving chapter 6, page 572, the tacks were spaced at 1.25cm (½″) intervals and the warp for the sampler was eight ends per 2.5cm (1″). If a set of four ends per 2.5cm (1″) is required, simply wind one warp thread around each tack with an extra thread each end to form the double thread of the selvage (fig.1).

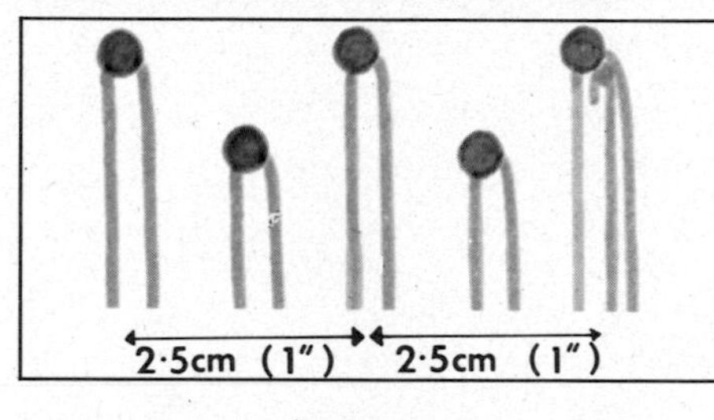

1. *A set of four ends per 2.5cm (1″) with the extra thread for the selvage.*

For twelve ends per 2.5cm (1″) wind three threads around each tack. (See Weaving chapter 6, page 572 for warping instructions.)

Weft yarn

Before starting to weave, a choice of weft yarn must be made. It is always extremely interesting to experiment with yarns of differing colors, thicknesses and textures (Weaving chapter 5, page 374).

A rough guide to the thickness necessary in tapestry is that the weft yarn should just fill the space between two consecutive warp ends with only a slight clearance on each side.

In the sampler, which was shown in Weaving chapter 7, page 600, a warp spacing of eight ends per 2.5cm (1″) was chosen and the weft used was 3-ply rug yarn. As the weft thickness is dependent on the warp spacing, a spacing of four ends per 2.5cm (1″) needs a weft of twice that thickness. Conversely, a closer warp needs a finer weft.

Combining weft threads

The required thickness of weft can be achieved by using several thin threads together instead of a single thick thread. When using several threads together be sure to wind them onto the bobbin with an even tension to prevent some threads becoming longer than others while weaving.

This technique can be particularly interesting when working with color if several different colors or tones of the same color are blended together. This can be used to create a shading effect between two dominant colors. Alternatively, you can use hatching. This is the term given to irregular lines and areas of color, a form which was used extensively on medieval tapestries. Hatching gives an indistinct shading effect (fig.2).

Victoria Drew

2. *Hatching, or joining two colors irregularly, produces a shading effect that is very effective.*

General tips

Try to keep your first design simple — to be over ambitious at this stage may well result in failure.

Avoid long, thin, vertical lines in the design. Shapes and lines are so much easier to weave across than upward that if a design has many upright features it should be woven sideways.

Do not weave individual shapes higher than about 10cm (4″) without filling in the background and always weave slightly higher than the outline on the cartoon to allow for beating down.

When weaving your own designs, begin the tapestry with a plain band of at least 2cm (¾″). This spaces the threads evenly across the warp and gives you something to turn under after the weaving has been taken off

Four variations on a landscape theme woven in the one tapestry and showing the subtle effects that can be achieved by using a multitude of closely related colors. Designed by Anna Goues.

the loom. If you want your design to have a fringe without the band, you can simply pull out the first few rows after the weaving is finished.

Keeping an even width

One of the commonest problems experienced by beginners is the gradual decreasing in the width of the tapestry. The narrowing process is so slow that it can go by unnoticed until it is too late. Keep a tape measure at hand and check continually as the only remedy is to rip out and start again.
The cause of this fault is usually too much tension in the weft. Do not forget that the weft thread must have enough slack to go around each warp end. Always leave the loop of weft thread as mentioned in Weaving chapter 7, page 600 before beating down. If you have problems, also check that you have a thick enough weft in relation to your warp spacing.

The tote bag

This is an excellent project to try after the sampler as it gives practice in weaving diagonals and curved shapes.

One side of the totebag is woven on the frame loom using tapestry techniques. It is backed with suede and has suede gussets. Instructions for weaving the tapestry are given below.

The weaving measures 54cm x 40cm (21½"x16") to make a bag 50cm x 40cm (20"x16").
You will need:
A 100gm (¼lb) skein in each of five different colors of 2-ply rug yarn. Orange, rust, brown, cream and slate gray were used in the bag illustrated, but as some suppliers only sell non-

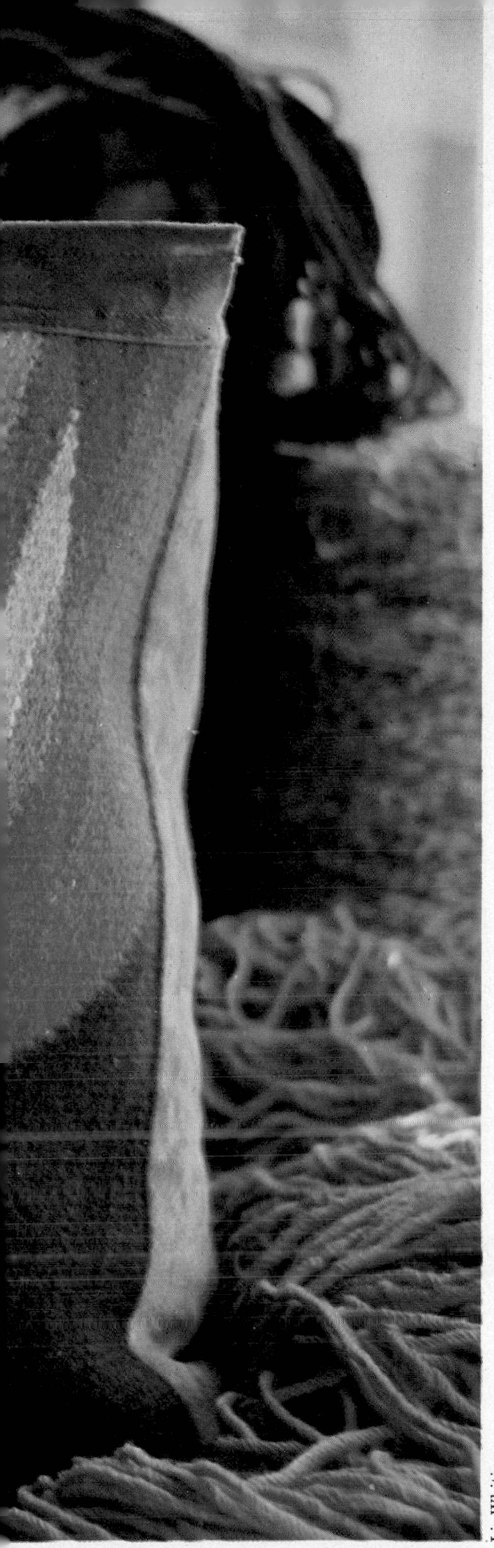

Liz Whiting

repeatable colors in order to keep their prices down you may have to adapt your color scheme and choose from suppliers' current stock.
Medium thickness cotton twine for the warp.
Frame loom (see Weaving chapter 6, page 572).
Finishing nails or tacks.
Upholstery needle.
Silk or synthetic sewing thread.

☐ As a set of six ends per 2.5cm (1″) is needed, knock another set of finishing nails into the reverse side of the cross bars on the frame loom. They should be 8mm (⅓″) apart and staggered as shown in Weaving chapter 6, page 572. It is well worth doing this, even if you do not plan to make up the tote bag as a set of six ends per 2.5cm (1″) is a very useful alternative to four or eight ends per 2.5cm (1″).

☐ Warp up your frame with the cotton twine taking the warp once around every finishing nail and remembering the extra selvage thread at each end. Your warp should measure about 42cm (16½″).

☐ Make a full size cartoon by copying the design (fig.3). Each square represents 2.5cm sq (1″ square).

☐ Weave 2cm (¾″) of plain tapestry weave. The color is irrelevant as this section merely spaces the warp threads evenly and will be lost in the turning when making up the bag.

☐ The bag is woven on its side. Follow the cartoon, remembering to weave slightly above the outline to allow for beating down.

☐ The curved shapes are woven using a combination of diagonals and vertical joining as in section 8, Weaving chapter 9, page 652.

☐ In the last section where there are vertical upright joins, weave the three areas A, B and C separately leaving slits.

As the areas build up, sew the pieces temporarily together, using an upholstery needle and a piece of contrasting yarn.

☐ Finish with 2cm (¾″) of plain tapestry weave.

☐ Cut the piece off the loom. No knotting is necessary as the weaving will be secured when sewing up the bag.

☐ Rip out the temporary stitches and sew up the slits on each side of B and C carefully using a strong, fine silk or synthetic thread.

☐ Use the tapestry as if it were a piece of material when making up the bag. Line the bag with strong cotton and use suede for the gussets at sides and bottom as well as for the back of the bag. The top suede pieces to which the handles are attached can be strengthened with a metal or wooden rod.

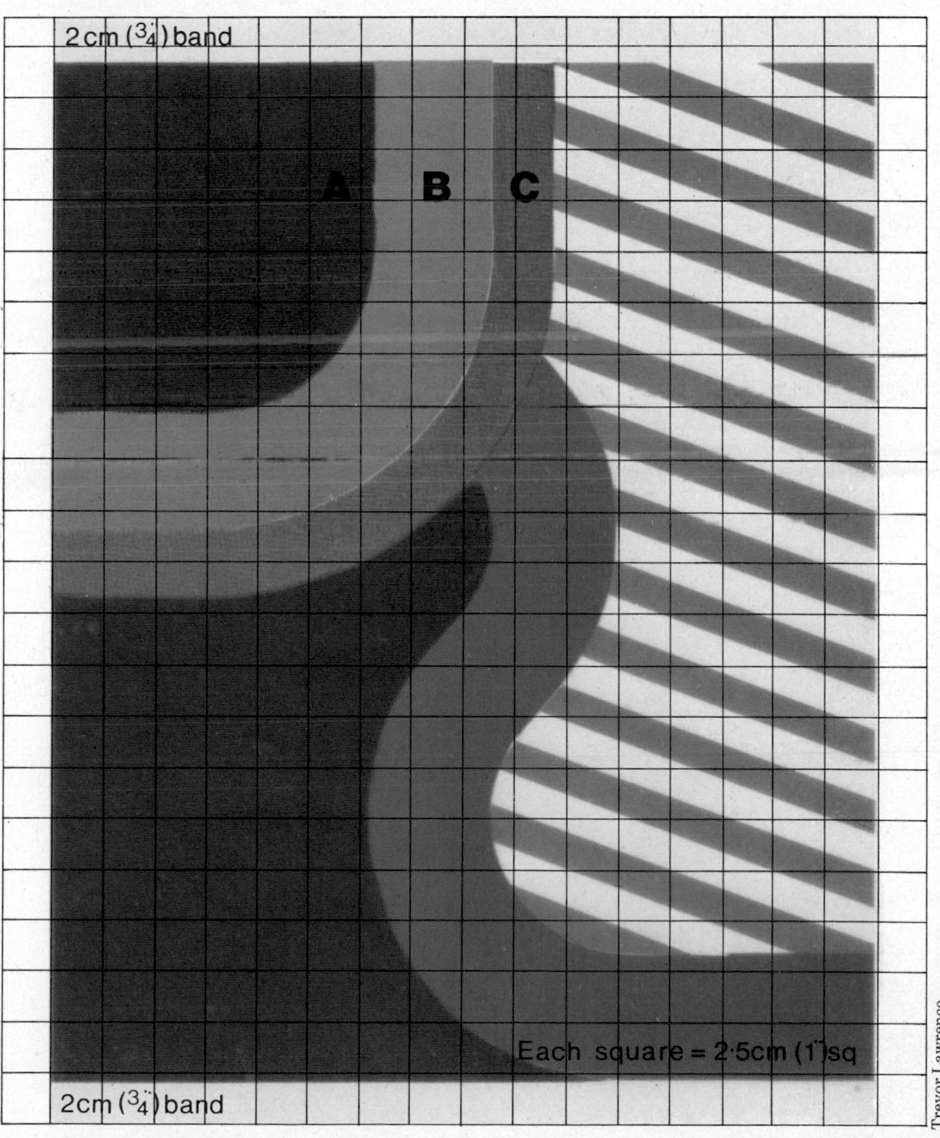

Trevor Lawrence

3. *Make a full-size cartoon to hang behind your loom as an accurate guide.*

Making a linoleum cut

Linoleum printing is derived from wood cuts, one of the oldest forms of printing and it works in much the same way. You make your design by carving away unwanted parts of a block — in this case, linoleum — then cover the surface of the block with ink and press paper against it to print the design. The sections that have been gouged out receive no ink and print white (or the color of the paper). The contrast makes the printed design. Linoleum is, of course, far easier to cut than wood and, nowadays, is cheaper as well.

Equipment

The equipment required for linoleum cutting is simpler than that required for other traditional forms of printing and all materials can be bought from art supply shops and some craft shops. Kits are also on the market containing all the basic tools and materials.

Linoleum cutters are gouging tools specially designed for engraving linoleum blocks. They are shaped to make U and V cuts and come in several sizes. To begin, you should have a small and medium-sized V-shaped cutter and a small and fairly large U-shaped one. Tools can be bought either with individual handles or with interchangeable cutters which fit into the same handle.

To sharpen tools use an oilstone preferably and rub it gently against the outside edges so as not to bend the blade. Inside edges can be sharpened with a slip, as very narrow oilstones are called. Triangular slips are available for V shapes.

Craft knife, such as a Stanley knife or linoleum cutting knife, is essential for cutting linoleum blocks to size.

A printing roller and a slab to roll out inks on are also needed and small, cheap rollers are available for this purpose. The slab can be a sheet of glass, Formica or Masonite.

Printing paper. Construction paper is suitable for linoleum cut printing and there are various Japanese tissues made especially for block printing but these are more expensive. It is worthwhile experimenting with all sorts of papers but avoid very shiny paper as this is non-absorbent and consequently does not take ink sufficiently well.

Linoleum should be the old-fashioned, canvas-backed matt finished type, not the vinyl flooring which is commonly used today. Genuine linoleum suitable for linoleum cutting can be bought in art supply shops usually in several

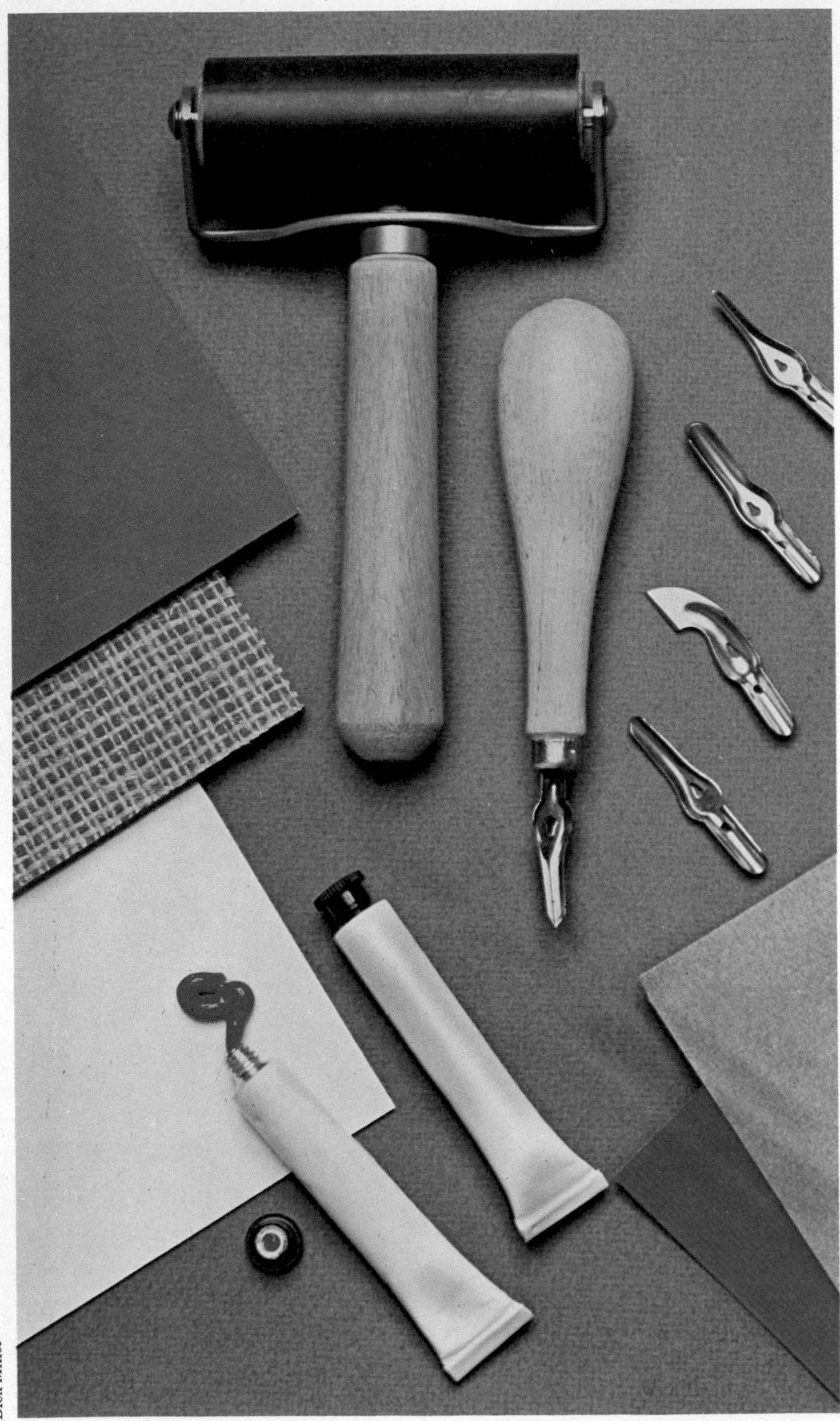

Dick Miller

Linoleum cuts are made by gouging out parts of a linoleum square, inking the surface and printing it. The materials needed are shown on the left: canvas-backed linoleum, roller and slab, cutting tool and inter-changeable cutters, ink and paper.

different sizes ranging from a small square the size of your hand up to a meter (yard) or so. The larger quantities can be cut to the size you need with a craft knife.

Inks. Use either oil-based printing inks which are cleaned up with turpentine or printing water colors, cleaned up with water. Both inks are available in a good range of colors. For mixing inks you will need a palette knife or old table knife and some rags for cleaning up.

Printing press or burnisher. To make a good print you will require pressure and this can be achieved either by burnishing or rubbing the back surface of the paper with the back of a tablespoon handle or the bottom of a glass. Alternatively, you can use a small screw-down printing press or for small prints, an inexpensive flower press.

How to cut a linoleum block

Before you begin to cut your first design experiment a bit with what sort of cuts your tools will make. See how many different lines and textures you can make and remember that the purpose of your tools is to gouge out the parts of the block that you do not want to receive ink. It is by recessing these areas that the ink is prevented from reaching them when it is rolled on to the surface of the block.

To cut: hold the ball of the handle against your palm and guide the tool with your thumb and forefinger, the V or U turned upward. Push the tool gently forward to make a groove.

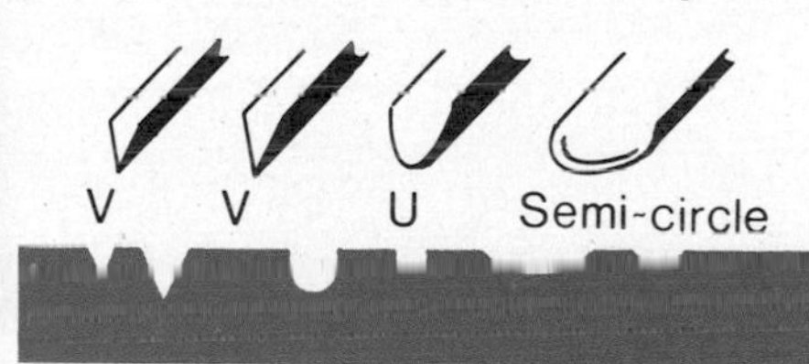

1. *Linoleum cutters are normally V- and U-shaped. The diagram above shows the grooves different cutters make.*

V-shaped tools will leave a pattern that will print a line the width of the V at the top. By turning the block as you go you will be able to make a curved line. U-shaped gouges give a wider line and can also be used to create a pebbled effect. Broad U or semi-circular gouges are useful for removing large areas. **The angle of the cuts** should slant upward as shown in fig.2 so that the printing surface of block remains firm. **To avoid cutting your fingers** in case the tools should slip, keep the hand holding the linoleum block behind the cutting hand as often as possible. **Begin with the peacock motif** shown and cut a piece of linoleum the same size as your design, in this case 8cm x 10cm (3⅛″x4″). It is easiest to cut through the burlap backing with a knife and then crack the linoleum apart. Trace the pattern (fig.3) onto the linoleum block and, using the gouges indicated in the diagram, cut away unwanted parts of the block as indicated with the small U- and small and medium V-shaped gouges.

2. *Always make the slanting type grooves (right), otherwise the printing area will be weakened from beneath.*

3. *Tracing pattern and cutting instructions for peacock shown below and next page. Short cuts render the pebbly background evident in the finished print.*

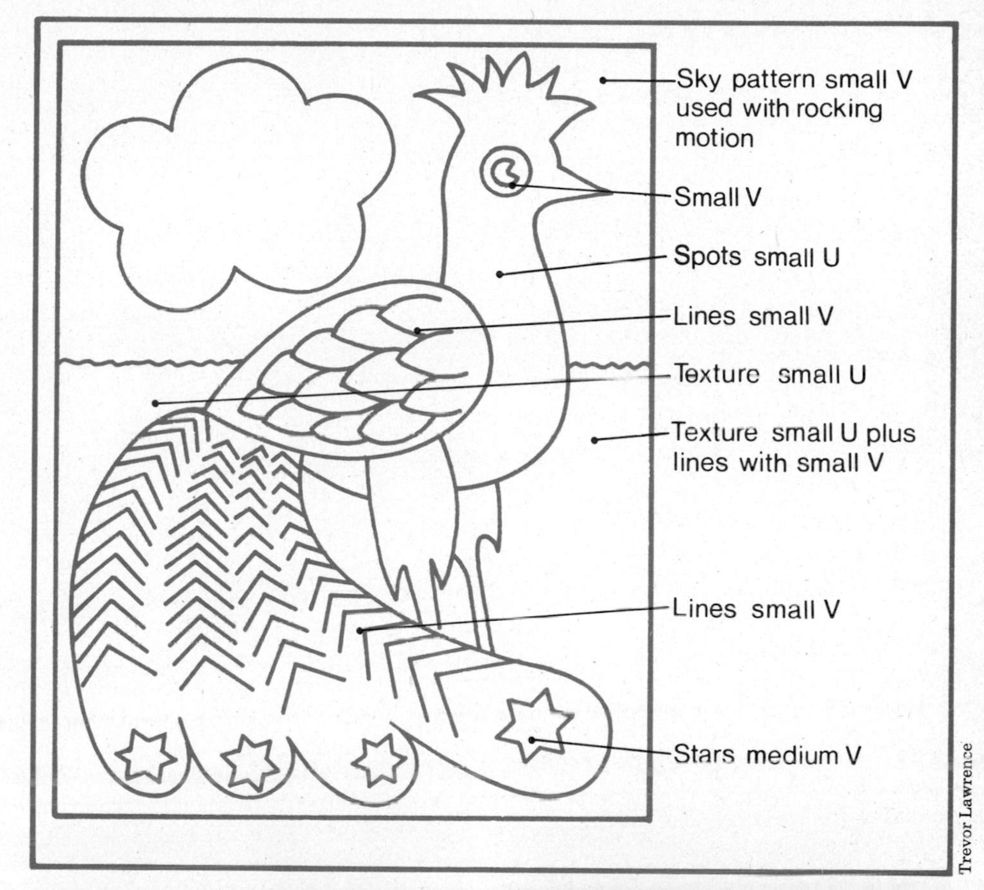

Trevor Lawrence

The peacock design must first be traced on a block of linoleum the same size.

The design is made by gouging out areas of the linoleum block.

When you have finished cutting your block always make sure there are no loose bits of linoleum left on the block as these will stick to the roller, mess up the ink and spoil your print.

How to print

Before you begin to ink your block make sure you have plenty of table space including an area on which your wet prints can be laid out to dry. Spread newspaper or old cloth over working surface. Once you have inked the printing block you will have to proceed to print so cut paper to size now, allowing a generous margin all around.

Preparing the ink. Squeeze a line of ink the length of your roller onto the inking slab. Now roll this out, rolling in several directions to make sure the ink is distributed evenly.

Roll ink from the slab onto the surface of your linoleum block, again rolling in different directions and re-charging the roller with ink as necessary.

To print by burnishing, place a piece of printing paper on the inked block and gently but firmly rub with a spoon handle or other burnishing tool, working from the center outward. If you are printing on delicate paper such as Japanese paper do not burnish directly on the printing paper as it may tear. Place a thin sheet of white paper on top and then burnish.

Do not rip the printed paper straight off the block. Lift a corner carefully to see if more burnishing is needed. The paper will flop back again into the right place.

To print in a screw-down press you will need two pieces of stiff cardboard which will fit inside the press. Put a flat pad of newspaper on top of one sheet of the cardboard. Then put your printing paper on this and put the inked surface of your block face down on the printing paper. Cover this with the other sheet of cardboard and put the whole sandwich into the press. Apply pressure by screwing down the top of the press. It is necessary only to nip or press it for a moment; there is no need to leave it sitting in the press.

Reprinting. After taking one print, simply re-ink the block and proceed again. You don't have to clean the block between prints. Proceed to make as many copies as you wish and when you have finished clean up all equipment and the block with the appropriate solvent.

Facing page: peacock note cards can be printed in a variety of colors by using different colored papers and printing inks. Alternatively a limited edition of prints can be made on white construction paper and presented as gifts. Peacock design is by Janet Allen.

To print, ink must first be rolled out evenly on a slab in different directions.

The ink is then rolled from the slab onto the surface of the linoleum block.

Paper is lowered onto the surface of the inked block and then burnished.

When the paper is gently peeled away the finished print is revealed.

All about power tools

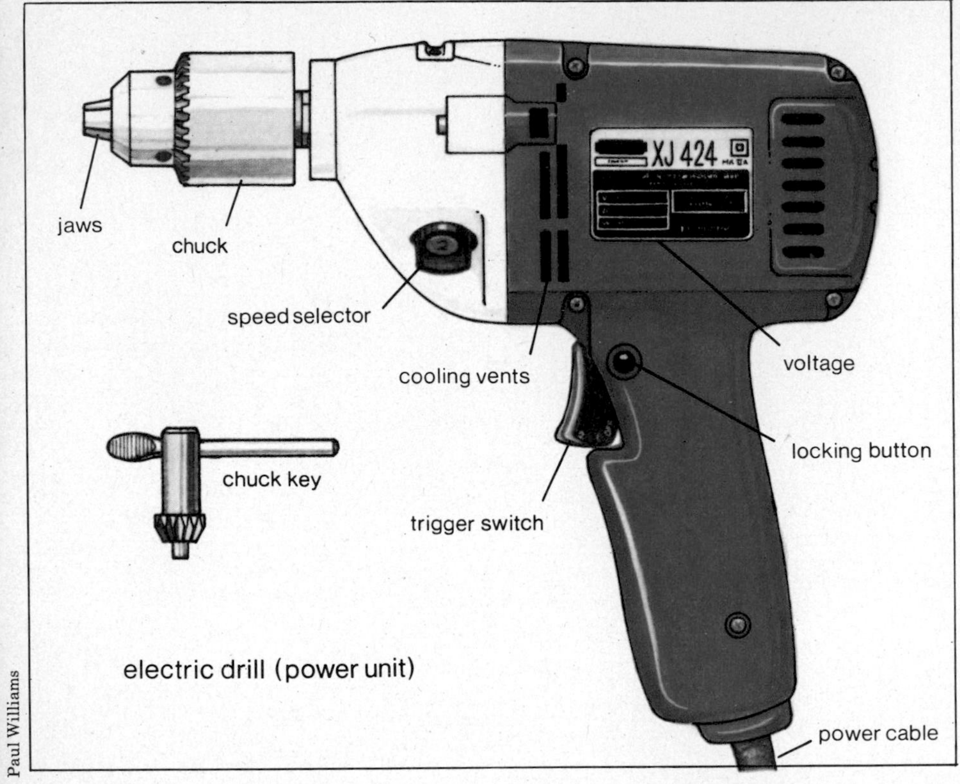

Paul Williams

1. The power unit or electric drill and chuck key which is used to open and close the jaws which hold the bits.

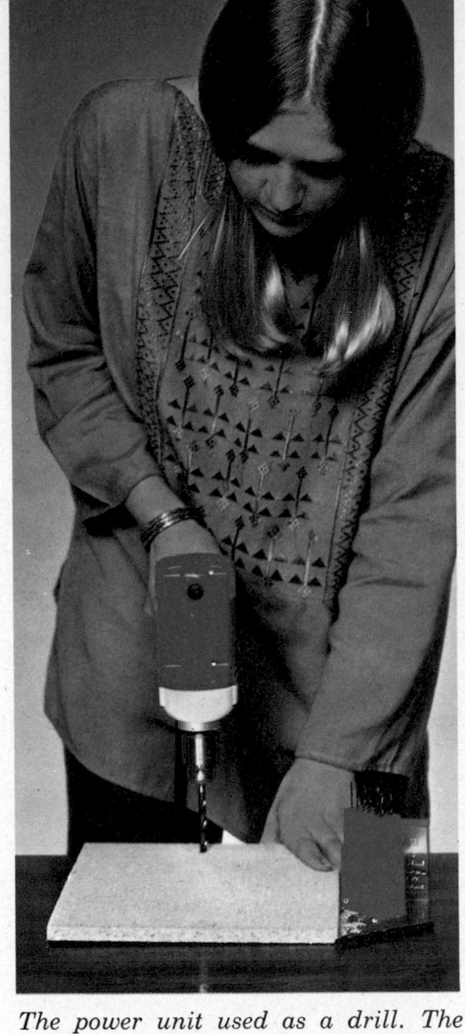

Peter Heinz

The power unit used as a drill. The correct bit must be used when drilling into wood, masonry and metal otherwise the bit will be damaged.

Most of the carpentry jobs around the house can be done well using hand tools and it is a mistake to imagine that very sophisticated machinery is needed to do things well. After all, the antique furniture much admired today was made entirely with hand tools, which allow you to retain a sense of feeling for the natural wood.

However, portable power tools save time and energy for the home craftsman or woman especially when repetitive work is planned. Women, especially, find that much as they may enjoy carpentry, the sheer physical effort defeats them. So a power tool, used properly, can take out a lot of the slog, enabling you to spend more time on the skillful and interesting aspects of woodworking.

There is no doubt that what is usually called an electric drill is a very useful object. A variety of attachments is available to make a drill more versatile. So, if you are purchasing one it is worthwhile spending a bit more to enable you to get the best possible use from the drill. This does not necessarily mean buying the most expensive drill, but one that is suitable for your particular requirements.

Think of the electric drill in terms of a power unit. The bigger motor has the most power. It drives tools more quickly and works longer without overheating but it is more expensive and heavier than smaller units.

Check too that the type of drill you buy can take the attachments you might want to purchase at a later date.

Choose a unit that will work on at least two contrasting speeds. The slower speed around 900 rpm, is used for heavy boring work, say into brick walls with a masonry bit, and the faster speed, around 3000 rpm, is used for most attachments.

The power unit

This is a compact electric motor with a shaft at one end on which a chuck is mounted (fig.1).

The chuck has jaws which hold the tools and attachments. The unit has a *pistol grip* handle that makes it easy to hold and through which the power cable passes. The unit has a *trigger switch* to start and stop the motor, and often a *locking pin* to keep the power on, so that both hands can be used on the unit or to steady the work if a drill stand is being used.

Behind the slots in the side of the power unit case is a *fan* which cools the motor — and on no account must these slots be covered up.

Basically the drill must be safe to use and this is assured if you buy the type which is *double-insulated.* If in doubt check with the shop assistant and make sure that the electric plug is correctly attached and wired.

The chuck size refers to the maximum size drill shank that can be fitted to the drill. The sizes vary between 6mm ($\frac{1}{4}''$) and 12mm ($\frac{1}{2}''$). An 8mm ($\frac{3}{8}''$) chuck size is a suitable choice for most jobs.

This basic unit can be adapted to many uses. Accessories will allow you to use it as a grass cutter or hedge trimmer.

A jig-saw attachment allows you to cut

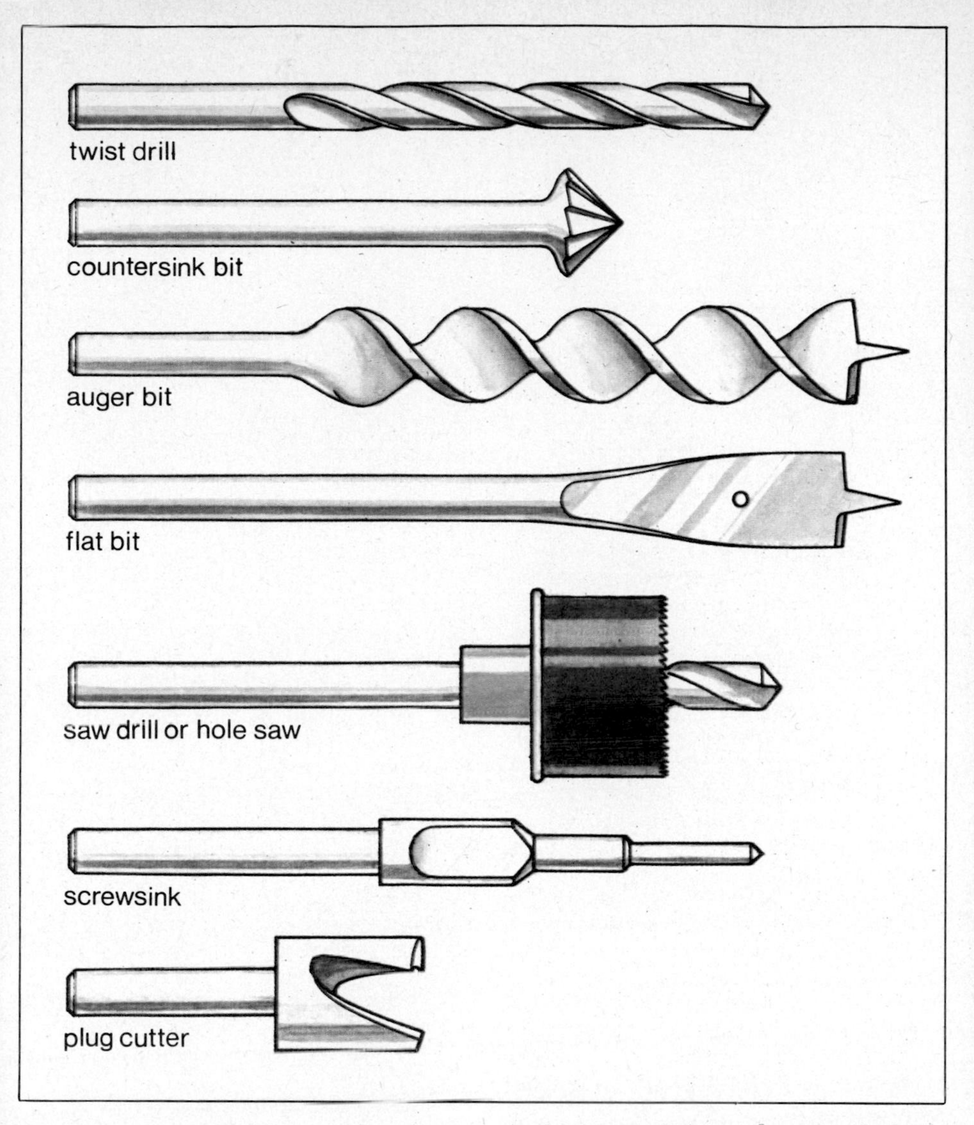

Special purpose bits for woodwork are not essential equipment. For the amateur a range of twist drill bits and a countersink bit are sufficient.

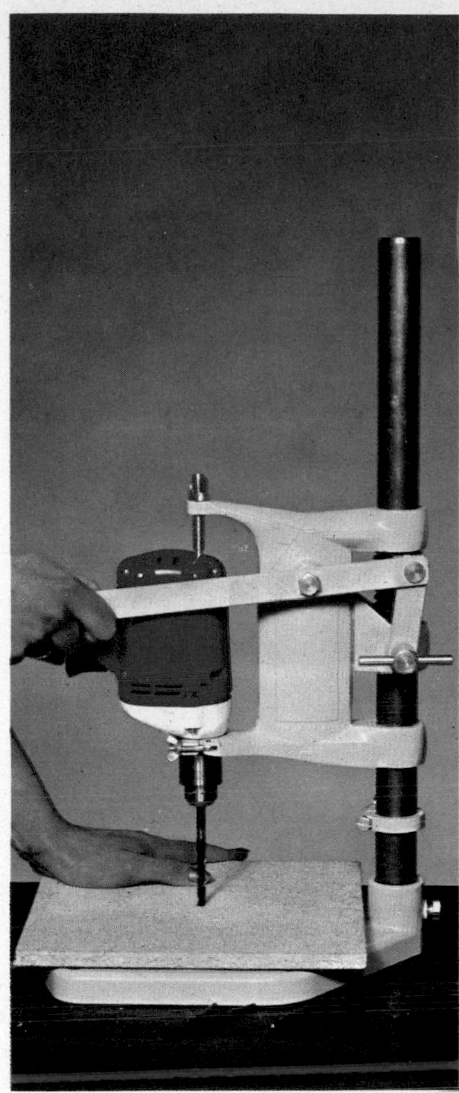

A drill stand makes it easy to handle the power unit and also ensures that a hole is at right angles to the surface of the wood.

curves. A variety of sanding and polishing attachments saves time and energy on large projects.

Each accessory has a specific function so treat each one as a special purpose tool and do not expect it to do a job that it is not made for.

To familiarize yourself with the electric drill (and attachments) use it on a piece of waste softwood. Work away from knots and make sure there are no nails or screws in the wood.

Accessories and attachments

From the many items available choose only those you need.

An extension cable is probably the first item you will need, since electric outlets are rarely sufficiently near to the work to be done. Do not buy or use anything other than the correct cable — it could be dangerous. Various lengths of cable can be purchased. For outdoor work a cable on a drum is useful but indoors a length of about 3m (10ft) is adequate. The extension cable must be fitted with rubber, not plastic, plugs and sockets.

Wood twist drill bits are used for boring small holes in wood. They are suitable for making screw holes and also for holes into which dowel rod is inserted. For example the projects in Carpentry chapter 5 could be done with a power tool.

Special drill bits, similar in appearance to the wood twist drill bits, are available for drilling holes in masonry and into metal. The masonry bit would make a much quicker and easier job of putting up shelves as discussed in Carpentry chapter 6.

The wood, metal and masonry drill bits are not interchangeable.

A countersink bit is used for shaping the hole into which a screw head is recessed.

An auger bit is used to bore deep and accurate holes through a piece of wood. The spiral feeds out the waste wood and keeps the hole straight.

A flat bit is used for shallow holes up to 32mm ($1\frac{1}{4}''$) diameter. It is suitable for making holes in egg racks.

A saw drill is ideal for boring holes up to 75mm (3″) diameter.

A screwsink and plug cutter are used to hide screw heads. The screwsink is driven into the wood to shape a hole into which the screw head, shank and thread fit. This is known as counterboring. The matching plug cutter is then used to produce plugs to be glued into the counterbore to hide the screw head.

Each set is for a specific screw size, for example a 38mm ($1\frac{1}{2}''$) screw sink and cutter for a No.8 screw.

Drill stand. To bore a hole at right angles into a piece of wood is not easy. If the drill is clamped to a drill stand there is no problem. Use one hand on the lever to pull the drill down to the wood and use the other hand to prevent the wood from revolving. This method is also useful when the holes have to be an accurate and constant depth. If you find the drill heavy to hold the drill stand will make it easier.

Creating feathered fabric

Normally, feather fabric is made by sewing or gluing a row of feathers onto a tape or a strip of cloth and then attaching each tape in rows to a larger piece of fabric so that the feathers overlap. (Sometimes the tapes are attached to one another.)

By these two methods feather fabrics can be built up fairly simply to make warm feather coverlets from curved body feathers or muffs and glamorous capes from flat shiny feathers. They can be applied to hats in the same fashion or used to make sleeves for a gown. A single row of feathers on a tape can be used to trim the hem of a garment or the edge of a neck or sleeve.

Buying feathers. Although small amounts of feathers can sometimes be purchased in numbers, feathers are generally sold by weight. Some will inevitably be below standard and have to be discarded so it is wise to order somewhat in excess.

Turkey feather fabric

Feathers are surprisingly resilient and spring back into position even after they have been trodden underfoot. They are also (as anyone who has slept in a feather bed knows) remarkably light yet incredibly warm, and when the feathers are on the outside instead of the inside they make a coverlet or rug of exceptional beauty. The feather sample illustrated is designed from a Victorian pattern for a lap rug and can be made to any size from a doll's cradle to a double bed, to make cuffs or a shawl. The sample is worked with turkey body feathers in three colors and it would be possible to work the same pattern in a geometric or other design.

To estimate feathers for fabric calculate 550 body feathers per 900 sq. cm (1 sq.ft.). This may seem rather a lot but in fact the work goes comparatively rapidly, at about the same speed as knitting.

Before you begin, dye the pale brown and chocolate tones from your supply of white feathers and sort different colors into separate plastic bags so that they will be easier to work.

To mount the feathers use ordinary 2.5cm (1″) binding tape cut into lengths the desired width of the fabric. For 900 sq.cm (1 sq.ft.) you will need about 24 rows or about 7.2 meters (8 yards) of tape.

The fabric is worked on overlapping tapes so that the sharp ends of the central shafts are sandwiched between

Alasdair Ogilvie

Sample of turkey body feather fabric: the top row is pulled up to reveal the construction on a tape base.

the tape to prevent them scratching. In any case you must cut off the point of every central shaft.

To work a row, place the feathers one at a time along the tape face downward so that the curved end sticks up and the hard tip is on the edge of the tape (fig.1). Quickly stitch each feather in place with cross stitch or attach with a dab of glue applied to the central shaft. Permanent adherence is not a factor since the stitches or glue will be covered by the next tape and machine stitched over for still more security. The feathers should overlap along the row and the shafts should be placed about 1.2cm (½″) apart.

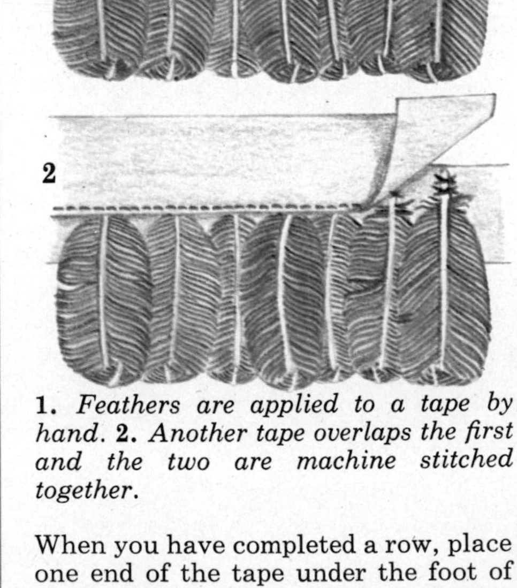

1. *Feathers are applied to a tape by hand.* **2.** *Another tape overlaps the first and the two are machine stitched together.*

When you have completed a row, place one end of the tape under the foot of the sewing machine, ready to begin, and lay another piece of tape over the feather tips so that it overlaps the first tape by about half (fig.2).

Machine stitch the two tapes together using a small stitch. This will not only encase the tips of the feathers, but

Lesley Fox

Rows of feathers mounted on tapes can be used to trim clothes or make a coverlet.

attach them even more securely to the tape.
Now repeat the first step and sew on or glue another row of feathers, this time of a different color, to the tape which is on top, then machine stitch a covering tape as before. Continue in this way until piece is desired size. When you have finished the fabric it will be wonderfully light yet warm and it will also be very thick because of the fluff at the base of the feathers and their way of sticking out.
To line the feathered fabric to make a rug or shawl choose a velvet or silk and cut it to the finished size plus a seam allowance, then turn in the raw edges and slip stitch it by hand to the feather fabric.

Feather cape

The brilliant green plumage in the 1930s cape illustrated is from dyed chicken hackle feathers. You can make a similar one yourself by building up feather fabric on a commercial paper pattern.
Choose a simple cape pattern that has straight rather than flared lines and resembles as much as possible the cape in the photograph. Cut out the shape *twice* so that you can eventually line the cape with the same fabric. Silk or a similar cloth is suitable. Make up the cape and the lining following the instructions given with the pattern but do not attach the two.
The feathers must be dyed first according to the method described in Featherwork 1. page 772. Chicken hackle feathers are slender back feathers and 1kg (2lb) should be more than sufficient to cover your cape.
The feathers are applied in rows on 2.5cm (1″) binding tape just as they are for the fabric but since these are longer and flatter (and curve in instead of out) the rows are more widely spaced, about 2.5cm (1″) between the tapes. The tape should be the same color as the cape and feathers.
To apply the feathers to the tape use milliner's glue. Since chicken hackle feathers are very fine, additional sewing to hold them in place is not required. Cut each tape the width of the cape at the point where each tape will be sewn (or a little longer since you can always snip off any excess). Measure right around from edge to edge but subtract the front seam allowances. (It may be easier to baste this back before you begin.) Tapes are applied from the hem line up.
Place the first tape on a working surface and spread a line of glue along it. Place a fairly thick row of feathers along the tape with the sharp shaft tips well into the glue. Spread more glue across the top of the feathers and lay another piece of tape on top to make a 'sandwich'. Press down along the tape with an old rag. Then prepare the next tape.
When the first tape is dry, stitch to the bottom of the cape fabric so that the bottom edge of the tape is just above the seam allowance for a hem and the feathers hang below the fabric. Use a large running stitch. Build up the fabric in overlapping feathered rows. Because you must follow the rounded contours of the shoulder it is best to work on a dress stand or at least a hanger.
At about 2.5cm (1″) below the neck turn the last row in the opposite direction so that the feathers form a 'collar'.
To complete, attach the lining by hand. Turn up and sew the hem and front edges and sew a matching ribbon around the neck under the last rows of feathers so the joins will be covered. Leave enough for a tie in front.
Using other kinds of feathers. If you wish to make the cape with other feathers remember that if they are not very fine then you will need to machine stitch them as in the fabric opposite and estimate the number of rows and amount of overlap to suit their particular size.

Steve Bicknell

Glamorous 1930s cape made from dyed chicken hackle feathers. The slender feathers curve gently around the wearer imitating the wings of a bird.

Cutting sheet metal decoratively

Various sheet metals, such as copper, aluminum and silver, can be used extensively around the house if they are cut out into decorative shapes. Silver is mostly suited to jewelry but copper and aluminum can be used to make name plates, number plates for the front door and also to make decorations around key holes or hinges.
The tools used allow you to cut complex and delicate shapes, the surfaces of which can be textured, engraved, painted or polished. So choose something with an interesting outline for your design.

Necklace cut from sheet silver and engraved to decorate the surface. Designed by pupils of Priory Park School.

Steve Bicknell

Sheet metal

Sheet metal is sold by weight and is available in various thicknesses.
Copper and aluminum are ideal to start with. (The copper shapes can also be enameled.)
Silver. Once you are familiar with the technique you can use silver, which is available from silversmiths and once again it is sold by weight and is available in varying thicknesses. Fine silver is too soft so use sterling silver. For small items you can buy scraps but if you have a number of designs a larger piece is more appropriate as you can fit the designs onto the sheet in a more economical way.
The thickness of the metal you will need depends largely on its function. For jewelry and most other small projects .9mm (20 gauge) is quite sufficient. Larger items that are mounted onto another surface such as wood can also be made from this particular thickness. For example, you can make decorations to put around drawer handles or hinges of an old chest of drawers or sideboard.

Tools

Jeweler's piercing saw frame and blades are used to cut the metal and are available from jewelers' suppliers and some hardware stores.
To insert or replace a blade clamp one end of the blade in the screw at the end of the frame — make sure that the teeth slope toward the handle — and at the same time tighten and tension the other end of the blade in position.
The saw is used as illustrated on p. 838.
The metal with the design on it is placed on the bench peg which is clamped securely. Hold the metal firmly with one hand and work the saw with the other hand. If you find it difficult to saw, increase the tension of the blade slightly until you can control the saw easily with a rhythmic movement.
The saw cuts on the downward stroke. Each downward stroke removes a small piece of metal, allowing you to follow an exact line. It is quite normal to break blades at first so do not worry — it takes a bit of practice to adapt to the rhythm of sawing. Do not handle the saw roughly.
Blades for the saw are available in varying sizes. The thinner the metal the finer the blade must be. To get the correct blade to cut a particular thickness of metal refer to the instructions supplied with the piercing saw.
A finer blade must also be used for scroll work, ie curved shapes. If a blade breaks when cutting a curve the chances are that the blade is too large to cut the curve so use a finer blade.
Practice on a piece of scrap metal before actually cutting out a design and use various blades to cut curves. You will find that the finer the blade, the finer the curve can be cut.
A hand drill is used with a metal bit to drill holes in the metal.
A bench peg (board pin) is used to place the metal on when cutting. The bench peg is secured with a C-clamp on the edge of a working surface — a table edge will do. A bench peg can be purchased from a jewelers' supplier, and is inexpensive. Or you can make

your own by cutting a V-shape into the thin end of a wedge-shaped piece of wood (fig.1).

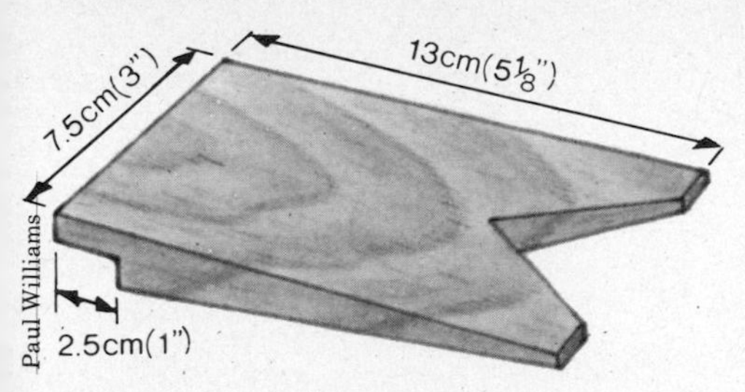

The bench peg is cut from a wedge shaped piece of wood and clamped to the working surface with a C-clamp. The cutting is done within the V-shape.

Cutting the metal

The metal is placed on the bench peg for support while cutting and the cutting is done within the V-shape of the bench peg so that the metal is supported around the area being cut.

To turn a corner continue with the sawing up-and-down action, but with less pressure, and ease the saw gently around so that the cut starts to follow the line of the curve indicated. Continue sawing as before. It is easier to work in stages. If the saw has to be held in an awkward position to cut then place the metal in such a position so that the saw can be held comfortably.

To cut on the inside of a design drill a small hole using a hand drill and a metal bit — large enough to let the blade pass through it. Open one end of the saw, pass the blade through the hole and tighten and tension the blade to the saw frame as before. Cut out the required shape so that it drops out then open and remove the saw blade from the metal.

Tools for decorating

Engraving is done with a flat engraving tool. First mark the line to be engraved on the metal with a pencil. Using the engraving tool place the point on the line and with a wrist movement wiggle the engraver from side to side, 'walking' it along the metal surface. Engraving tools can be bought from jewelers' suppliers. They are available in various sizes and shapes. Alternatively, a small jeweler's screwdriver is inexpensive and also makes a suitable engraving tool. You can file it down to sharpen it if necessary but you will not be able to use it as a screwdriver again. You can also make do by flattening and then shaping a nail with metal files.

Punching. The surface can be textured with a center punch (nail punch). Hold the punch in position and tap it with a hammer to indent the metal surface.

Drilling. Clusters of holes made with a hand drill and a metal bit can form part of the design. Alternatively use the drill to make indentations by drilling only part of the way through the metal.

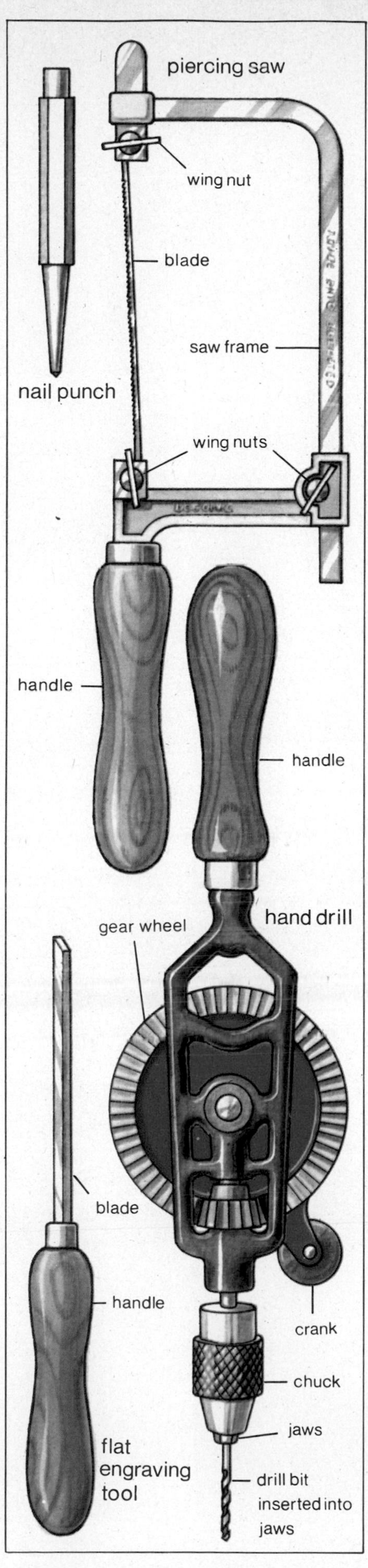

Polishing. Use metal polish to shine the surface. If a satin finish is desired rub the metal in one direction with fine wire steel wool. The use of metal varnish is optional.

Designs

Inspiration can be drawn by observing and copying shapes and patterns from man-made and natural objects such as spike-like flowers, frost patterns on windows, intricate machine parts and even letters of the alphabet.

Draw your ideas on paper so that you can see the exact shape, form and size clearly. Try combining various shapes until you are satisfied with the results. You can further enhance the design by texturing the surface.

You can drill holes or texture parts of the surface by using a center punch or a nail punch, or you can engrave and paint the surface.

Transferring a design onto metal can be done in various ways. The point is to transfer the design in such a way that it will not rub off while the metal is being handled.

Draw the design on a piece of paper (tracing paper will do) with a ball-point pen. Cut out the design slightly larger than the outline and glue it to the metal with any household glue.

Leave to dry, then shade in the parts of the design that are to be removed. This will prevent cutting the wrong pieces from an intricate design.

Another method is to paint the metal with poster paint. Transfer the design onto it using carbon paper. Use a ball-point pen or felt-tipped pen to shade in parts of the design to be removed.

To make the bird brooch

The instructions explain how to make a nesting bird but you can use any design you like to make a brooch and glue a brooch pin to the back once the design has been completed. The overall size of the design is 7mm x 5.5mm ($2\frac{3}{4}$"x $2\frac{1}{4}$"). Two pieces of metal are used and then glued together to complete the brooch.

You will need:

Jeweler's piercing saw frame: blades (shown here and next page).

Bench peg (board pin).

C-clamp.

Tin snips.

Mallet — a plastic one or a wooden one with a hide head.

Needle files.

Hand drill with metal bit and center punch or nail punch.

Flat engraving tool — available from jewelers' suppliers. This is optional

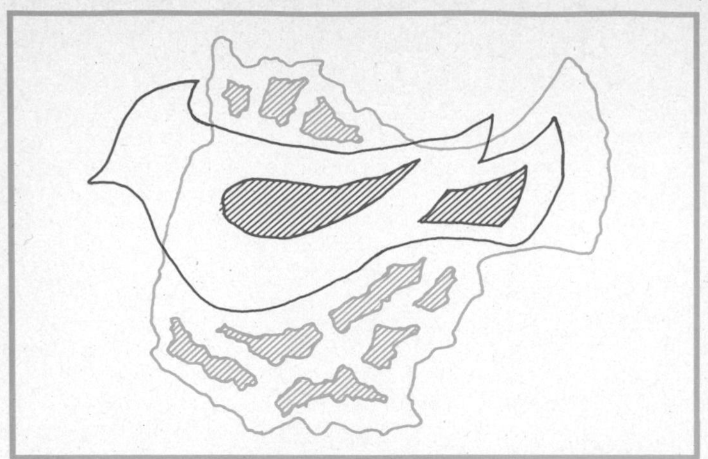

Tracing pattern for brooch made up of two separate pieces.

1. *The metal with the design on it is cut with tin snips.*

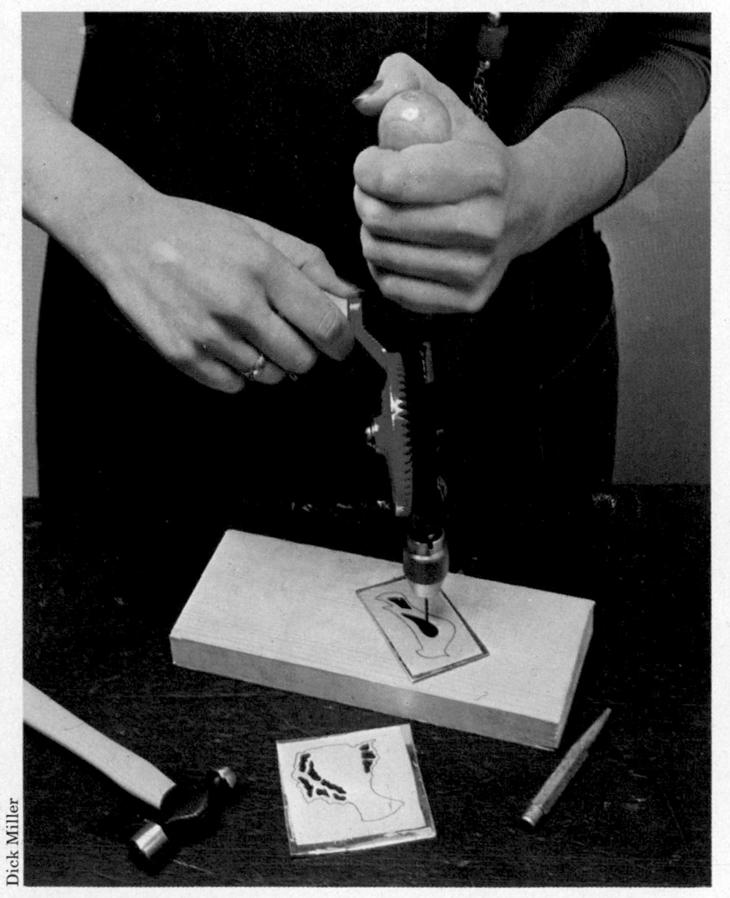

Dick Miller

2. *Hole drilled on waste side of design to hold saw blade.*

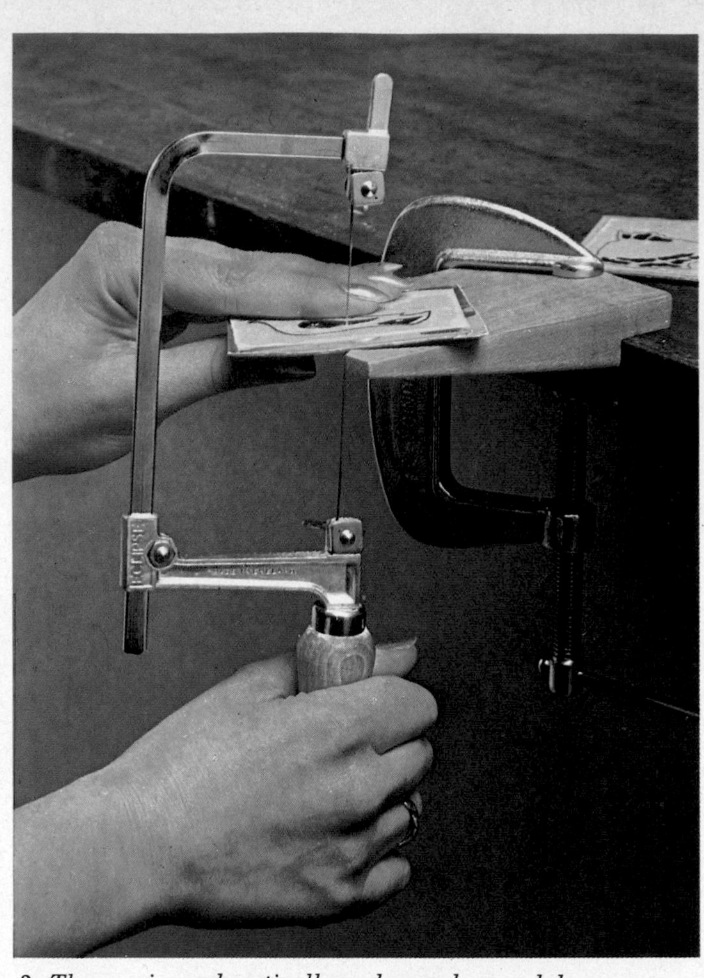

3. *The saw is used vertically and moved up and down.*

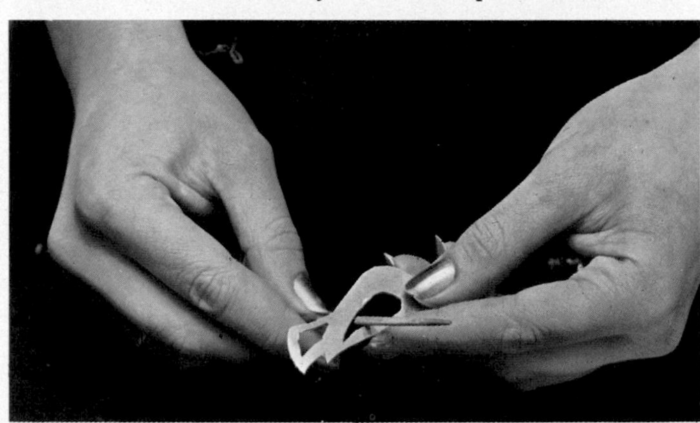

4. *The cutting completed, the edges are smoothed with needle files. Use a triangular file to reach into corners.*

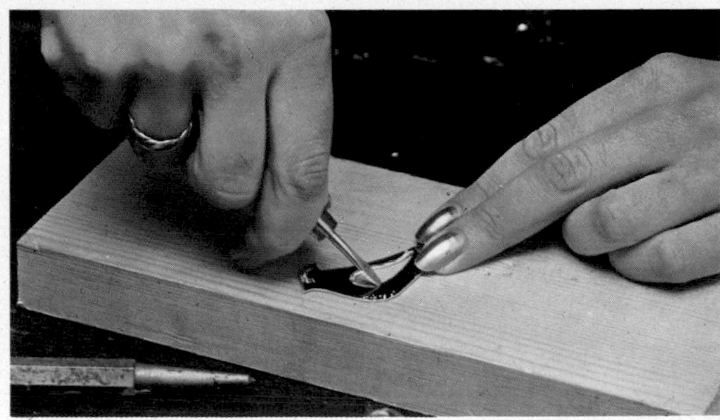

5. *The surface being decorated with an engraving tool.*

but it is useful for decorating the metal surface.
.9mm (20 gauge) 10mm x 7.5mm (4″x3″) copper, silver or aluminum sheet.
Brooch pin, epoxy resin adhesive and metal polish.
☐ Transfer the design onto the metal.
☐ Using the tin snips cut the design from the metal allowing for a waste area around the design.
☐ On a solid surface gently flatten the metal with the mallet.
☐ Use the center punch to make marks on the waste side of the metal for each cut ie the shaded part of the design.
☐ Drill a hole through each mark. The hole must be just large enough to let the blade pass through it.
☐ Using the piercing saw cut away the waste areas starting with the parts inside the design. Cut out the outlines last.
☐ Wash off the poster paint or tracing paper from the metal.
☐ Use the needle files to smooth all the edges.
☐ Decorate the metal using the engraving tools.
☐ Glue the bird shape onto the other piece of metal to form the design illustrated.
☐ Polish the brooch.
☐ Glue brooch pin to the back.
Complete all engraving, punching, drilling and polishing first and then to finish use adhesive for gluing on the brooch pin.

Other decorating ideas

Enamel paints, opaque or transparent, can be used on the surface. Clean the surface with metal polish before applying the paint.
The paint can be used very effectively if another piece of metal with the same outline as the design is glued to the back of the design so that recessed areas are formed by the cut out parts within the design. Paint is then used to fill the recessed areas.
Resin can also be used on the surface. If you have used two pieces of metal on top of each other clear-cast resin with color pigments can be added to the recessed parts of the design.
Curving the metal. You are not limited to flat surfaces. If, for example, you have cut out a flower shape you can use a pair of round-nosed pliers to curl the individual petals. This must be done before painting the surface but after any engraving or punching has been completed.

Right: leaf designs in aluminum decorated with resin and wire. Designer Kit Gladwell. Bottom left: design for pendant cut from aluminum. Designer Tony Harper. Right: the petals of the flower are shaped with round-nosed pliers. Designer J. Mumby.

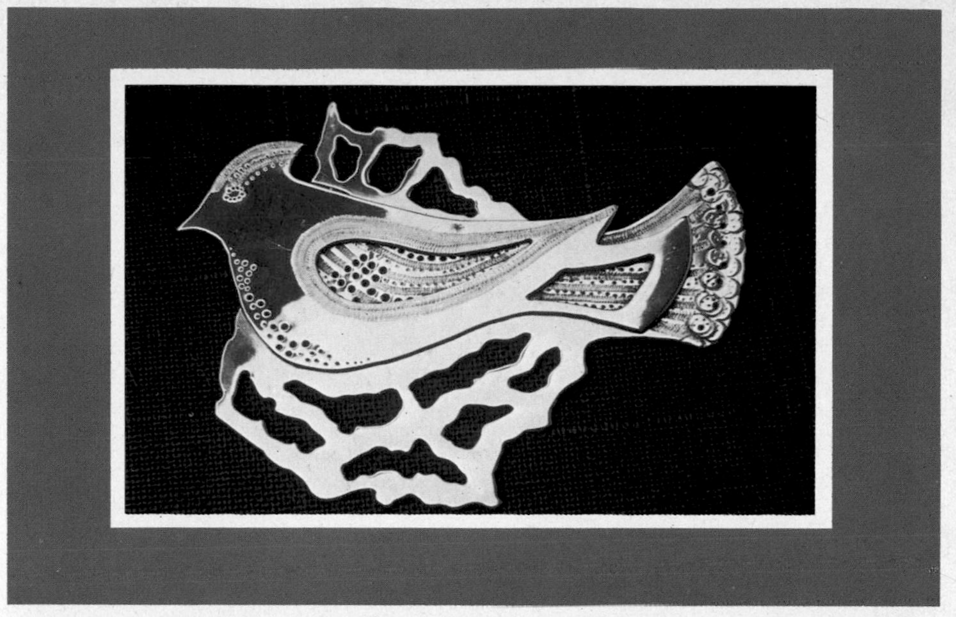

Above: bird brooch with punched and engraved surface. Designer Kit Gladwell.

Dick Miller

Pattern next to pattern

One pattern can be combined very successfully with another provided that you follow two principles of good design: unity and contrast.
Contrast. Several patterns together will naturally contrast but they work most successfully if the contrast in pattern is definite and unambiguous. At the same time you may find that the patterns need a focal point such as one dominating pattern at center of design.
Unity. When two or more patterns are used in juxtaposition you will need to find something which holds them together. It could be a similar color or material. It could equally well be a single pattern in several colors or one pattern repeated on different scales. There is nothing to be gained by throwing each and every pattern together in a medley; the result will be a mess.
Patchwork. The most notable example of pattern next to pattern is in patchwork where different patterns are deliberately set next to each other to create an overall design. The shapes of the different materials are important; they are mostly, with the exception of crazy patchwork, very regular, controlled and geometric. Color also holds patchwork together. You will find that the most effective patchworks are often quite restrained in color, a variety of blues for example.
You can use pattern next to pattern for all kinds of craft projects besides patchwork: marquetry, where different woods create a design, appliqué and collage, the wrapping of gift boxes or the design of a woolen rug or hanging. Even something as everyday as teaming a skirt with a blouse may need a decision on whether to use one pattern with another. Bear in mind that a rich variety of patterns works best set against a plain, even an austere background to show it off.

Patchwork: a multi-patterned arrangement which is held together by a common design (a kite shape) and color.

Chris Legee

Experiment
To make a decoration using various patterns
You will need:
Package of plain, white postcards.
Variety of colored paper to be stuck with paper glue, or gummed squares of paper.
An assortment of small gummed shapes such as squares, circles and stars.
Scissors, needle and thread.
From a postcard cut two identical shapes such as squares and circles. Stick a different colored paper on each side of the shapes.
Decorate all four sides with small gummed shapes, keeping to circles on one side, stars on another, stripes on another and so on.
Find the middle of each card and make a small hole with the needle. Cut from the outside to the middle (fig.1).
Slot together the two shapes (fig.2).
Hang the three-dimensional shape from thread sewn into one side of it.
You can make any number of decorated, patterned shapes to make a mobile. Experiment to see which patterns look pleasing together.

1. *Cut from the outside to the center.*

2. *Two decorated circles are slotted together to make a sphere-like shape.*

Victoria Drew

Creative ideas 30

Glittering jewelry never goes out of fashion and is easy to make with brightly colored enamel paints. The small jars of enamel paint that model makers use are ideal, together with glittering beads, sequins, diamanté—anything that sparkles.

Draw the shape of your design onto a piece of wood veneer which is about 2mm ($\frac{1}{16}$") thick, either free-hand for abstract shapes or using tracing patterns for geometric shapes (cookie cutters are handy for this).

Cut the shapes out with a coping saw and smooth down the edges with sandpaper. Glue the pin fastener onto the back with a clear glue and leave to dry thoroughly.

Holding the brooch by the pin, apply an even coat of enamel paint to the front surface and the edges. Leave to dry completely.

Now apply the 'jewels' using a small amount of glue. Use toothpicks to apply glue and position the jewels. This is much neater than using your fingers.

Above: A pair of pert penguins painted in complimentary colors. A heart-shaped cookie cutter was used as a pattern for this pin. A cluster of 'diamonds forms the head of the comet.

Right: Make a barrette by gluing a diamond studded motif to a simple metal bobby pin.

Below left and right: This jewelry teams well with casual clothes.

Photos: Camera Press

Beginning with glaze

Clay 19

You will have noticed that most pots are decorated with a durable, non-porous material which can be matt or shiny, clear, translucent or opaque, and can be used in a variety of ways to create an enormous range of decorative effects.

Glaze composition

This surface material is called glaze, and it is a special kind of glass which is chemically formulated to adhere to the surface of the clay when heated.

The chemical composition of glazes is highly complex and the basic material varies according to the type of clay the glaze is to be used on.

Glazes for earthenware clays are basically lead or borax; and for stoneware, ground felspar or other stones are used.

A flux, which affects the color and texture as well as the temperature at which the glaze liquefies.

A refractory, which aids the application of the glaze and also makes it more durable.

A variety of other ingredients must also be added to lend particular qualities such as extra color, or shine opacity.

Buying glazes

Glaze mixing requires a great deal of skill and experience—studio potters generally mix their own glazes, but for the beginner or the hobby potter, ready-mixed, bought glazes are perfectly satisfactory.

These can be obtained from a potters' supplier, who provides charts of the color ranges available and comprehensive instructions for their use.

The type of glaze that you buy should be suitable for the clay body being used—stoneware glaze for stoneware clay, earthenware glaze for earthenware clay and so on.

Earthenware glazes are usually shiny and heavy because of their lower firing temperatures.

Stoneware glazes are often more matt, paler in color with a look of natural stone about them.

Porcelain glazes, because of the purity of the clay body, usually look refined and delicate.

Purchased glazes usually come in liquid or powder form. Liquid varieties need only be stirred thoroughly before use, powder ones should be mixed with water according to the maker's instructions. Other materials—such as powdered metallic oxides and stains for a particular effect—may also be added at this stage.

Once the glaze is mixed with water to a creamy consistency, it should be sieved and stored in a plastic container with a well-fitting lid and labeled with details of glaze type, color, and firing temperature.

Safety! Remember that some of the ingredients in glazes are toxic, so always wash your hands carefully afterward and store glazes well out of the reach of children and away from foodstuffs.

Applying glaze

Once a pot has been biscuit fired, it is ready to be covered with glaze and fired again. This second type of firing is called a glaze firing.

Brush the pot thoroughly inside and out with a damp sponge to remove any fine clay dust which would prevent the glaze from sticking and might cause flaws in the finished piece.

Make sure there are no grease marks on the pot either as the surface must be porous. It absorbs the glaze by sucking up the water in it, leaving a powdery coating of glaze on the surface. Just the right thickness of glaze is needed to give a good finished effect, and this depends on the porosity of the pot (a less porous pot needs a thicker glaze), and the type of glaze used.

As a general guide, the thickness of the glaze applied should be about 2mm ($\frac{1}{16}''$)—observe how your glaze goes on and the effects of firing, and keep a notebook of results for future reference for your pottery work.

Ken Kirkwood

This small-town scene, designed by Tessa Fuchs, is built up on a curved slab panel. The lowering clouds and small houses are also cut from rolled out slabs and are applied to the basic structure to build up a perspective. The sunset is in strong reds and yellow opaque glazes, offset by the neutral grays and browns of the rest.

If a glaze is too thick it may run or 'crawl', and if it is too thin the surface will be dry and uninteresting. Consistent results can only be achieved with practice and experience, but it is also exciting to open the kiln door after a glaze firing and see the result of a particular experiment.

Melvin Grey

Above. Three examples of faulty glazing. The glaze on the tall vase is flaking off in strips, probably because the clay was dusty. The slab dish has been over-glazed, and the glaze is dribbling off at the bottom, and the glaze on the pitcher has not 'taken' on greasy areas.

Glaze can be applied to pots by dipping, pouring, spraying, trailing, painting and splashing—but always remember to stir it before use, as the ingredients settle at the bottom even if the mixture is left standing for only a short while.

Dipping. This is the best and simplest way to glaze a pot. Stir the glaze thoroughly with your hands (fig.1).

1. *Stir the glaze well with your hands.*

2. *Dip the pot quickly into the glaze.*

3. *Then lift it straight out again.*

4. *Quickly pour away surplus glaze.*

Nelson Hargreaves

Dip two fingers in the glaze, hold the pot with these fingers as lightly as possible and dip the pot into the glaze (fig.2)—there should be enough glaze in the vessel for the pot to be completely submerged. Dip it in sideways, sliding it from side to side to avoid airlocks, then lift it straight out again (fig.3).

An immersion of a few seconds should be long enough to give the pot an adequate coating of glaze. Quickly pour out any surplus (fig.4), and stand the pot on its base to dry. Touch up finger marks by gently dripping glaze on them from a fingertip.

Do not touch the pot until it is completely dry, or you will smudge it. It should be dry in a few moments.

The bottom of the pot must be cleaned before it is put into the kiln. Glaze melts in the heat and sticks to the surfaces it touches, so the bottom must be glaze-free, otherwise it will stick to the kiln shelf, spoiling the pot and the shelf. Wet a flat piece of sponge, stand the pot on it, press down gently and twist. This should clean the glaze away neatly and quickly.

Safety

It may be dangerous to add metallic oxides, particularly copper, to low temperature glazes. This accelerates the release of lead from the glaze when brought into contact with acids.

Almost all the glazes are slightly soluble in acid, and because of this most countries have established detailed specifications indicating the legally tolerated levels of lead and other heavy metals released from any glazed article intended to come into contact with food.

When glazes are used properly there is not likely to be any problem, but when you are producing pots for use in eating, drinking or storage the manufacturer's instructions must be followed carefully, and it is advisable to check that the glazes you are using comply with your country's tolerated limits.

When you are using any glazes for any purpose it is wise to treat them as though they were toxic.

5. *Swill the glaze around inside pot.*

8. *Wax patterns can be brushed on.*

6. *Pour the glaze over outer surface.*

9. *Wax forms a glaze-resisting area.*

7. *Splash on glaze to form a design.*

Below. This group of pots illustrates the different effects achieved by using the glazing techniques described in this chapter. The stripes decorating the two pots on the left, and the bold stripe across the plate, are all made by painting on a wax design and then glazing the unwaxed areas. The pattern can be as free or controlled as you wish. The third pot from the left is an example of 'dribbled' glaze—the upper portion is glazed, and trickles have been allowed to run down onto the unglazed portion. Of the two bowls, one is splashed with cobalt and other is simply dipped. Pots designed by Val Barry.

Nelson Hargreaves

Pouring. If the pot is large or irregularly shaped, glaze can be poured onto the pot.
Deal with the inside of the pot first. Take up some glaze in a jug, pour it into the inside of the pot, and swill the pot around until the glaze completely covers the inside surface (fig.5).
Quickly pour away the surplus. Allow the pot to dry slightly before glazing the outside. To do this you will need a bowl with two sticks resting across it. Stand the pot upside down on these two sticks, then pour the glaze around the pot until the surface is completely covered (fig.6). It needs practice to get the glaze on evenly, but it can look attractive if a decorative feature is made of the pouring runs.

Painting, dribbling, splashing. Glaze can be painted on with a brush, or dribbled and splashed on to form a design (fig.7). It is difficult to paint glaze onto a pot evenly, so apply several coats for a smooth effect, or use just a few brush strokes to form a design. Always let the first coating of glaze dry before applying a second, and make sure that the coatings are not too thick.

Trailing. Glaze can be trailed onto the surface of a pot as described for the technique of slip trailing (Clay chapter 16 page 704). Take some glaze up into a trailer and work patterns across the pot. You can do this straight onto the biscuit surface, or apply it as a second coating of dark glaze on a pale glaze base.

Waxing. Wax can be painted onto the pot to form patterns before applying a glaze (fig.8). The wax resists the glaze (fig.9), forms a patterned effect and melts off in firing to expose the raw clay body beneath.
As a variation, the pot can be glazed all over in one color then partially waxed on top of the glaze and dipped in a second color to give a two-color glaze effect.

Spraying. This process is not very successful unless expensive pressurized sprays are used, and you must also spray into a special 'spray booth' to protect your lungs. It is perhaps a technique best avoided by the beginner.

Glaze firing

Care should be taken when loading your kiln that the glazed pieces do not touch each other or the sides of the kiln. The kiln should be packed evenly so that the temperature distribution is even, and the temperature inside the kiln is gauged with cones and/or the pyrometer in the same way as for a biscuit firing.
Temperatures required for a glaze firing can be very high indeed. The graph given here, for example, shows how a final temperature of 1250°C

(2282°F) should be gradually achieved over a ten hour period for a stoneware firing.

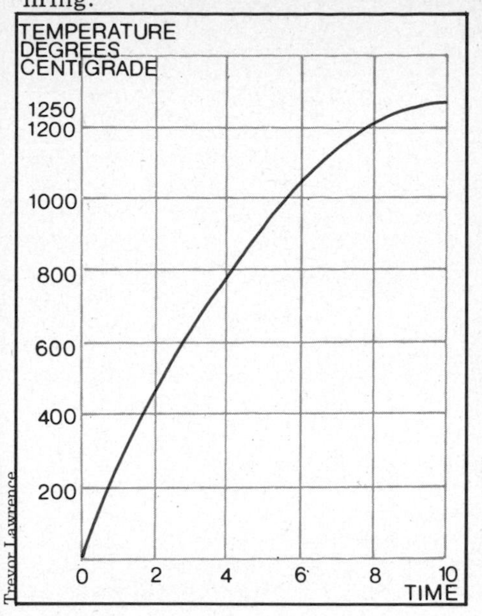

Temperature/time ratio for a glaze firing.

Summary of points

When you are preparing to glaze your pots and experiment with glaze firing, bear the following points in mind.

Read your suppliers' catalog. Any supplier will post you a catalog listing his products and prices. These catalogs include comprehensive descriptions of glaze types, colors and firing temperatures.

Always read the manufacturer's instructions and information carefully. Order small experimental quantities of glaze to start with.

Match glaze type to clay type. Earthenware clays require earthenware glaze. Earthenware glazes are specially formulated to fire at low temperatures—if low firing clay is subjected to higher temperatures it becomes dehydrated and distorts.

Stoneware clay takes a higher firing temperature, and stoneware glazes are formulated accordingly.

Decide what effect you want. Low firing earthenware glazes are generally thick, shiny and opaque.

With these glazes aim for bold, colorful or rustic effects.

Stoneware glazes can give more subtle effects. You can choose from paler, matt or translucent shades.

Porcelain glazes are the most delicate, but they fire at such high temperatures that they are beyond the range of the beginner.

To mix and apply glaze. Make sure that your glaze is well mixed then apply it in any of the ways described in this chapter.

Remember that the presence of oxides and staining agents makes *no* difference to the way the glaze is applied or the temperatures at which it fires. They merely affect the color of the finished piece.

Remember that unless you are using a very opaque glaze, the color of the clay body will show through the glaze and affect the finished color.

Glaze fire. Load the kiln as described in this chapter.

Check the glaze manufacturer's instructions again for the right firing temperature.

Use firing cones and/or the pyrometer to gauge the temperature during the firing.

Keep records. Keep a notebook listing the types of clay and glazes that you use.

Ordinary white ceramic tiles can be overglazed to achieve widely different effects. The green/gray glaze and the yellow, red and brown are fairly simple to use, and are commercially available.

Make a note of the colors and effects achieved with each firing, and how you obtained these effects. This will provide an invaluable reference system for when you want to repeat or improve upon a particular type of glazing.

To begin with, every pot and every firing will be an experiment. You will, however, soon become familiar with what can be done and how to do it. A future chapter deals with further techniques in the use of glazes.

Making a leaded terrarium

Once you have tried your hand at leading up a few pieces of glass and have perhaps made one or two of the small window hangings described in Glass chapter 7, page 798, you will be able to construct something larger.

In this chapter a terrarium (or mini-greenhouse) is made with clear window glass and lead cames. Once planted with a variety of small plants you will have a miniature garden which can be hung from a wall, either indoors or out, or stood on a table or shelf. The terrarium needs very little attention and is an ideal way of displaying your plants all the year around or even of growing a tiny herb garden.

The terrarium

Terrariums come in all shapes and sizes: square, cylindrical or conical. Some are completely glassed over with a removable lid, some are partially made of colored glass and others are open at the sides. The terrarium in this chapter is open at the back for easy access and planting. It has five straight sides and a conical top made of five tapered pieces of glass. A back piece of glass retains the soil.

You will need:

Tools

See Glass chapter 7, page 798.

Materials

Window glass, 55cm x 40cm (22″x16″) or other similar area of glass, eg 60cm x 35cm (24″x14″). Buy more glass if you need some for practice.

Lead cames: 3.8m ($12\frac{1}{2}$′) double-channel, round type, 8mm ($\frac{5}{16}$″) wide. 0.6m (2′) single-channel, round type, about 6mm ($\frac{1}{4}$″) wide. Both types of leading should be high enough to accommodate the thickness of glass. See Glass chapter 6, page 702, for a table of lead types and sizes.

Solder, 8mm ($\frac{5}{16}$″) thick.

Flux or a tallow candle.

Steel wool or wire brush.

Lasting nails, finishing nails or other similar nails.

Small hammer.

Felt or thick cloth for padding the glass while cutting it.

Masonite or smooth piece of wood at least 50cm x 50cm (20″x 20″).

Lampblack.

Medium grade sandpaper.

Linseed oil-based putty (optional).

Epoxy glue (optional).

Masking tape.

Thin cardboard the size of the sheet of window glass.

Pencil, pen, protractor, metal ruler and scissors for cutting the cardboard.

Strong wire or chain for hanging the terrarium. Remember that when it is filled with earth and plants the total weight will be about 3.2kg (7lb).

□ Make a set of templates from the cardboard as a pattern for the terrarium. To do this follow the measurements in fig.1, making sure that you have the angles correct. Draw each template onto the cardboard using pencil, ruler and protractor to measure the angles. Cut out the twelve templates. You have five side pieces, five top pieces, a base and a back support.

The finished but empty terrarium. It is a strong, solid construction. Designed by Anthony Wilson.

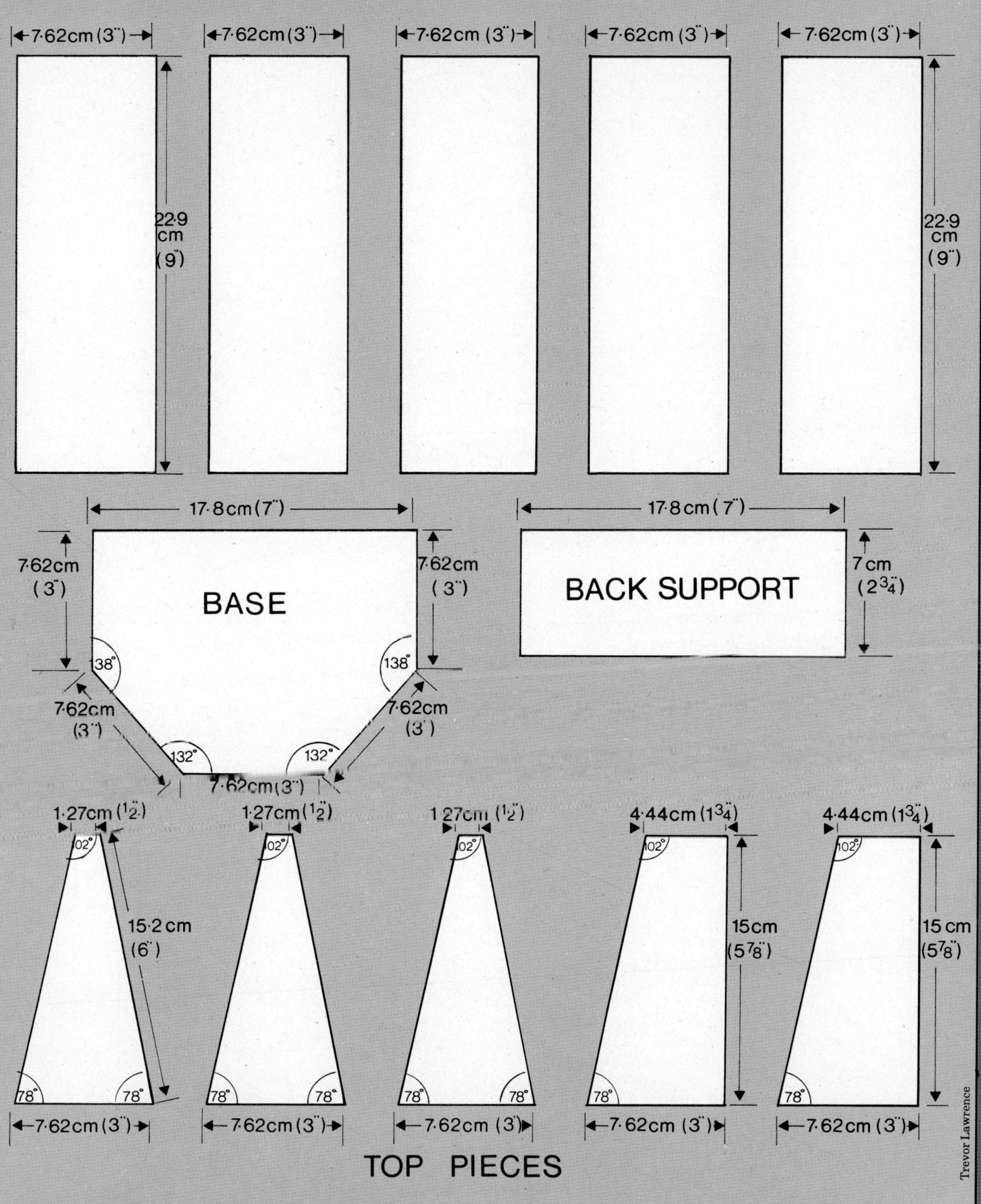

1. *Precise drawing of the templates is the key to good work. Make sure this step is accurate before proceeding.*

Cutting. Lay the felt on a flat working surface and place the glass on top.

☐ Arrange the templates on the glass. They do not have to be arranged in any particular order so long as you get them all in. Leave enough space around the templates to allow for minor errors when cutting.

☐ Carefully draw around the templates with the felt-tip pen before removing.

☐ Take the glass cutter in one hand and score the glass along the lines of the templates using a ruler to keep the lines straight. Turn the glass over and, with the end of the glass cutter, tap along the score line until the glass cracks. Follow the instructions in Glass chapter 4, page 450, for cutting glass. Sand the corners of each piece of glass.

Leading. Untwist the lead, then stretch and straighten it using the method described in Glass chapter 7, page 798.

☐ When the lead is quite straight lay it on the working surface. With the cutting knife cut off sections of lead sufficient to hold the pieces of glass together. You will need the following lengths:

Double-channeled lead:
Six lengths 22.9cm (9″), for the sides.
Two lengths 38.1cm (15″), for top and bottom of sides.
Six lengths 15.2cm (6″), for top pieces.
Two lengths 17.8cm (7″); two lengths 6.5cm (2½″), for back support.
One length 12.6cm (5″) long, for 'horseshoe' shape around top pieces.
One length 3.2cm (1¼″) long, to join up two ends of 'horseshoe'.

Single-channeled lead:
For the inside of the base,
One length 17.8cm (7″) and one length 38.1cm (15″).

☐ Open the leaves of the lead with an oyster knife or other strong, blunt knife. The handle of a pair of pliers can also be used for this process.

☐ Slot the pieces of glass into the appropriate lead cames and lay them flat on the Masonite as in fig.2. Do not slot in the base or back at this stage. You may find that you need to trim the lead at the corners of the glass with a cutting knife. Make sure that the pieces of lead lie neatly against each other at the joins. There should be no gaps between lead and glass although it does not matter if the glass rattles slightly so long as it is securely inside the leaves of the lead.

☐ Smooth the lead flat over the glass with a piece of softwood or other small piece of wood.

☐ Using the hammer place lasting nails or other suitable nails at intervals around the leaded glass to hold it firmly in position. You are now ready for soldering.

Soldering. Before soldering clean the end of the soldering iron and all the lead joins with steel wool.

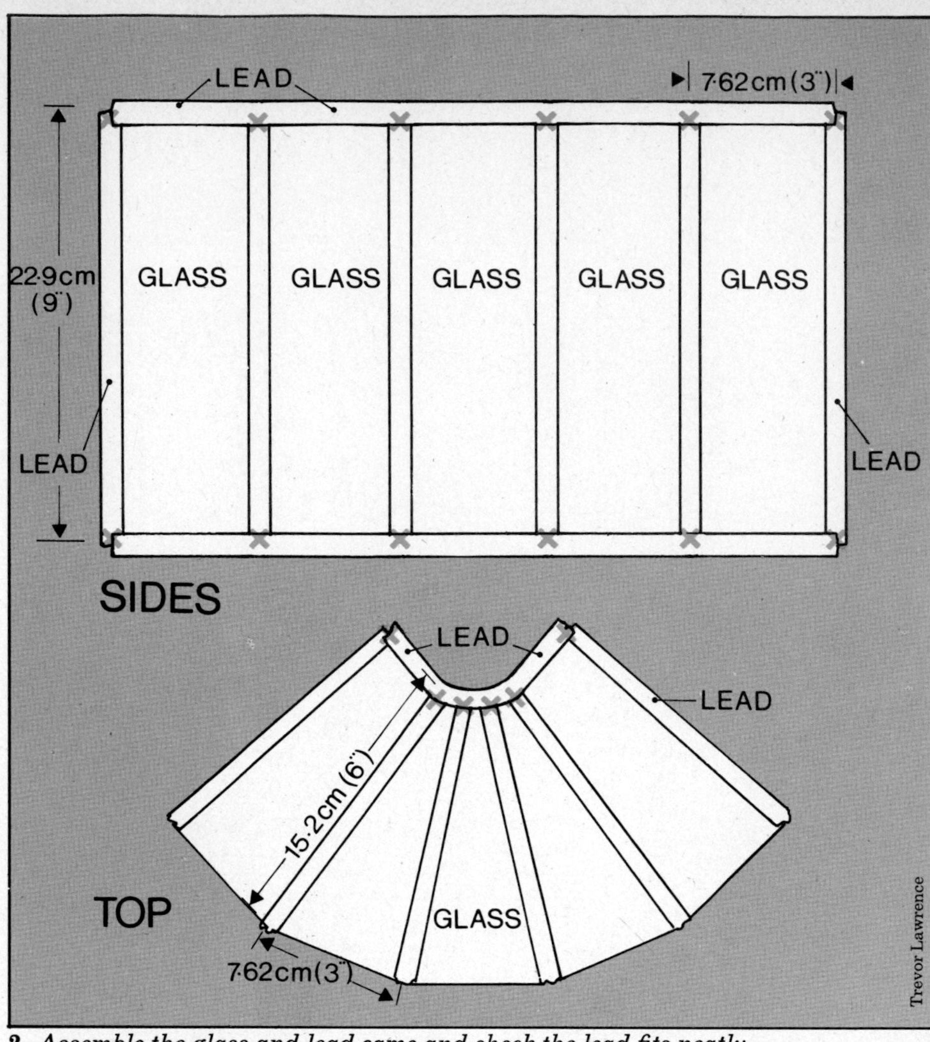

2. *Assemble the glass and lead came and check the lead fits neatly.*

☐ Heat up the soldering iron and, following the method described in Glass chapter 7, page 798, solder all the joins of the lead surrounding the five side pieces of the terrarium. In fig.2 the soldering points are marked with an X.

☐ Pull out the lasting nails, turn the glass over, replace the nails and solder on the other side.

☐ Next, solder the lead surrounding the top five sections of the terrarium. You will only need to solder at the top.

☐ When all the sections are soldered lift the side pieces upright and very carefully bend them into position around the base glass. Do not force the lead; it will bend if you are firm but gentle.

☐ Wrap masking tape around the sides to hold them in position.

☐ Similarly bend the top section and place in position above the side pieces. The glass of the top sections will slot into the double-channeled lead of the side pieces.

☐ Solder the top sections to the side sections at the lead joins.

☐ The short strip of lead 3.2cm (1¼″) long connects the back of the 'horseshoe' shape at the top of the terrarium. Stretch across the back just inside the outer edge and solder.

The base. The glass base must be attached to the main structure of the

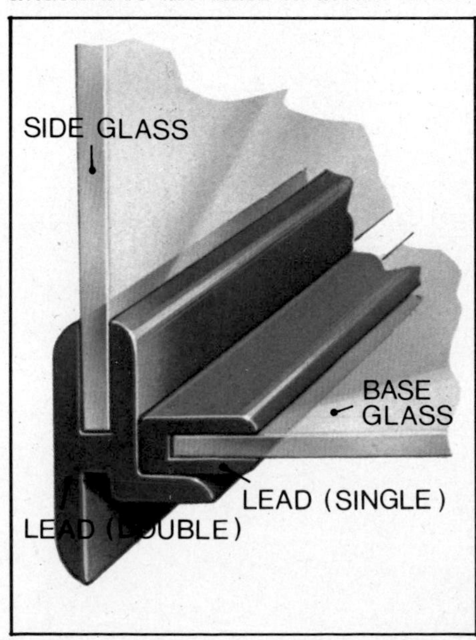

3. *The position of base and side lead.*

terrarium.
☐ Use the pliers to bend the inner leaf of the double-channeled lead at the bottom of the sides, inward and upward to form a right angle (fig.3).
☐ Bend the 38.1cm (15″) strip of single-channeled lead around the curved edge of the glass base, and slot in the glass. Take the remaining 17.8cm (7″) strip of single-channeled lead and slot along the back edge of the base. Trim the lead at the corners if necessary.
☐ Solder the two joins together.
☐ Place the leaded base inside the terrarium so it fits snugly on top of the right-angled lead (fig.3).
☐ Smooth under the outer edge of the double-channeled lead toward the center of the terrarium for a neat finish.
☐ For an extra strong finish turn the terrarium over and solder base to sides at intervals.

The back. The back support is made from the remaining rectangle of glass.
☐ Fit 17.8cm (7″) of double-channeled lead along one long side of the glass and repeat for the other side.
☐ Slot the two short sides of the rectangle into the remaining leading.
☐ Trim the four corners of the lead so they fit neatly against each other.
☐ Solder the corners together.
☐ Fit the back onto the terrarium.
☐ Temporarily remove the glass base and solder the joins where the inner side and back leaves meet.
☐ Replace the base and solder the four points where the back leading meets the side leading.
☐ Any uneven edges should be finally smoothed over with a piece of wood.

The terrarium is perfectly usable as it is but water will run out of the bottom. If you prefer the terrarium to be waterproof, mix up a little lampblack with putty. Using an oyster knife press the putty between lead and glass around the base, the back and 7.5cm (3″) up the sides. Make sure that the putty fills the gaps for a tight seal. The lead of the base should also be firmly glued to the lead upon which it is resting. Use an epoxy glue for this.

The hook. The terrarium can be hung from a chain or a couple of twisted strands of strong wire soldered to the top. In the terrarium illustrated two lengths of solder were soldered to the top. Remember that the terrarium is quite heavy, especially when full of plants and soil, and will need a strong support.

To finish. Rub down the lead and clean up the joints with medium grade sandpaper, then polish with lampblack for a good shine.

Plant the terrarium as you would plant a pot but remember that terrarium plants will probably need less water than you expect.

Martin Chaffer

The terrarium looks very effective against a plain background such as this white outside wall. Grow small plants inside for a miniature garden which will look after itself most of the time. Designed by Anthony Wilson.

Tent stitch projects

Tent stitch is one of the oldest and most well known needlepoint stitches. Its name probably comes from tenter, an old word for the frame on which the work was stretched.
On the right side of the canvas, tent stitch looks like half cross stitch (see Needlepoint chapter 4, page 544). On the wrong side, however, when it is worked horizontally or vertically it slopes across two holes of canvas. This gives a much greater coverage on the wrong side and the extra padding has a cushioning effect so the needlepoint is more hardwearing than with almost any other stitch. Because of this it is particularly suitable for carpets and upholstery.
Tent stitch was known in the 13th century when small areas of it were worked on the needlepoint border of the Syon cope, a beautiful semi-circular cloak named after the convent at Syon in Middlesex, England, where it was kept for a long time.
The stitch became more common after the 16th century when the creation of the steel needle made it possible to work intricate detail.
Tent stitch was popular because it could be worked in such fine detail that it has the effect of a painting. In old pieces of pictorial work the areas of detail were done on fine gauze and inserted or woven into the less detailed background which was worked on canvas. Wool and silk were often combined to give a rich effect.
Double canvas. With the development of double-mesh canvas in the 19th century, it was possible to work areas of detail and coarser background on the same foundation. Because of its construction, with threads woven in pairs instead of singly, the threads can be moved apart with the needle in order to make much smaller stitches where required. Tent stitch when worked like this is often known as *petit point*, as opposed to *gros point* where the stitch is worked over the double threads as if they were one thread.
The effect of needlepoint worked in tent stitch is similar to a woven tapestry. This is probably why double-mesh canvas is also known as Penelope canvas, after the legend of Penelope, the wife of Ulysses. (While Ulysses was away she wove a tapestry all day and secretly ripped it out at night in order to prolong her work and thus repel unwelcomed advances from suitors.)

Using a frame

Because the diagonal pull of tent stitch distorts the canvas, it is advisable to mount the canvas onto a frame. Use a slate frame for large pieces of work (see Needlepoint chapter 3, page 120), or for small pieces, such as the lighter case shown on page 852, you could mount it into a round frame.
Round frames. The canvas can be mounted into a round frame as for regular fabric (see Embroidery chapter 1, page 260) but, as the pressure of the frame distorts the canvas, you should not work over the area enclosed by it.
Mounting canvas. If you prefer not to waste this amount of canvas, you can mount a small piece onto a larger piece of fabric. You can also use this method with a slate frame.
Cut the canvas at least 2.5cm (1″) larger all around than the area to be worked. Place it onto the fabric and stitch around using a wide zigzag.
Mount the fabric on the frame in the normal way and check that it is really taut. Cut away the fabric underneath the canvas to within 1.5cm (½″) of the zigzag stitching (fig.1).

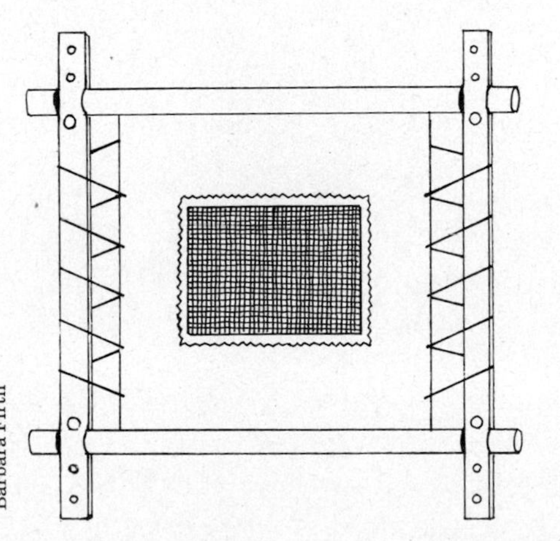

1. *Small piece of canvas, stitched to fabric, mounted onto a slate frame.*

Stretching the canvas

If, in spite of using a frame, you find that the canvas is distorted, when finished, you can restore its shape by stretching. Stretching is also essential if you intend to frame the work for a picture or if you are going to use it for upholstery because it makes it really flat.
To stretch the canvas, find a piece of wood which is larger than the canvas. If you have no scrap or board of the right size, you could use the back of a cupboard or door or even the floor. Check that the wood is really clean and free from any water-soluble stains or paints.
Cover the wood with absorbent fabric such as a thin towel or with several layers of blotting paper.
Remove the canvas from the frame and dampen it thoroughly from the wrong side with a wet sponge. Apply the sponge with several dabbing motions rather than spreading it over.
Lay the dampened canvas, right side down, onto the chosen wood surface. Pin one edge, through the unworked section, to the wood with thumb tacks, making sure that it is quite straight and taut. Space the tacks so that they are 3mm (⅛″) apart.
Pull the opposite edge firmly to keep it taut and to straighten it and tack it in the same way. Check that the corners are square by measuring diagonally between opposite corners; the measurement should be equal, so correct if necessary. Then tack the two remaining sides (fig.2).

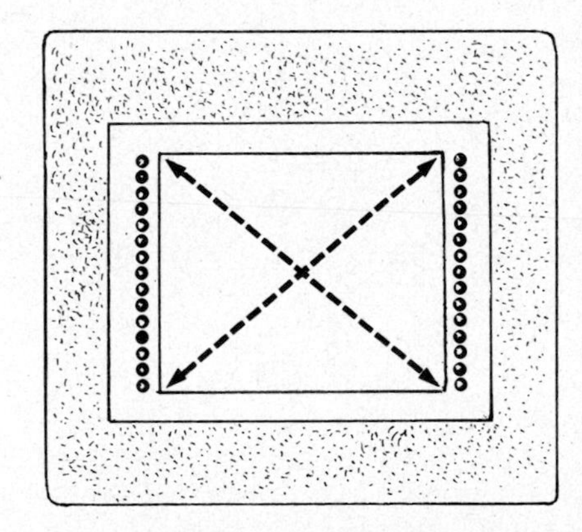

2. *Dampened canvas tacked to wood to stretch it and restore its shape.*

Dampen again evenly with the sponge and remove any wrinkles with your fingers. This dampening loosens the stiffening gum in the canvas and makes it pliable. When the canvas dries again it resets the threads in the correct position and keeps the work flat.

Tent stitch designs

Before you start on a major project in tent stitch, it is a good idea to practice it on a small item first and to try working it in different directions. If you combine the methods, be careful to

Tent stitch

Tent stitch can be worked horizontally, vertically and diagonally to suit the direction of the pattern you are using.

Of the three methods, working it diagonally produces less distortion on the canvas because the needle passes parallel to the threads on the wrong side rather than diagonally as with the other two methods.

To work tent stitch horizontally (fig.3a), start at the right hand end of the row and bring the needle through to the right side of the canvas. Insert it at hole 2 and bring it out at hole 3. Continue in this way to the end of the row.

For the next and following rows, finish the last stitch of the row and take the needle through to the wrong side of the work. Bring it through the hole immediately above, turn the canvas around and work the stitches from right to left as before (fig.3b).

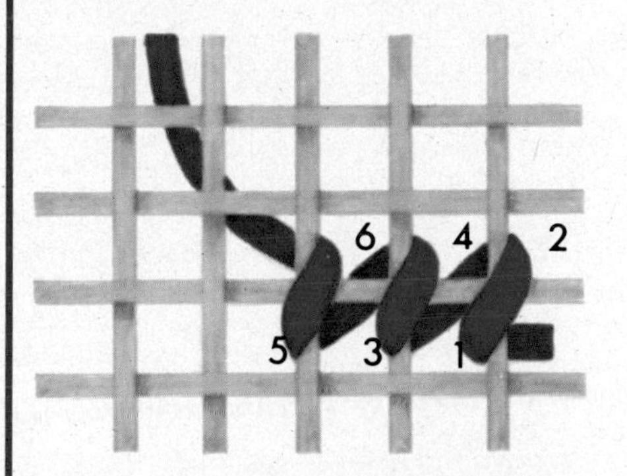

3a. *Tent stitch worked horizontally.*

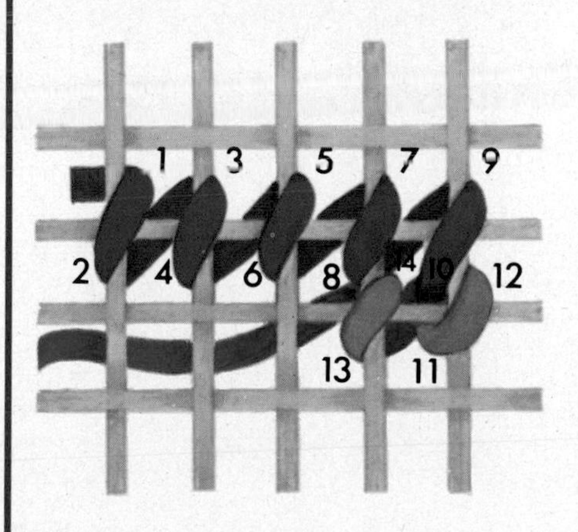

3b. *Canvas turned for row 2.*

To work tent stitch vertically (fig.4a), bring the thread through to the right side of the canvas and insert it at hole 2. Bring it through at hole 3, immediately below hole 1. Insert it at hole 4, next to hole 1. Continue in this way to the end of the row. Take the needle through to the back of the canvas and turn the work around. Bring the needle through the hole immediately to the left of the last hole and continue the row as before (fig.4b).

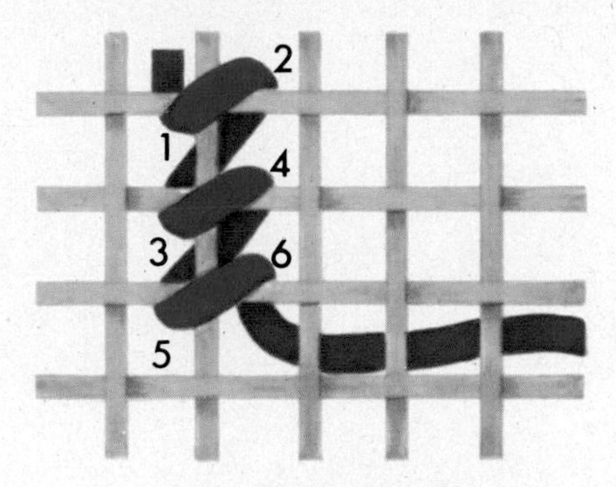

4a. *Tent stitch worked vertically.*

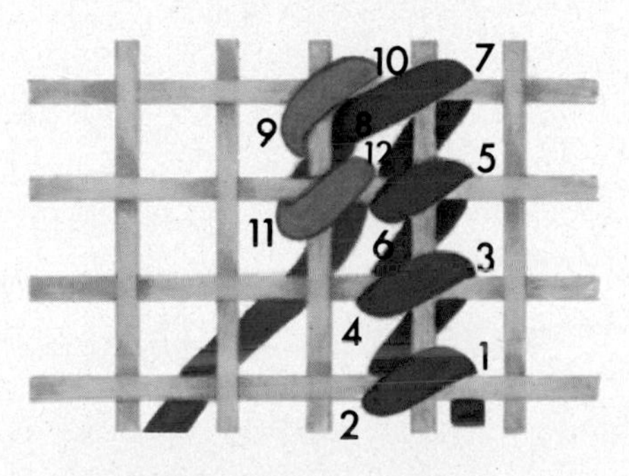

4b. *Canvas turned for row 2.*

6. *Wrong side of diagonal tent stitch.*

To work tent stitch diagonally (fig.5a), start at the bottom right-hand corner of the first row and bring the needle through at hole 1. Insert it at hole 2 and bring it out at hole 3, two holes to the left. Continue in this way to the top left hand corner of the row. For the next row, do not turn the canvas around but bring out the needle in the hole immediately below the last one. Insert it diagonally as shown, pass it vertically down the canvas and bring it out two holes below (fig.5b).

Work the third and every alternate row as for the first row and the fourth and every alternate row as for the second row. As the work progresses you will notice how a basket-weave effect develops on the wrong side of the canvas (fig.6)

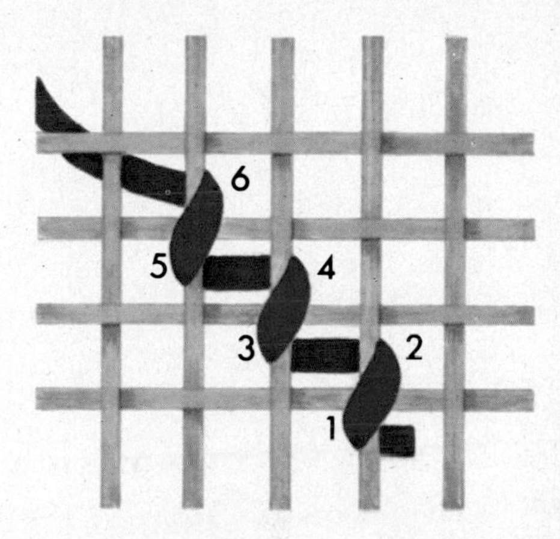

5a. *Tent stitch worked diagonally.*

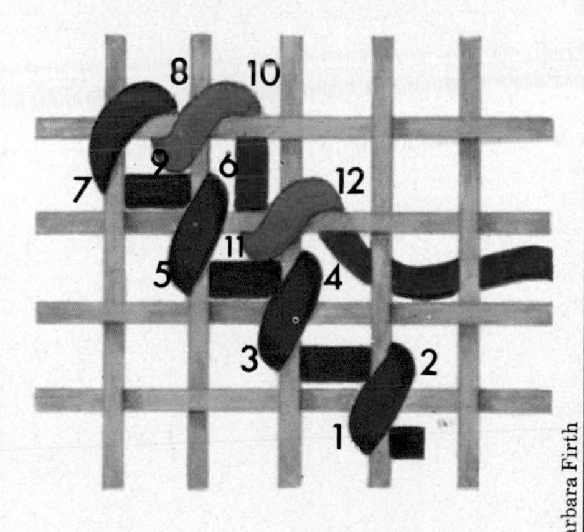

Barbara Firth

5b. *Starting the second row.*

keep the stitch sloping in the same direction on the right side.

The designs worked next page show how tent stitch can be used for backgrounds because it throws into relief more important areas of texture, such as the heart which is worked in satin stitch (see Needlepoint chapter 3, page 120).

If you intend to make more than one of the cases, you can save on the amount of canvas you need by working them on one large piece. Allow at least 2.5cm (1″) between the amount allowed for each case with 5cm (2″) around the outside. Mark the area for each case on the canvas with basting or with felt-tipped pen and then the centers of each in both directions in basting. The yarn quantities are the amounts you need per case but if you are making more than one in the same colors you will probably have some left over which can be used for the next case.

Theo Bergström

Tent stitch glasses case

Completed size: 9.5cm ($3\frac{3}{4}''$) x 16.5cm ($6\frac{1}{2}''$)

You will need:

Single canvas 16 threads per 2.5cm (1″), measuring 15cm (6″) x 20cm (8″).

Yarn, 2 skeins Bucilla crewel wool in background color, 1 skein in main contrast color for the heart, $\frac{1}{2}$ skein for the second contrast color.

Felt to match the heart for lining and backing the case, measuring 30.5cm (12″) x 16.5cm ($6\frac{1}{2}''$).

Piece of non-woven iron-on interfacing, 9.5cm ($3\frac{3}{4}''$) x 16.5cm ($6\frac{1}{2}''$).

Tapestry needle.

Matching sewing thread and needle.

☐ Mark the center of the canvas in both directions with basting and mark the dimensions of the glasses case to come exactly in the center of the canvas.

☐ Mount the canvas into a frame.

☐ Using four strands of the main contrast color in the needle, count ten threads in from the left hand side of the marked area and three threads up from the center. Bring the needle through and start working the outline of the heart following the chart, working in a clockwise direction.

When the outline is worked, fill in the middle.

☐ Next work the flowers, positioning them as shown on the chart and using four strands of yarn in the needle. Work the centers of the flowers first in cross stitch (see Needlepoint chapter 5, page 568) and fill in the petals in satin stitch.

☐ Using three strands of yarn in the needle, work one row of cross stitch across the base of the case in the main contrast color and three rows across the top using the main contrast color for the inner row, then the second contrast color with the background color on the outer edge.

☐ Work the background in tent stitch, using three strands of yarn.

Finishing. Remove the canvas from the frame and stretch to shape if necessary. Alternatively, pin it to shape on an ironing board and press under a damp cloth. Leave to dry thoroughly.

☐ Trim the canvas to within 1.5cm ($\frac{1}{2}''$) of the worked area. Fold the turnings onto the wrong side, mitering the corners, and herringbone to the back of the needlepoint (see Needlepoint chapter 2, page 62).

☐ Cut the felt into three equal sections, each 9.5cm ($3\frac{3}{4}''$) x 16.5cm ($6\frac{1}{2}''$). Place one section onto the wrong side of the needlepoint and slip stitch in place. Place the interfacing onto one of the remaining pieces and iron on.

Lighter case, glasses case and pin cushion with satin stitch motifs thrown into relief by tent stitch background. Designed by Pearson Gorman School.

Place the third piece of felt onto the interfaced side of the second piece and hem neatly along one short side. Put this double piece onto the wrong side of the needlepoint with the hemmed edge at the top. Hem the remaining three sides neatly to the needlepoint to form a firm back for the case.

Pin cushion

Completed size 9.5cm (3¾″) x 8cm (3¼″).

You will need:

Single canvas 16 threads per 2.5cm (1″), measuring 15cm (6″) x 14cm (5½″).
Yarn, 1 skein Bucilla crewel wool in background color, 1 skein in contrast color.
Felt for back of the cushion, measuring 10.5cm (4¼″) x 9.5cm (3¾″).
Small amount of sawdust or bran for stuffing the cushion. (Sawdust or bran must be used if you will be using the cushion regularly because the pins can be pushed in easily.)
Tapestry needle.
Matching sewing thread and needle.

☐ Prepare the canvas in the same way as for the glasses case and work the heart in the middle using four strands of yarn in the needle.

☐ Using three strands of yarn in the needle, work a border of cross stitch around the outside of the case, in the main color, leaving a hole between each stitch. Go around the border again, filling in the gaps with cross stitch in the contrast color.

☐ Using three strands of yarn in the needle, work a border of tent stitch in the contrast color along the inner edge of the cross stitch and then fill in the background in tent stitch.

Finishing. Remove the canvas from the frame and press it as for the glasses case.

☐ Trim to the same size as the felt and place the felt onto the right side of it. Machine stitch around three sides as close to the cross stitch as possible. Trim the corners diagonally and turn right side out. Press the seams with your fingers.

☐ Fill the case well with the stuffing, fold under the turnings along the opening and slip stitch the folds firmly together, making sure that none of the stuffing can leak out.

Chart for glasses case. Use the motifs for the other designs.

Lighter case

Completed size: 7.5cm (3″) square.

You will need:

Single canvas 16 threads per 2.5cm (1″) measuring 12.5cm (5″) square.
Yarn, 1 skein Bucilla crewel wool in background color, ½ skein each in two contrasting colors.
Piece of felt, 16.5cm (6½″) x 7.5cm (3″)
Tapestry needle.
Matching sewing thread and needle.

☐ Prepare the canvas as for the glasses case and work a flower in the center using four strands of yarn in the needle. Work the remaining flowers, following the color arrangement shown in the photograph.

☐ Work a border of satin stitch over two threads of canvas in one contrast color around the edge of the case and then a border of cross stitch over two threads along the inner edge of the satin stitch.

☐ Work the background in tent stitch using three strands of yarn in the needle.

Finishing. Remove the canvas from the frame and press it. Trim the unworked canvas to within 1.5cm (½″) of the stitching and fold the turnings down on the wrong side, mitering the corners. Herringbone to the back of the needlepoint.

☐ Cut a 7.5cm (3″) square from the felt. Hem the square to the back of the needlepoint. Turn under one of the shorter edges of the remaining piece of felt for 1.5cm (½″) and hem neatly. Place the piece onto the back of the case and hem neatly around three remaining sides. Finish off securely.

Cats and dogs from one pattern

The previous Toys chapter shows you how to make a pony from felt which has a soft filling and is machine stitched. This chapter gives instructions for making two more felt toys—a dog and a cat—from one pattern. These toys are 10cm (4″) high (excluding the tail) and stitched together by hand using a small, spaced blanket (simple buttonhole) stitch.

The dog

You will need:
30cm (12″) square of brown felt.
Matching, single strand, embroidery thread, such as Coton à Broder.
Scraps of white, black and cerise felt for tail bow, eyes and nose.
Acrylic stuffing.
Clear, general-purpose glue for attaching nose, eyes and eyelids.

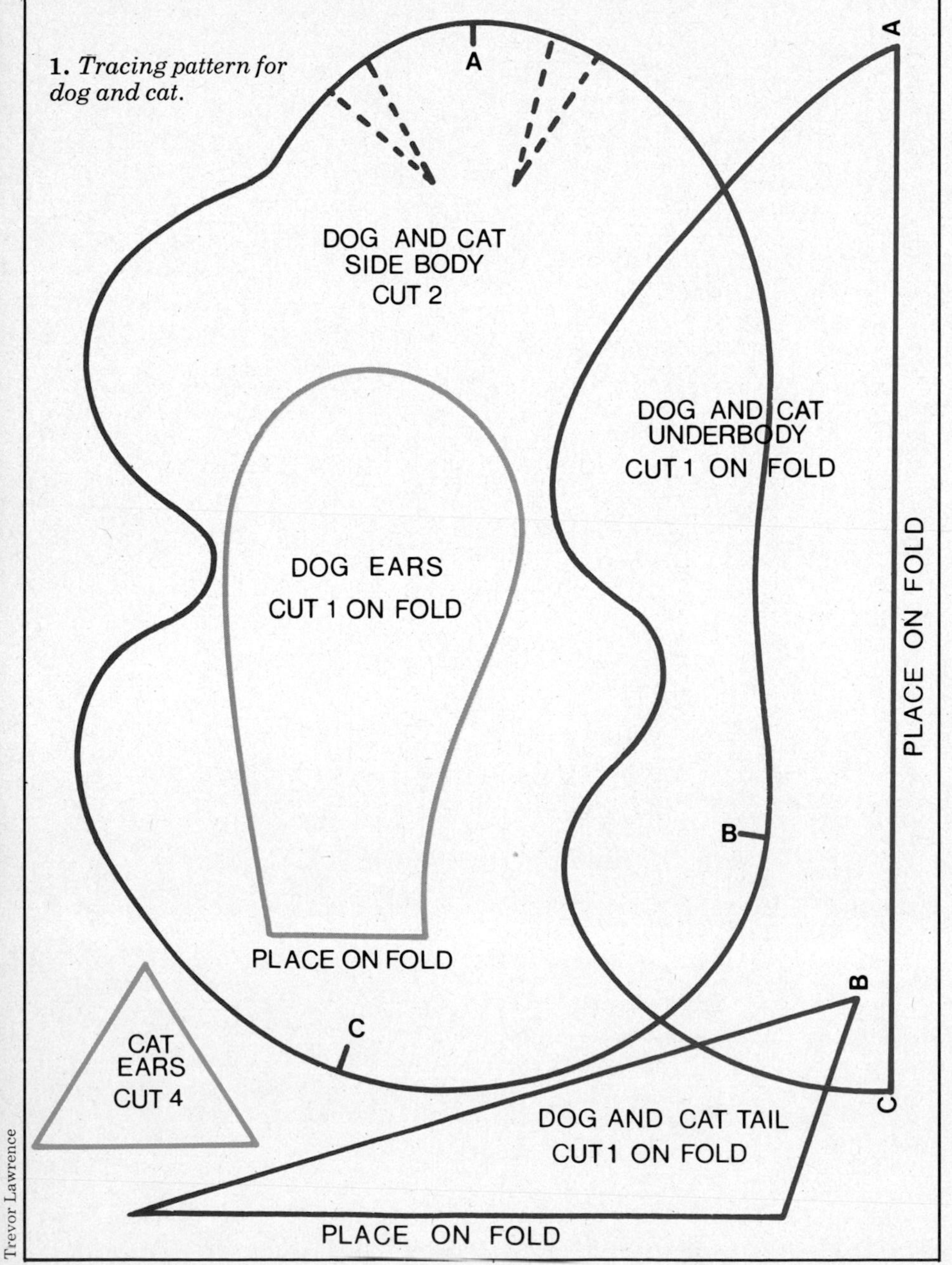

1. *Tracing pattern for dog and cat.*

Trevor Lawrence

□ Following fig.1 trace the appropriate pattern pieces for the dog. In brown felt, cut out two side body sections, and cut one tail, an ear section and an underbody on the fold. Mark in the darts on each side body section.
□ Stitch in the darts of the wrong side.
□ Baste the two side body sections together along the top from A-B, wrong sides together. Sew with a small blanket stitch.
□ Baste and blanket stitch underbody to sides, matching points A and C. Leave the back of the animal open between B and C.
□ Fold tail in half lengthwise, wrong sides together. Baste and blanket stitch along long edge.
□ Stuff tail, pushing filling down with a knitting needle.
□ Stuff the body firmly, pushing the filling in with a pencil or knitting needle.
□ Slip stitch tail into the back opening matching tail seam to point B.
□ Push more stuffing into the body if necessary. Then baste and blanket stitch the opening.
□ Cut out circles of white and black felt for eyes and nose, using small coins as patterns. Using brown felt cut half circles for eyelids with a diameter slightly larger than the white circles.
□ Glue on nose, eyes and then eyelids.
□ Back stitch center of ears in place on head, over the center seam. Bend each ear forward and secure fold with a dab of glue (fig.2).

Victoria Drew

2. *Securing fold on ear with glue.*

□ Cut a strip of cerise felt 27cm x 1cm (11″x⅜″) and tie around base of tail in a bow. Glue in position if desired.

The cat

You will need:
20cm (8″) square of orange felt.
15cm (6″) square of white felt.
Matching, and black, single strand, embroidery thread, such as Coton à Broder.
Scraps of green and black felt for tail bow, eyes and nose.
Bristles cut from soft broom for whiskers.
Stuffing and glue as for dog.

Roger Phillips

This delightful, hand stitched dog and cat are made from one basic pattern. Designed by Ruth Beard.

☐ Following fig.1 trace the appropriate pattern pieces for the cat. Cut out two side body sections, and two ears, and cut one tail on the fold in orange felt. From white felt cut out two more ears and cut one underbody on the fold.

☐ Make up body and tail as for dog.

☐ Cut circles for eyes in green felt, using a small coin as a pattern.

☐ Make a long straight stitch down the center of each circle with black embroidery thread, then glue in place.

☐ Cut half circles for eyelids in orange felt, with a diameter slightly larger than the eyes. Glue in place.

☐ Glue or stitch center of whiskers to center of face.

☐ Stitch mouth with black embroidery thread, making three long straight stitches.

☐ Cut a small heart shaped nose in black felt and glue in place over whiskers.

☐ Take one orange ear and one white one and blanket stitch together along two sides. Stitch the other two together in the same way. Overcast to head above eyes along the third side.

☐ Cut a strip of green felt 27cm x 1cm (11″x$\frac{3}{8}$″) and tie around base of tail in a bow. Glue in position if desired.

Texture, stripes and leashes

Yarn — weaving 11

To relieve the flatness of a tapestry you may want to incorporate areas of textural contrast. This can be done by experimenting with fancy yarns or unusual materials (see Weaving chapter 5, page 374) or by using ordinary yarn in an unusual way. Never be frightened to experiment as there are no hard and fast rules.
Here are some long established techniques to start you off.

1. *The Ghiordes knot creates a pile.*

2. *An upward knot falls the other way.*

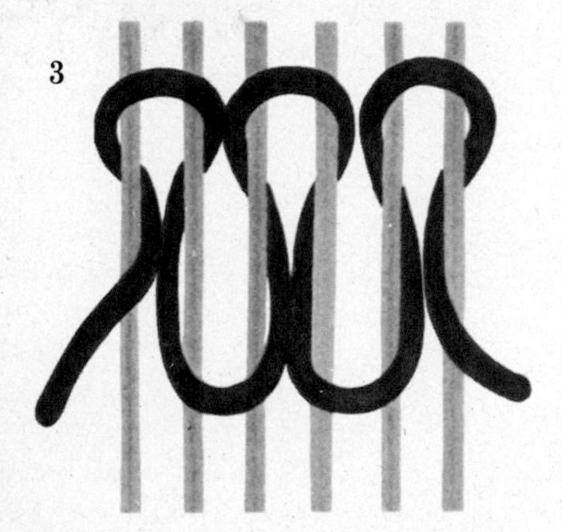

3. *Row of knots made with one thread.*

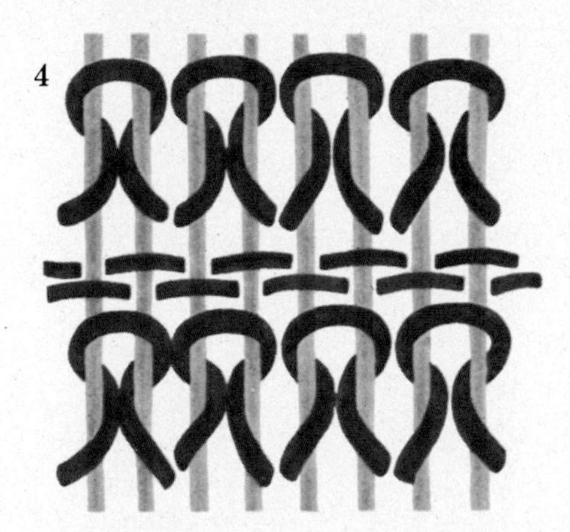

4. *Strengthen with rows of weaving.*

The Ghiordes knot

The Ghiordes or Turkish knot is more commonly associated with rugs but it can give an interesting tufted effect when incorporated with tapestry.
Loop the yarn as illustrated (fig.1) over two warp ends and pull it down to the weaving. Do not pull too tightly or you will alter the spacing of the warp threads. If you wish to get the tuft lying in the opposite direction, make the knot in the reverse way (fig.2).
A row of knots can either be made separately using short pieces of yarn or several can be made with a continuous thread (fig.3). Irregular tufts can create a shingled effect especially if made with an unusual material such as thin strips of suede. Usually, however, a thick, multi-ply yarn is used so that a firm shaggy tuft is created.
Always weave at least one and preferably two rows of ordinary tapestry weave between rows of knots. Traditionally, knots are always made over the same two warp ends however many rows of knots are made (fig.4).

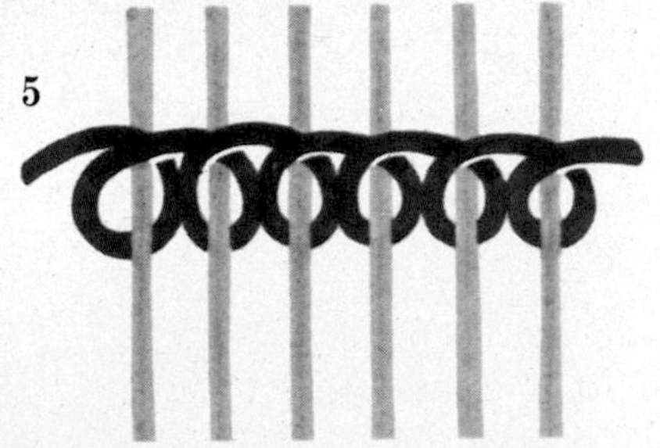

5. *Soumak gives a nice raised area.*

6. *Missing out warp ends.*

Victoria Drew

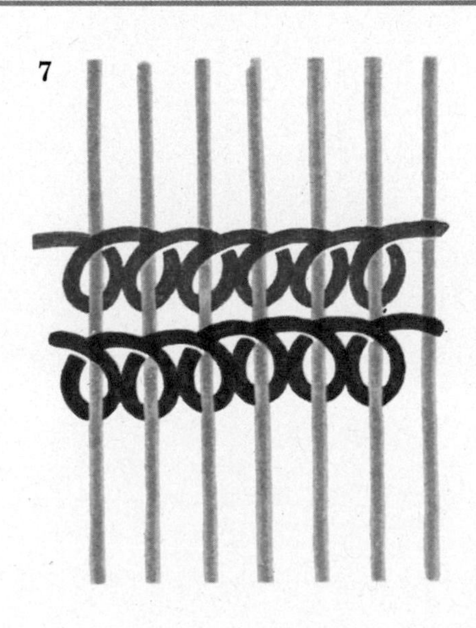

7. *Two rows in different colors.*

Soumak

Soumak gives a nice raised contrast to tapestry weave. It can be woven over every warp end (fig.5) or you can miss out a regular number of warp ends (fig.6). Two consecutive rows of soumak can be woven and if the direction is altered an interesting braided effect, rather like knitting stitches, is created (fig.7). Strengthen your weaving by inserting a pick of tapestry weave between rows of soumak.

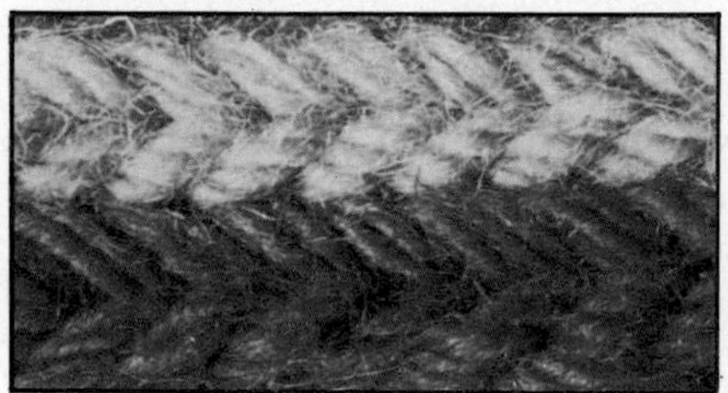

Dick Miller

Effect of two rows of soumak.

Twining

Another technique is to twist two weft threads between the warp ends (fig.8). Again, you can miss out warp threads (fig.9) or do two rows together, alternating the colored wefts (fig.10).

8, 9 and 10. *Twining is another technique that gives a textural contrast to a flat tapestry. Missing out warp ends or using two different colors are interesting variations.*

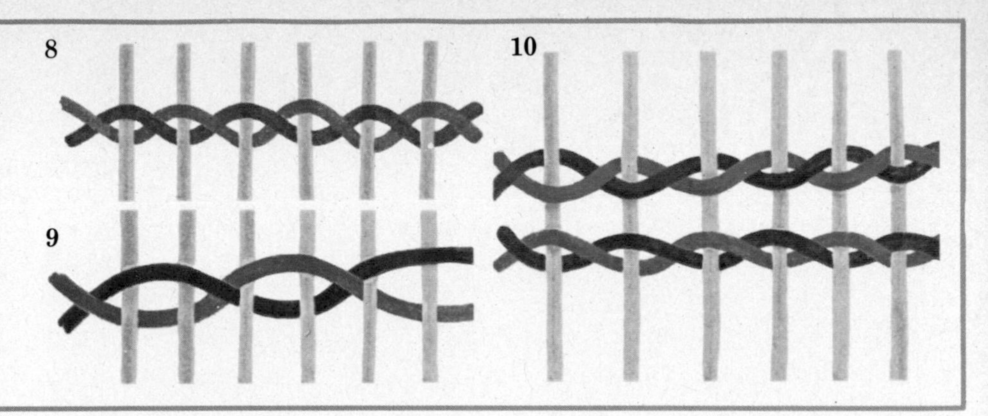

Stripes

Bands of plain color which cover the whole width of the warp can be woven quickly if the process of making a shed is mechanically operated. To do this you need two additions to your loom—a thin piece of wood to lift the even threads up and a system of leashes or heddles to lift the odd warp ends.

Shed stick

A piece of pinewood 1.25cm x 3.75cm x 61cm (½"x1½"x24") should be inserted near the top of the frame under the even warp ends and over the odd ones, just like a row of weaving. When the shed stick is stood on its side it lifts the even warps and the bobbin can be passed straight through the shed completing one pick of weaving.

Leashes

There are two methods of leashes suitable for the small frame loom:

Simple method. Cut lengths of cotton yarn 38cm (15") long. You will need enough cotton lengths to lift up half of the number of warp ends in your frame.

☐ Pass each yarn length around an odd warp end below the shed stick.

☐ Gather them together into groups of six.

☐ Tie them together in groups of six so that the knot is about 6cm (2½") above the warp (fig.11).

With this method the number of warp ends lifted at a time is six and each row has to be woven in small chunks. This method is useful for small areas of solid color but the leashes have a tendency to slide down and obstruct the weaving.

Advanced method. A more satisfactory way of dealing with leashes is to tie them onto a rod which is placed across the warp.

You will need:

Two 10cm (4") C-clamps.

Dowel rod, 61cm (24") long and 2.5cm (1") in diameter.

Cotton yarn.

Frame loom (Weaving chapter 6, page 572).

☐ Screw the two clamps to the outside of the frame loom uprights, about one third of the way down from the top.

☐ Tie the rod securely to the C-clamps.

☐ Push the two cross sticks up the warp so that they lie about 2.5cm (1") below the dowel rod.

☐ Tie them to the sides of the frame. The cross sticks ensure that the leashes will all be of the same length as they keep the warp threads even.

☐ Cut the cotton yarn into 38cm (15") lengths. You will need enough lengths to cover every other warp thread.

☐ Pick up an odd warp end from between the cross sticks and pass a leash around it (fig.12).

☐ Tie the leash to the dowel rod with a reef knot.

☐ Repeat this with all the other odd warp ends. The leashes should all have the same amount of slack.

☐ Untie the cross sticks and return them to their normal position.

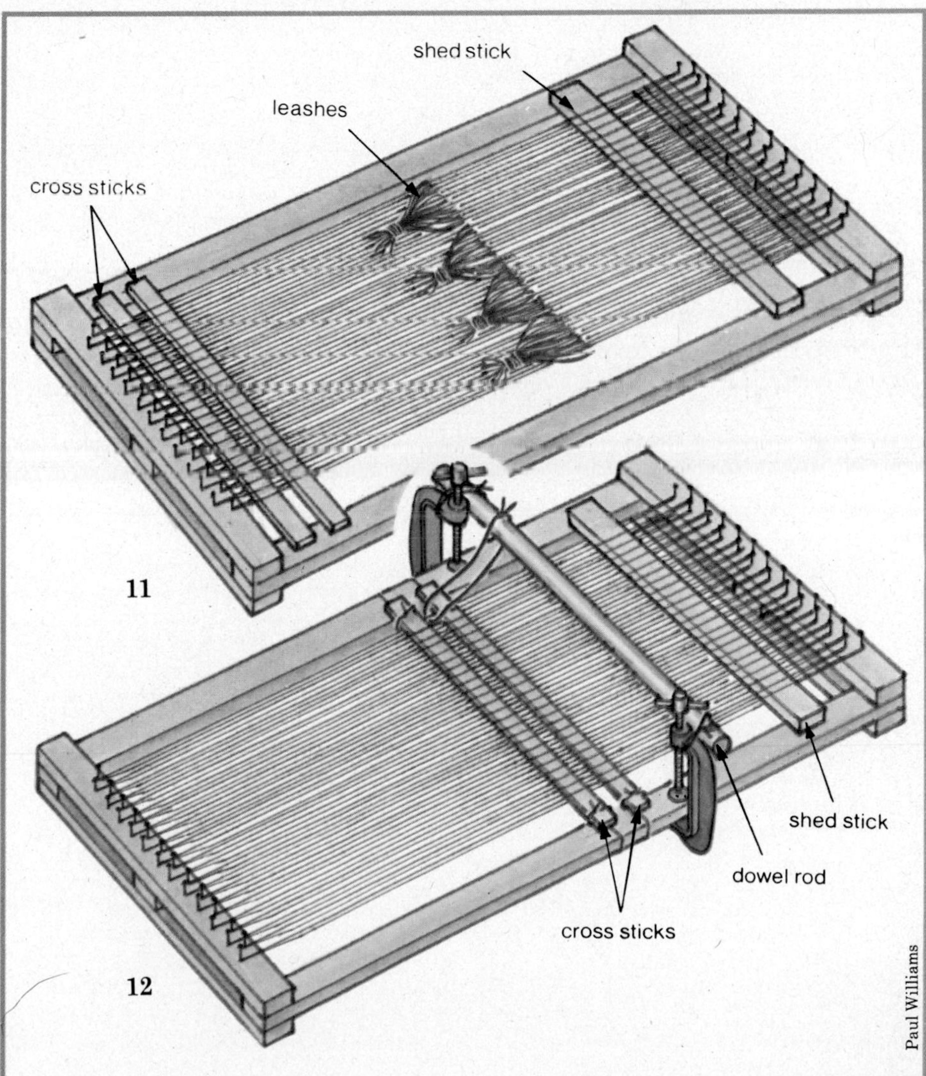

11. *Simple method of putting leashes on the frame loom.* **12.** *Tying leashes around a dowel rod using the cross sticks to keep them even.*

Weaving with leashes

To weave a horizontal stripe or solid area of color, all you have to do is pass the shuttle through the sheds made first by standing the shed stick on its side and then by pulling on the leashes. The shed stick will lift all the even threads and after the stick has been returned to its horizontal position, the leashes will lift the odd warp ends as you pull them.

Dick Miller

Pull the leashes to lift the odd warps. The shed stick lifts the evens.

The pillow cover

The pillow cover uses all of the techniques described already. The striped flat area in the middle is 30cm (12″) square and was woven using leashes for speed. The textural area at each end of the cover includes soumak, twining and Ghiordes knots. The final pillow cover measures 30cm x 45cm (12″x18″).

You will need:

One ball of linen warp with a count of 8/3.

Five different colors of 3-ply rug yarn. The colors used in the pillow cover illustrated were not bought commercially but were obtained by dyeing raw wool. The beige wool was dyed in cold tea, the mauve in lichen and all the others in commercial dyes (see Dyeing chapter 3, page 382).

Three colors of 6-ply rug yarn for the textural area. If you prefer you can use the normal 3-ply, doubled.

Frame loom (see Weaving chapter 6, page 572).

Extras for the leashes as listed above.

☐ Warp up 31cm (12½″) of your frame loom so that you have a sett of eight ends per 2.5cm (1″).

☐ Put leashes on using either method described above. As you will be weaving 30cm (12″) of tapestry going from selvage to selvage it is probably advisable to adopt the advanced method using the C-clamps.

☐ Weave about 1.25cm (½″) with any waste yarn you have available. This area of weaving simply brings the threads together and spaces them easily—it will be pulled out after the pillow cover is finished. It also gives you a nice straight edge for the real first row of the pillow cover.

☐ Choose any color yarn and weave about 6mm (¼″). Although this area will be part of the final cover, it will be covered by the overhanging tufts.

☐ Cut 15cm (6″) lengths of two colors of 6-ply rug yarn (alternatively use 3-ply doubled).

☐ Miss out the double thread of the selvage and using alternate colors, make a row of downward Ghiordes knots on each pair of warp threads (see fig.1).

☐ Take your weft thread from the previous area of weaving and wrap it twice around the selvage so that it is covered. (You can of course change the color, but do remember to bind the selvages.) When you get to the other side bind that selvage.

☐ Weave two picks of tapestry weave in 3-ply yarn.

☐ Do a row of knots using 12.5cm (5″) lengths of yarn. Make the knots around the same warp ends as were used in the previous row and keep to the same color scheme to achieve the striped effect.

☐ Weave two picks of tapestry weave in the 3-ply yarn.

☐ Do a row of knots using 10cm (4″) lengths. Do not forget to wrap around the selvages of each row of knots.

☐ Weave a few rows of plain tapestry weave in 3-ply until your weaving measures 2.5cm (1″) from the top of the waste yarn (ie the beginning of the weaving proper).

☐ Do two consecutive rows of soumak using only one color 6-ply yarn. Go over four and back two warp ends as in fig.6 and reverse the direction of the rows to achieve braided effect (fig.7).

☐ Weave a pick of plain tapestry weave with 3-ply yarn.

☐ Weave two more rows of soumak using a different color yarn.

Dick Miller

Detail of the textured area of the pillow showing the final effect of the knots, soumak and twining.

The pillow cover has a textured area at each end framing the stripes. Stripes are woven with leashes for speed. Pillow designed by Jane Moran.

☐ Weave 6mm (¼") of plain tapestry weave.
☐ Do two rows of twining using two colors of 6-ply yarn in each row to achieve the braided effect (see fig.10).
☐ Weave two picks of plain tapestry weave.
☐ Do two more rows of twining.
This should bring you up to about 7.5cm (3") from top of the waste yarn.
☐ Using the leashes, weave plain bands of color for the next 30cm (12"). Either make regular stripes or avoid all pattern making by going for irregular areas of contrast. Use as many colors as you like.
☐ After you have completed 30cm (12") of the striped area, you simply repeat the first 7.5cm (3") only in reverse. The knots should be made upward (see fig.2) so that they fall in the opposite direction to the ones the other end.
☐ There is no need to weave the area of waste yarn at the end.

Finishing off

☐ Cut the piece off the loom and cut the warp loops.
☐ Rip out the area of waste yarn.
☐ Using a darning needle, thread each warp end up inside the back of the weaving. This creates a nice, clean straight edge at each end.
☐ Fray out the tufts of the knots so that they have a nice velvety effect. Trim them if you prefer them shorter or less regular.
☐ Make up into a pillow cover with a contrasting, plain material as the reverse side.

Linoleum printing on cloth

Linoleum cut designs can be successfully printed on cloth as well as on the paper surfaces already described. The linoleum cut is in fact derived from the earliest form of printing on cloth, the wood block, and the methods for printing remain virtually the same for both.

Designing for fabric printing

This is a fascinating occupation in itself and the practical application can be even more rewarding since you can transform the linen cupboard, the clothes you already have or those you intend to make.

On clothing, a single motif printed on a patch-pocket or a handkerchief is decorative but you can take better advantage of the printing medium by stamping your design repeatedly along the hem of a skirt or all over some napkins.

Household linens are excellent printing surfaces, but remember you will be working with colors that 'take' on natural fibers, eg silk, linen, cotton, wool, and on viscose rayon, and not on mixed fibers or other synthetics.

Suede, another natural fiber, can also be embellished with linoleum designs and a tan suede coat, for example, with a dark brown motif printed on a pocket or a delicate border decorating the edges would look very original.

Fabric: to best exploit the potential of linoleum decoration on clothing, however, it is best to print the cloth before the garment is made up. Either print a length of cloth in an all-over pattern of your own design or cut out the cloth and then print motifs that follow or complement the contours of the pattern. By following the shape of the cut out pattern you can decorate the curve of a shoulder line or a neckline and by printing a garment before it is sewn you can position motifs more accurately.

To position motifs on garments it is wise to print the motif (or motifs) on paper first and cut it out. Then you can arrange it exactly where you want it to go and either mark or outline the position with tailor's chalk.

Colors

Fabric can be printed using either fabric printing inks or cold water fabric dye in paste form. Both work equally well but the methods of printing are slightly different so choice depends largely on personal preferences and availability. Fabric printing inks do tend to give a slight stiffness to cloth but this can be quite effective. Both ink and fabric paste dyes can be bought at most art supply and craft shops.

Printing with inks

There are two ways to print using fabric printing inks; the first, a straightforward stamping technique, is very similar to printing on paper while the second requires mounting the linoleum block on wood and striking it with a mallet to print. This method is easier to use if the motif is to be repeated.

To print by stamping, you will need the same equipment as for paper printing, eg a roller and slab, turpentine and rags for cleaning up and a palette knife or old dinner knife for mixing colors.

Place the fabric on a work table, roll up the linoleum with a generous coating of ink, place it face down on

Dick Miller

A linoleum cut printed on a variety of fabrics: suede, burlap, rayon, velvet, cord, silk and cotton. The design is by Barbara Pegg.

the fabric and press carefully and firmly all over the back. Then gently peel the linoleum away from the fabric.

Printing from a mounted block. When you have cut your design into the linoleum, glue it with a strong glue to a block of wood the same size as the linoleum and at least 9cm (¾") thick.

For your working surface use an old blanket stretched over a table, and pin a piece of cotton or plastic sheeting to the blanket. The blanket gives a resilient printing surface, and the article or pattern pieces you are printing can be pinned to the backing which can be changed when necessary for a clean piece. Pin the fabric all around the edges, stretched as flat as possible, so they cannot lift while the block is being moved to the next position.

If you are printing a motif which has a correct way up, it is helpful to mark the back of your block with an arrow at the top.

Print by positioning the block on the cloth and then striking it with a mallet or stick. If the block is a small one then one tap will be sufficient but larger surfaces need several strikes. The wood backing spreads the pressure of the blow and insures a clear print. An unmounted block would have a darker area of color at the point you hit it.

Block printing in this way, using cut wood blocks, is still a flourishing business in India and Persia and the famous 19th-century textile prints of William Morris were also made using this method.

Using fabric dyes

Fabric dyes, even in paste form, are more liquid than inks so it is necessary to give the linoleum an absorbent surface. This is done by a process known as flocking.

Melvin Grey

Above: When linoleum printing with fabric dyes it is necessary to coat or 'flock' the surface of the linoleum cut with powdered fibers so that it will become absorbent and hold the dye.

Right: elegant caftan in apricot silk by designer Penny LeRoy is entirely handprinted with linoleum blocks.

Sandra Lousada

Simple repeating printing with linoleum cuts is illustrated in this design for table linen by Barbara Pegg.

Flocking involves the use of special powdered fibers and a flocking mordant or glue to make it stick. Both are available from art supply shops along with fabric dyes.

To flock: put some flocking powder into a jar and make a number of small holes in the lid or use a salt shaker.

Roll the flocking mordant onto a linoleum block that has been cut and mounted on wood. You can use your clean printing roller for this purpose, rolling on the mordant just as you would the color.

If the glue is water soluble, the roller can be cleaned with water and detergent. Otherwise use the solvent indicated by the manufacturer for cleaning.

Sprinkle the flocking powder liberally onto the sticky mordanted surface of the block to make a thick velvet layer. Shake off the surplus powder and repeat the process three times.

Leave to dry overnight and then brush off any surplus powder with a stiff brush. Your printing block is now absorbent enough to hold the dye.

To print, put a blanket underneath the cloth as described.

Make a stamping pad by soaking either a pad of fabric or a thin dish-washing sponge cloth in a dish of dye.

Press the block into the pad and then onto the fabric you wish to print. When the block is in place on the fabric strike it with a wooden mallet or stick.

Always use the stamping pad to collect fresh dye before each printing.

When printing is completed, clean the block with water. If the brand of mordant you are using is not water soluble

then you can re-use the flocked printing block. Otherwise you will have to re-flock in order to print more later.
If you wish to remove the flocking powder from the block and the mordant is not water soluble then use the spirit solvent recommended by the manufacturers.
Dye manufacturers give instructions for fixing dyes on the fabric, usually by ironing on the back of the printed area for about five minutes with a fairly hot iron.

Tracing pattern for table linen motif.

Pony design by Janet Allen could be used to print a single motif on a child's garment or to make a border.

Janet Allen

Janet Allen

Walls for work and storage

One of the main obstacles to doing carpentry, making jewelry or doing pottery is not having the right place to work. Most people are not lucky enough to have a garage or basement workshop where they can leave the work spread out for as long as it takes to finish it. But it doesn't take a great deal of space to have a work area specially for your craft work. With enough storage space near your work surface it is easier to keep things tidy. Most houses, and even flats, have a corner of a room, or an empty hallway, or a shed or basement that has space enough for a small work area. And then all you need is a work top and a few shelves. Failing that, there is always the possibility of building a bench which can double as a kitchen table and fold away when not in use. Before you start buying or making a work table, see how far you can clear the decks by using wall space.

Basically what is needed is a work surface which is tough and sturdy to work on, and places to hang up tools and keep leftover material. But bear in mind that most crafts cause a certain degree of disorder so, when choosing a site, think ahead along these lines: will there be filings, sawdust, odors that may permeate nearby food storage, such as a pantry adjacent to a kitchen?

Is the area's floor surface sufficiently wear-resistant, water-proof, easy to clean, non-slip for work envisaged? The most obvious places to choose are those already mentioned, but keep in mind that you need good light when you work so place the work area either by a window or by a power point.

The power point must be in a good condition and safely earthed. If there isn't one, and you know you will need one, get it put in before you install your work surface. A convenient height is about 30cm (12″) above the proposed work surface. Place it slightly to the side so that it will not obstruct any tools that you may want to hang above the work surface.

If you are going to hang tools against a wall or make a work table that folds away against a wall make sure that the wall is suitable—most walls are. But sectional concrete garages are not suitable as these are generally reinforced with steel rods which make drilling difficult. Another disadvantage with concrete garages is that they are cold and encourage condensation, so it is not advisable to hang tools in this atmosphere unless they are coated with oil or lacquer to prevent rust. When drilling into a wall make sure that there are no power cables or plumbing pipes within the wall around the area where you are drilling. Start with shelves for storage space. See Carpentry chapter 6 page 354, for shelf ideas.

Battens are upright supports suitable for simple shelves. In a garage it is very simple to screw a few battens to the wall (providing they are not concrete sections), to which you can attach shelves by nailing small triangular pieces of plywood (called gusset plates) (fig.1). Screw fixing is preferable to nails, more because you can easily move them about, than for reasons of strength. If you use the gusset plates for supporting loose lumber tilt them up a bit at the front so that nothing can roll off. Shape the gusset plates so the vertical ends are flush with the battens against the wall.

Camera Press

Steve Bicknell

Above: each tool has its place and comes to hand easily when required.

Left: making the most of a small area to provide maximum storage space.

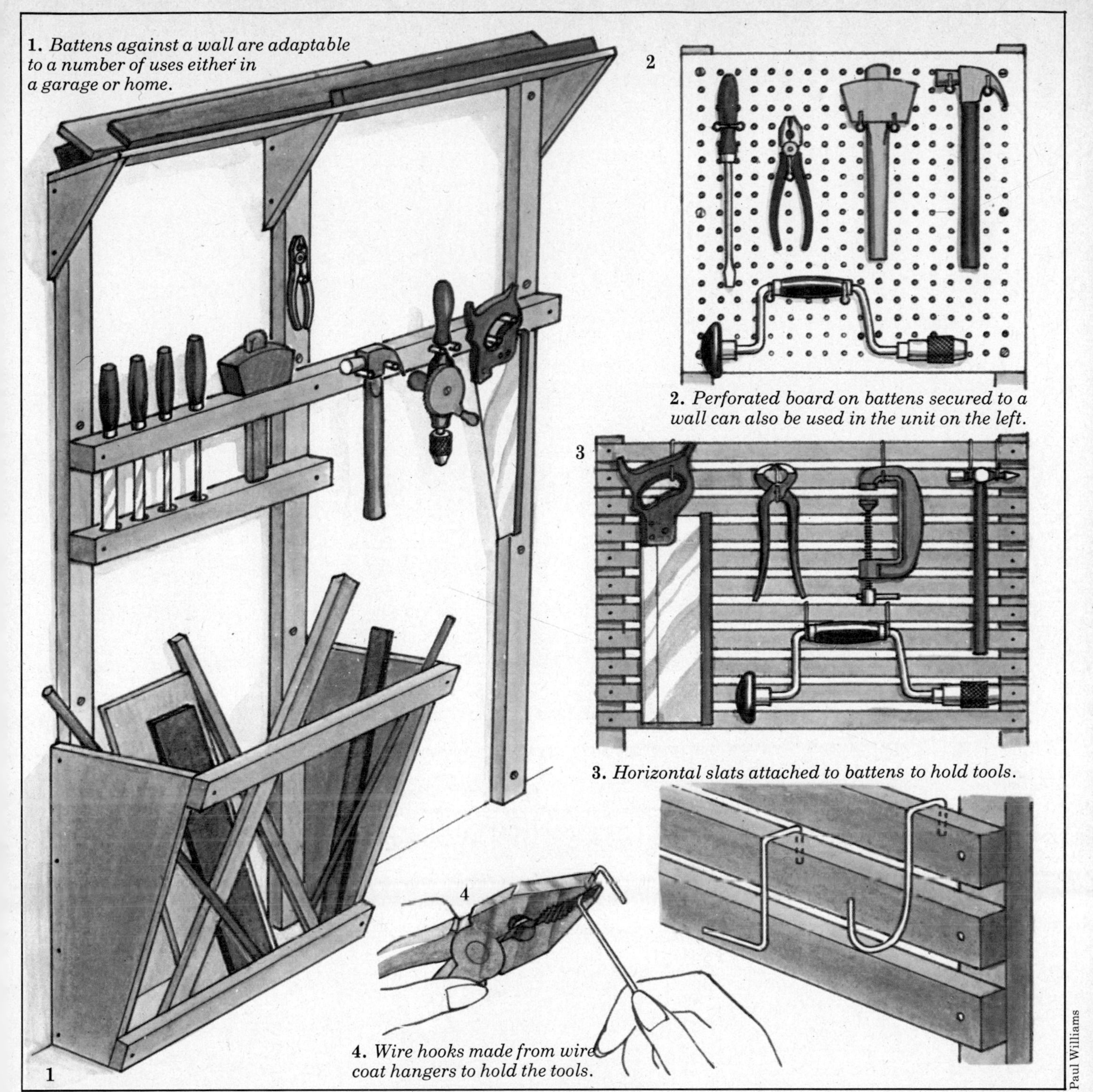

1. *Battens against a wall are adaptable to a number of uses either in a garage or home.*

2. *Perforated board on battens secured to a wall can also be used in the unit on the left.*

3. *Horizontal slats attached to battens to hold tools.*

4. *Wire hooks made from wire coat hangers to hold the tools.*

Storing tools
Chisels are inserted through a piece of wood so that the sharp ends fit into holes drilled in another piece of wood. This protects you and the edges of the chisel.
If you hang a saw make sure the teeth are protected by a plastic scabbard.
Small odds and ends can be put in an improvised 'bin' which is easily made from plywood; say 25cm (10″) wide at the top and about 10cm (4″) at the bottom. Nail it to the upright supports and attach a couple of battens along the front to hold the odds and ends (fig.1).

Perforated hardboard panels

Another useful idea is to screw a perforated Masonite sheet to the battens and then buy special hooks to hold your tools (fig.2).

Horizontal slats

Alternatively you can devise your own hanging space by nailing or screwing 12mm x 25mm (½″x1″) horizontal strips to the battens, leaving a space of about 12mm (½″) between them (fig.3).
You can then fashion hanging hooks in any shape by bending lengths of wire coat-hanger with a pair of pliers (fig. 4). File the ends of the wire smooth or double up the hook so that both ends will be at the back.
Another possibility is to drill holes at a downward angle into the slats and insert pieces of dowel rod so that they slant upward.
The advantage of using the horizontal slat method is that it is attractive enough to put up in a kitchen or hallway, and it can be used to hang up anything. In the kitchen it makes a wonderful place to arrange your utensils, in the study you can hang pencil containers and small boxes for other odds and ends.

Above: this versatile hang-up unit is suitable for the kitchen or workshop. It consists of a frame held together with lap joints. Right: a smaller unit is useful for sewing materials.

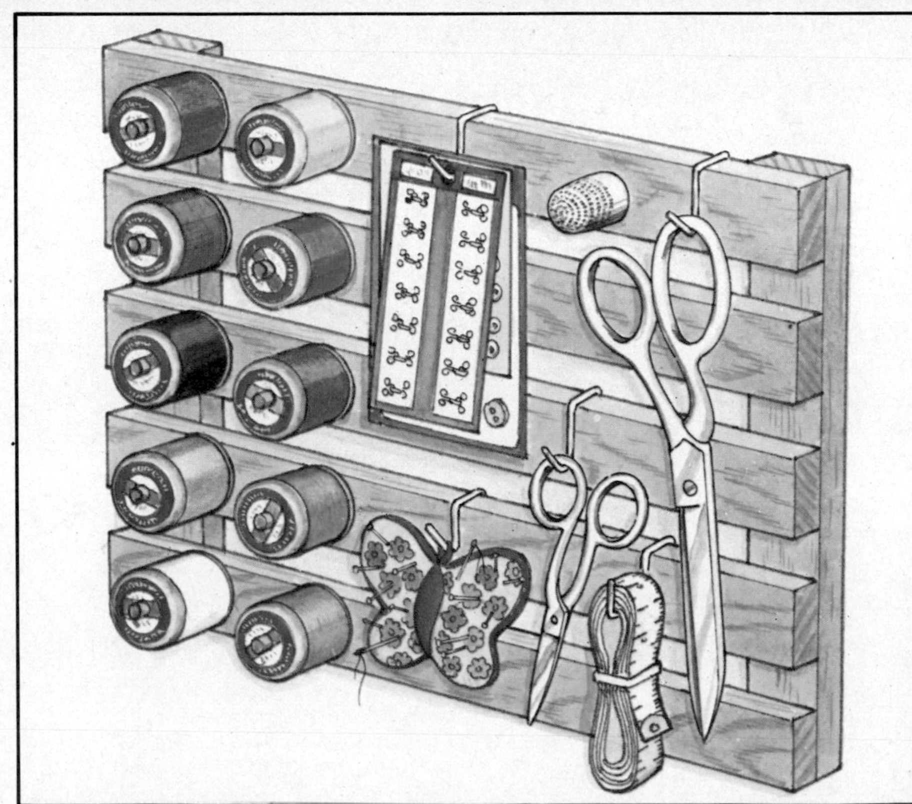

A hang-up unit

This versatile storage unit can be used in a kitchen, study or garage. The overall size is 91.4cm x 68.6cm (36″x27″). It consists of a framework, cross slats and back supports. The frame is joined together by lap joints.

You will need:
Panel saw.
Carpenter's square.
Screwdriver and hammer. Hand drill.
4 screws 31mm ($1\frac{1}{4}$″) long.
32 screws 25mm (1″) long.
Wood glue and sandpaper.
Polyurethane varnish, finishing nails.
Softwood 51mm x 19mm (2″x$\frac{3}{4}$″), 3.3m (11′) long.
Softwood 76mm x 19mm (3″x$\frac{3}{4}$″), 1.42m (56″) long.
Softwood 51mm x 51mm (2″x2″), 22cm ($8\frac{3}{4}$″) long.
Softwood 25mm x 19mm (1″x$\frac{3}{4}$″), 15m (16yd) long—from which to cut 16 horizontal slats each 87cm ($34\frac{1}{4}$″) long.

1. To make the frame cut the lengths of softwood indicated.
A lap joint is used to join two pieces of wood together.

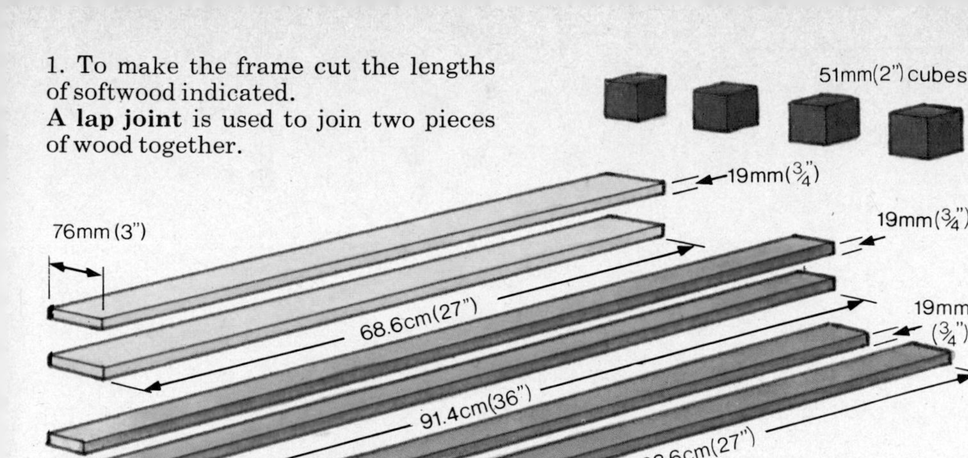

2. To make the lap joint place two pieces at right angles to each other and mark the width of each piece of wood onto the other. The mark on the vertical piece will be on the front and on the horizontal piece it will be at the back.

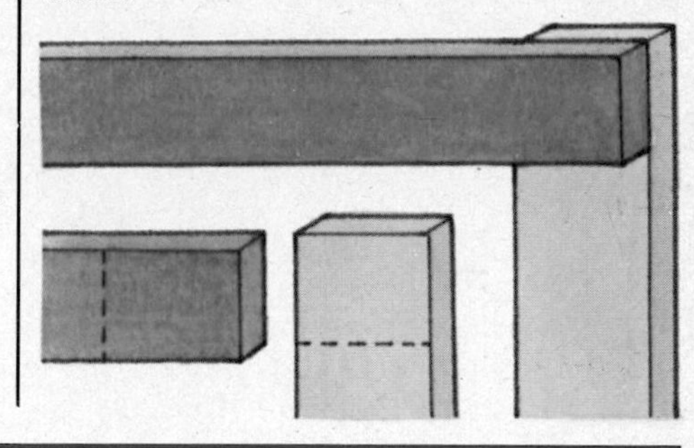

3. Using the saw cut along this line through exactly half the thickness of the wood.

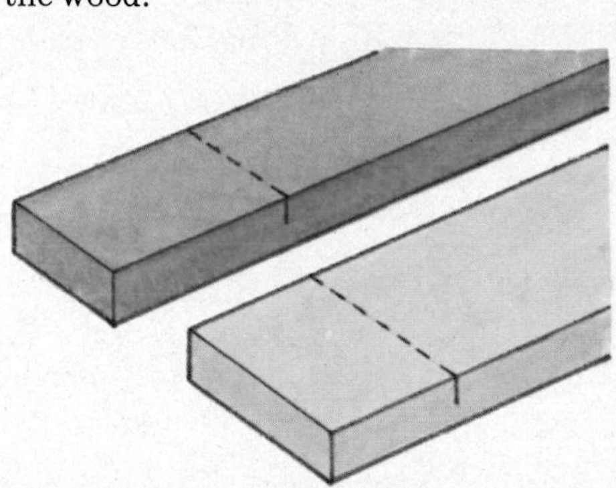

4. Along the width of the cross section draw a line to halve the thickness and cut down this line to the previous saw cut.

5. Repeat this with the other ends of the frame. Assemble the frame as shown.

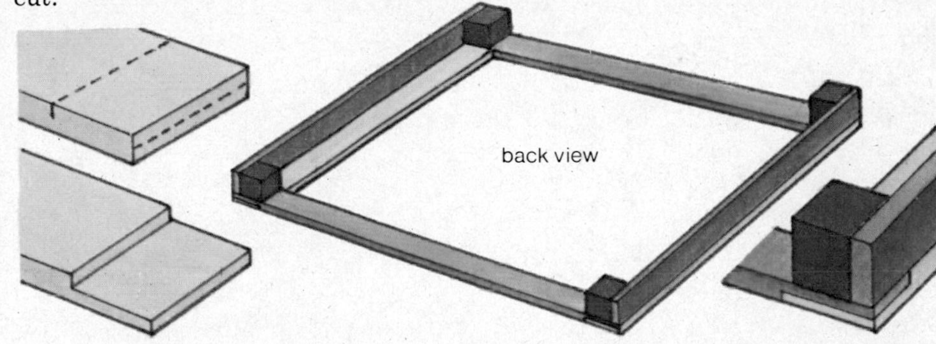

6. From the front drill a hole at each corner. Glue the frame together. Insert 31mm (1¼") screws through the joints and into the square pieces to secure it.

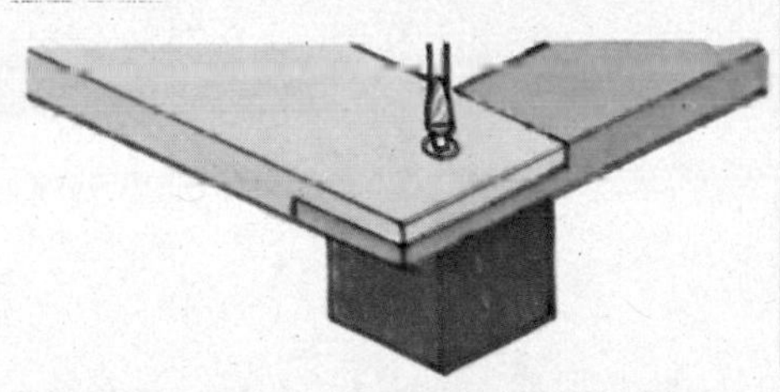

7. Nail the side pieces (also known as fillets) to the square pieces.

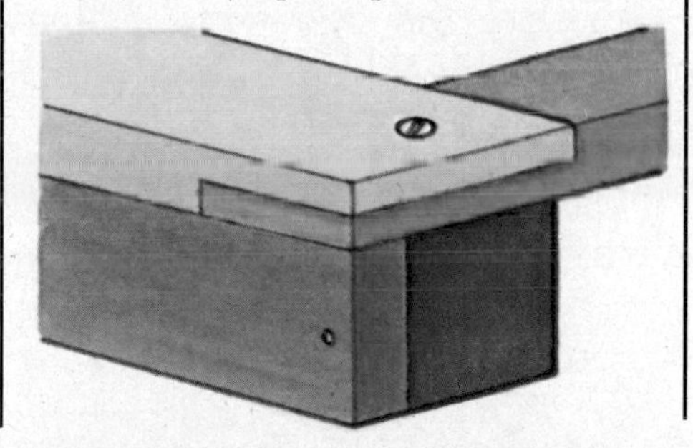

8. Cut 16 lengths as shown.
9. Drill a hole through each end of these pieces.

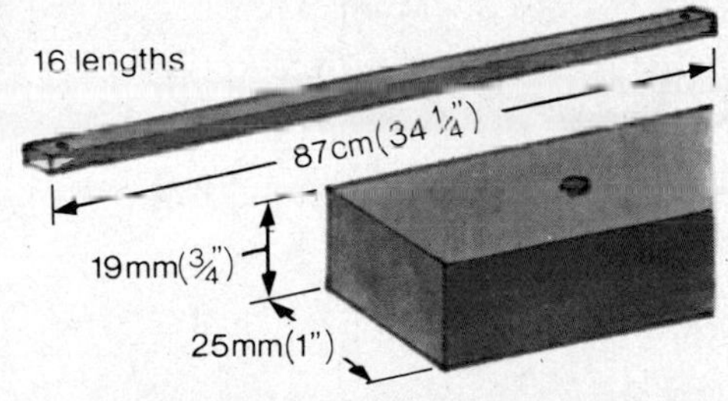

10. Glue and screw the 16 pieces to the back of the frame. Make sure that the slats are parallel and evenly spaced.
11. Drill a hole 25mm (1") deep in each of the square pieces along the top of the frame. Measure the distance between the two holes and drill corresponding holes in the surface on which the frame will hang. Plug the holes and insert 50mm (2") screws so that half the length of the screw protrudes from the wall and hang the unit.

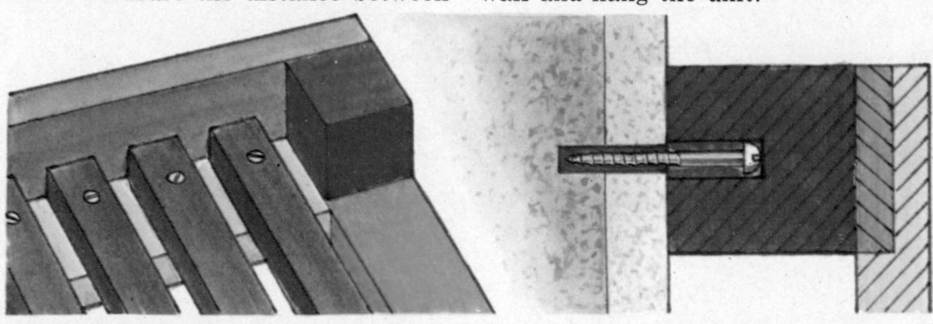

A simple box construction to hang on the unit. Glue, nail or screw it together and add metal brackets to the back to hook box on to the slats.

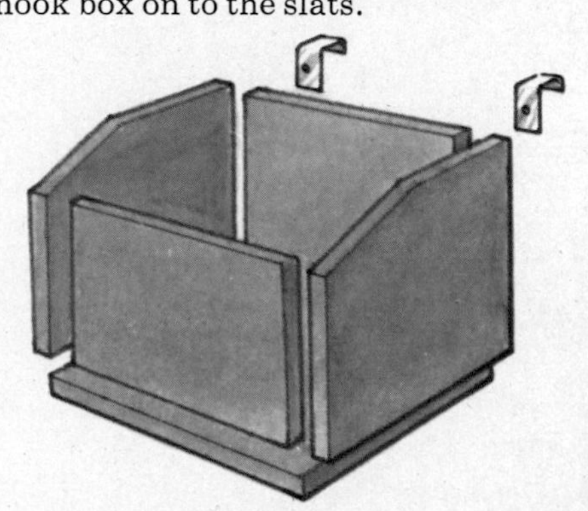

Paul Williams

Repeating patterns

A number of patterns can be made from a simple shape of three curved lines set within a square (fig.1). This shape can be repeated and rearranged within adjoining squares to make a variety of patterns (figs.2,3,4,5) which you can use for decorating your craft work. The shape can either be drawn straight onto the wood, tile, fabric, or whatever material you have chosen, or you can make a stencil to use again and again. There is no need to limit yourself to one shape. With a little practice you will be able to draw and use a number of shapes to make repeated patterns.

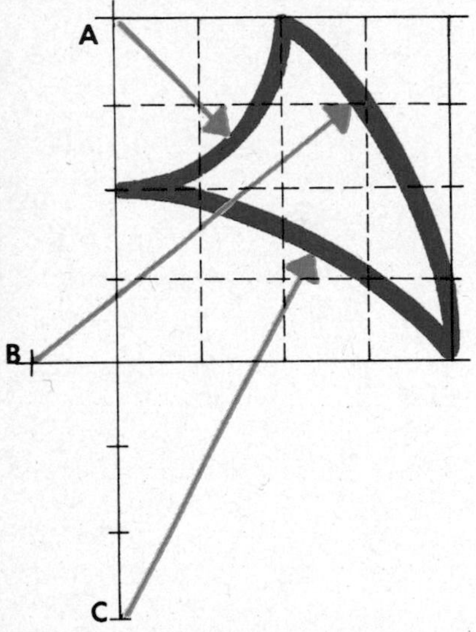

1. *Construction of the basic shape.*

2. *The shape can be repeated to make a mirror image pattern.*

The basic shape

You will need:

Piece of thick white paper or thin cardboard 20cm x 20cm (8″x 8″).
Pencil, ruler, compass, protractor.
Crayons or other colors.
Scissors (optional).

☐ Draw a square 10cm x 10cm (4″x 4″) toward the center top of the paper or cardboard using the protractor to make the right angles.

☐ Make a small pencil mark along all four sides of the square at 2.5cm (1″) intervals.

☐ Extend the bottom horizontal side left for another 2.5cm (1″) and the left vertical side down for another 7.5cm (3″) as in fig.1.

☐ With the compass draw in the curved lines. To do this place the point of the compass at point A in fig.1 and draw a curved line with 5cm (2″) radius. Draw a line from point B with 12.5cm (5″) radius and another from point C with 12.5cm (5″) radius.

You can either cut out the shape to make a stencil or continue to draw the shape within adjacent squares, altering the position of the shape to make a repeating pattern. Try reversing the shapes in a 'mirror' image, turning them upside down and leaving blank squares within a pattern. Once drawn, color in the pattern.

3. *Rearrange the shape to make a pattern for a border.*

4. *A pleasing egg pattern, simple but effective.*

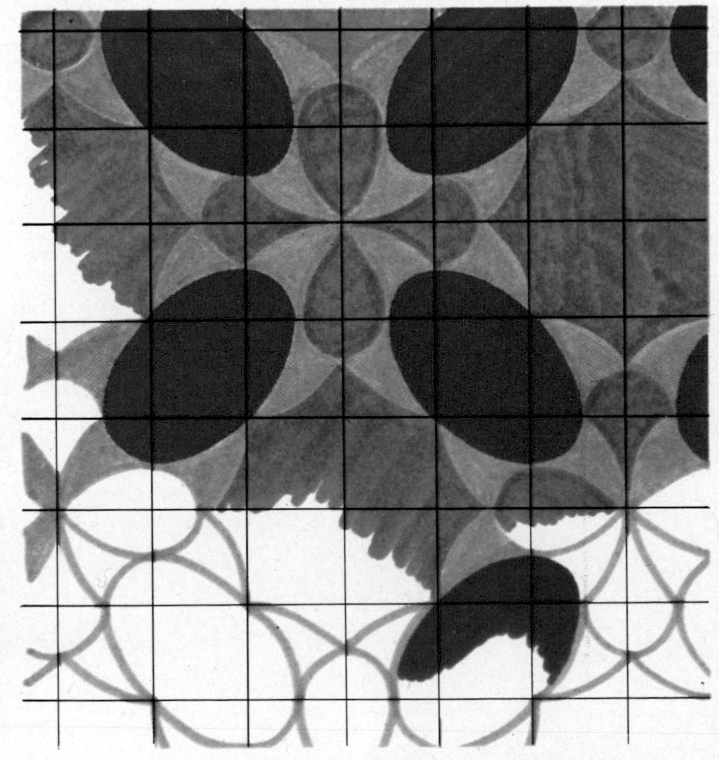

5. *This more complicated pattern has some squares empty.*

Victoria Drew

Creative ideas 31

Make something useful that is also decorative. These potholders are a good example—no more scorched hands and they make an attractive addition to kitchen decor if hung on the wall in a group.

You will need:

Scraps of cotton fabric for patchwork.
Terry cloth for lining.
227g (8oz) synthetic sheet batting for padding.
Contrasting bias binding.
Small brass ring.

The photograph shows various ideas for patchwork shapes. Cut out and make up the ones of your choice, using the techniques described in Patchwork chapter 3, page 208.

Using the finished patchwork as a pattern, cut out the terry cloth lining.
Cut batting the same shape and size.

Pin and baste batting to the wrong side of the patchwork then zigzag stitch along seam lines to hold in place.
Baste lining to the back.
Pin and baste bias binding around edges and zigzag stitch in place.
Sew a ring to the edge for hanging finished potholder.

Liz Whiting

Use patchwork, quilting and zigzag stitching to make these potholders.

Intricate cut-outs

Paper 23

Paper cutting has a long history in countries as far apart as China, Mexico, Poland and Germany. The skill and artistry lavished on these fragile creations is worthy of more than passing attention.

19th-century Polish paper-cutters were practiced at working with sheep shears, cutting scenes from rural life on folded paper with amazing talent.

In Mexico, where elaborate decorations are still cut from thin, colored tissue papers, these cut-outs once had a spiritual and magical meaning. Paper dolls cut from layers of tissue represented the spirits of the seeds and crops. Figures of men holding corn or chickens or other farm produce were buried in the fields to ensure a good harvest the following year. In some parts, cut-outs were also made for funerals and buried with the departed to speed the spirit on its way to eternity. Nowadays in many villages in Mexico, large sheets of brilliantly colored tissue paper are cut or punched into designs of flowers or animals and used at local festivities as decorations or even as tablecloths.

Trevor Lawrence

Left: a Mexican family displaying colorful tissue paper cut-outs.
Above: a pretty Mexican design to enlarge and cut. The white area represents the paper.

Maison de Marie Claire/Dirand

Wiggins Teape

This angel is typical of Central European cut-outs—length: 24cm (9½").

Melvin Grey

Left: A fish cut-out, mounted behind a plain glass table mat 20.5cm (8″) in diameter. Using the tracing pattern below make a cut-out from firm paper. Position it face down on the 'wrong' side of the glass.
Cut out a sheet of clear adhesive film to approximately the same measurements as the table mat. To stick, start by removing a strip of the backing from the center of the film, position the film over the fish and then press down the film firmly to anchor the fish in position. Then—very, very carefully—start to pull away the backing material from one half of the sheet, rubbing down the front surface as you go with a small, soft cloth to ease out any bubbles or wrinkles. When you have completed one side, remove the other piece of backing and stick down film. With a sharp pair of scissors or a sharp-bladed knife trim the spare film from around the edges. The cut-out is now securely sandwiched between identical transparent circles.

Full-size tracing pattern. You will find it simpler to start by cutting one motif at a time from firm paper.
Cut-out designed by Jan Mitchener.

The craft of paper cutting has been known in China for about fifteen centuries. 'Window flowers' are pasted on windows as ornaments to symbolize joy at the New Year or other festivals and designs for cut-outs are also used for embroidery patterns, on fabrics, and as decorative printing motifs.
The Chinese are fond of red, a color which shows up well and which they associate with courage and dignity, but other colors can look just as effective.
Chinese multicolored cut-outs are made by dyeing the layers of designs

Trevor Lawrence

after they have been cut, mixing the dyes with alcohol so they don't run into each other.

Modern uses to which these cut-outs can be put are as window decorations, for greetings cards, to decorate packages and notepaper and to make pictures. Finely-cut, colored silhouettes would also make a delicate decoration for a lampshade (they could be stuck on the shade and then varnished) or several could be mounted under glass for an unusual table top.

Making cut-outs

Try some experiments until you become skilled in the necessary techniques. Start with simple shapes, perhaps one detail from the motifs illustrated.

You will need:

Scissors with thin sharp blades.

Sharp knife.

Tissue paper.

Thicker paper (for single cuts or to keep multiple cuts from slipping).

Sharp knife.

Cutting board.

Staples or needle and sewing thread.

There are several methods of working. One is by cutting the thin paper with sharp-bladed scissors, when two or three copies at the most can be made in one cutting.

Or a very sharp knife can be used. It will cut about 20 sheets of thin paper, sewn or stapled together and worked on at once.

Some craftsmen like to cut out the inside shapes of a pattern with a knife then finish off the outside cuts with scissors.

Whichever method you use, it is essential to keep the papers from slipping while you cut. When making a lot of cuts together, place a sheet of lightweight paper underneath the several layers of tissue paper, then put another sheet of lightweight paper on top, on which the traced design is drawn. Staple or sew the sheets of paper together in several places out of the way of the design.

When preparing the design, make sure all points and lines in the drawing are interconnected, otherwise the design will drop out of its frame. Draw the design lightly on the top piece of paper. To cut, start at the center of the design and travel outward to the edges. It is usually best to cut smaller details first. Turn the paper to the scissors or knife rather than trying to manoeuvre the scissors or knife in and out of the paper.

When working with a knife, cut slowly without too much pressure, for if you press too hard it is difficult to control.

These delicate, modern Chinese tissue cut-outs follow the ancient tradition. Note how all pieces are connected.

Simple slab pot techniques

Clay can be rolled out to make tiles, and these rolled out slabs can be curved around cylindrical molds to make vases as described in Clay, chapter 3, page 90 and chapter 17, page 762.

Pieces of rolled-out clay can also be used to build up square or rectangular pots and boxes. Pots like this are made by joining together carefully measured stiff slabs, and are called slab pots.

Peter Heinz

Preparing the clay

The walls of slab pots need to be straight and rigid, so it helps if the clay is strengthened by the addition of sand or grog. Knead in 10-15% by weight of either of these when you prepare the clay so that the shape will support itself.

Rolling out the slab

You will need:
Prepared clay with grog or sand added. For a dish like the one described below you will need about 1.5kg (3lb) prepared clay, and 150g (5½oz) grog.
Canvas- or burlap-covered working surface.
Ruler.
Sharp knife.
Guide sticks.
Thick slip prepared from the same type of clay, but without grog or sand.
Try making a simple square shape first. Roll out the clay in the usual way, using guide sticks to keep the slab even to a thickness of about 6mm (¼").

Making a simple slab pot

Decide on the size and type of pot that you want, draw it on a piece of paper and mark in all the dimensions. This will help when you come to cut out the sections of the pot.
A square plant pot measuring 10cm x 10cm (4"x4") is a good size to begin with.
Base. Make the base first, rolling the clay in all directions so that you stretch it evenly.
☐ Measure the sides out with a ruler, to mark off the square base. Use the corner of a piece of newspaper or a try square to make sure the corners are at right angles. If the angles at the corners are not measured absolutely accurately, the finished pot will be misshapen and twisted.
☐ Use the sharp knife and ruler to cut out the base slab. Put the base on one side and allow the clay to stiffen. There are different types of boards which can provide an ideal surface on which to rest slabs for stiffening up evenly and quickly—these are available from lumber dealers.
Sides. Next cut four sides. Make them to fit the edges of the base and to the required depth. You may find it easier to use a paper template for cutting these pieces (fig.1). If you wish the completed pot to have a rough cast look, sprinkle the clay with a mixture of coarse grog and sand as you roll it out (fig.2). The base need not be treated in this way.
☐ Put these aside with the base and allow them to stiffen.
Assembling the dish. The clay pieces should be at the leather-hard stage—stiff enough not to bend when they are handled, but still moist enough to stick and hold together.
If the pieces buckle when you lift them you will not get a good straight finished shape, and if they are too dry the finished sections will not stick properly and will come apart in firing.
☐ Score the top edge of the base with a dampened toothbrush, and add a liberal coating of thick slip. Repeat this process with the under edge of each side piece, and press each side in turn firmly onto the edge of the base.

Two slab pots, textured with coarse sand and grog for a 'rustic' look and crenelated at the top, are joined together to make a small indoor garden. With drainage holes cut in the bottom, garden pots like these are ideal for growing herbs on a sunny windowsill.

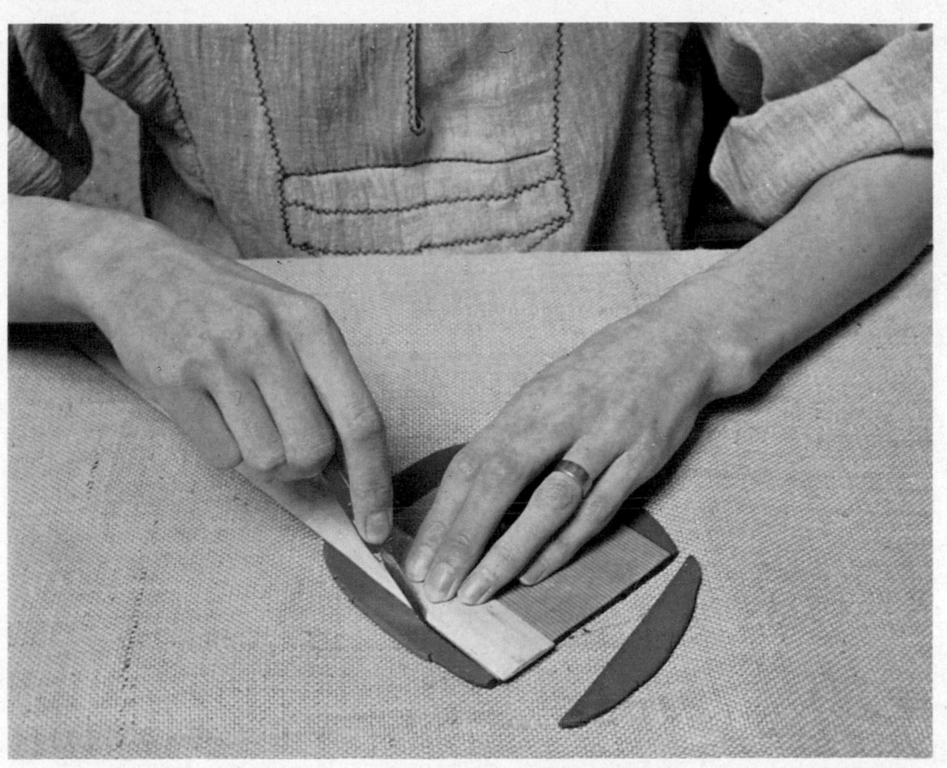

1. *Cut out the base and sides using a ruler and utility knife.*

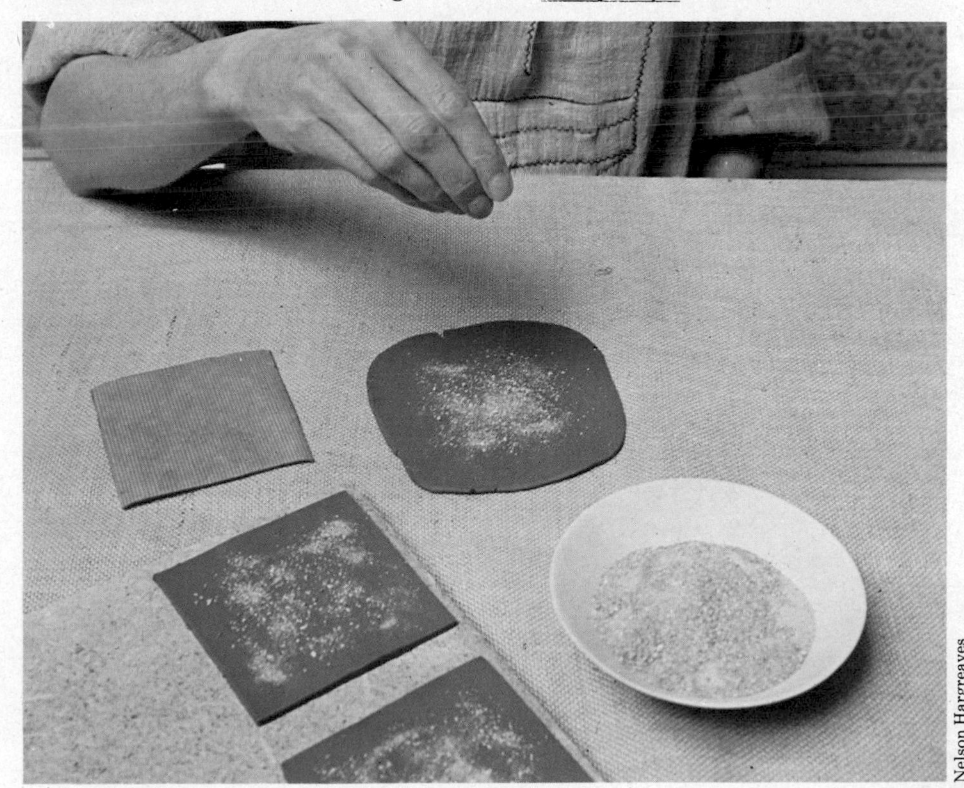

2. *Sprinkle the clay with grog and sand for a rough effect.*

Nelson Hargreaves

3. *Moisten edges with slip and join the pieces together.*

4. *Use a final coat of slip to completely seal all joins.*

Nelson Hargreaves

5. *Mark the position of the four strips on the dish base.*

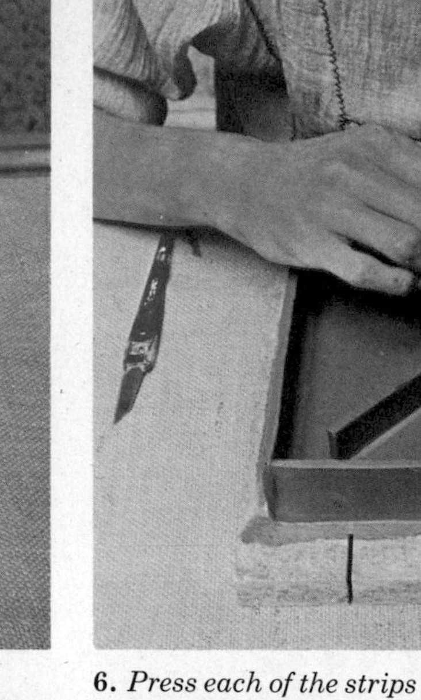

6. *Press each of the strips firmly into the marked position.*

7. *For a bonsai pot, add feet and cut out drainage holes.*

8. *Smooth away any rough edges with a piece of rasp.*

Score the side edges that are going to touch each other, add slip and press the edges firmly together as you build up the dish (fig.3). Paint slip down the seams of the pot as a final sealing process (fig.4).

□ Allow the completed dish to dry out slowly. Any slip that has oozed out of the seams should be scraped away when it is stiff.

□ If the edges need to be smoothed or evened off this can be done with a rasp before the pot has completely dried out.

Ideas for using slab pots

Hors d'oeuvre dishes. One addition to the basic slab dish makes an attractive container for hors d'oeuvres, candy or nuts—simply add cross strips to divide the dish up into convenient sections. The basic dish shown here measures 20cm (8″) square, and is 3.5cm (1½″) deep. Make it in the same way as described above.

□ Cut strips about 2cm (¾″) wide and 9cm (3½″) long. Position the strips as shown, and mark around them with a knife (fig.5). Score the center of the dish and the underside of the strip,and press it firmly into place.

□ Position the other three strips in the same way (fig.6). The dividers should neither touch each other nor the outside walls, or the pot may crack and pull out of shape as the clay shrinks.

Bonsai pots. Square or oblong slab pots make ideal containers for bonsai. Try making an oblong shape this time —the sides can be whatever depth you need to accommodate your plants, but keep them absolutely straight so that soil and plants can easily be removed. This kind of pot must be raised off the ground to allow the soil to drain. When you have assembled the pieces and the pot has stiffened turn it upside down and add small feet.

Make four small blocks of clay, about 1cm (¼″) square and 1.5cm (½″) in from the corners so that the pot is lifted but has a feeling of lightness (fig.7). The pot must also have drainage holes—bonsais need about three per pot or the roots of the plant will become waterlogged. Cut the holes at the same time as you add the feet.

Indoor gardens. Two or three different slab pots can also be joined together to form the container for a small indoor garden.

Make two or three square pots of different dimensions—try a small group with one 7.5cm (3″) square, one 10cm (4″) square and one 7.5cm x 5cm (3″x2″) and of varying depths.

The sides of these pots should be about 6mm (¼″) thick, strong and sturdy, without cracks so that they hold plant roots securely. Each pot should have a drainage hole cut in the base.

Arrange the pots to form an attractive group and join them by scoring the surfaces that touch and coating them with slip.

Try cutting strips out of the top edges to give a towered effect, and tidy up any rough edges with a rasp (fig.8).

You can develop this technique to make any shape or size of garden that you like, whether it is a small one or a much larger one for a terrace.

Decorating slab pots

Plant pots do not need to be glazed—they look natural and attractive with a rough, earthy finish. This effect can be heightened by rolling coarse grog or sand into the surface as you roll out the slabs.

The pots can also be decorated in any of the ways described in preceding chapters. The sides can be incised or impressed, or the inside of a large shallow dish can look most attractive with a slip trailed design.

If the dish is to be used for food it must be glazed—choose a clear glaze if you want a slip trailed design or oxide patterning to show through, or an attractive opaque glaze to enhance the shape of a cactus pot or vase for a table centerpiece.

The simple slab shape is infinitely adaptable—here a shallow square pot, with the addition of small cross-pieces, becomes a serving dish in which to arrange a selection of hors d'oeuvres.

Peter Heinz

Texture effects with stitches

One of the fascinating aspects of needlepoint is the way in which the same stitches can change their character to suit the type of design. When they are used for picture-making, the stitches are less important than the design and the colors and often you may not even notice which stitch has been used unless you look at the work closely.

But needlepoint can also be used to create texture where the stitches, and sometimes the yarns in which they are worked, become all-important and the colors and design, while still essential elements, take a secondary role.

Combining stitches. When several stitches are combined in a design, they create a pattern of their own. When they are worked in one color as in the clutch bag shown in the photograph, the strength of the design lies in the

Melvin Grey

contrast of texture between the stitches.

The pillow on p.881 demonstrates how color and texture are used equally in the design. The color is used to emphasize the characteristics of the stitches as seen in the color contrasts used for the squares worked in Florentine stitch and rice stitch.

The attractive texture of this elegant clutch bag is created by the use of bulky stitches, thrown into relief by flatter stitches. The bag and the pillow shown on p.881 were designed by the Pearson Gorman Needlepoint School.

Varying the yarns. Both of these designs are worked in crewel wool but you could also experiment and vary the texture by introducing different types of yarn such as one with a silky finish. You could treat the design as a sampler and make notes as you work about how much of a specific yarn you use to cover the square. Keep the notes as a reference for when you plan future designs. Or, if you do not plan to work the pillow at once, wait until you learn more stitches and introduce squares of these.

The stitches used are:

Cross (Needlepoint chapter 5, page 568).
Florentine zigzag (Needlepoint chapter 2, page 62).
Double cross (fig.1).
Rice (fig.2).
Knitting (fig.3).
Padded satin (fig.4).

Cream bag

Size of bag: 16.5cm x 23cm (6½"x9").

You will need:

Single canvas, 14 threads per 2.5cm (1"), measuring 32cm x 40cm (13"x16").
Yarn, 75gm (3oz) crewel wool in off white.
Cream linen fabric for backing and lining the bag, 65cm x 25cm (25½"x10").
Non-woven iron-on interfacing, 14.5cm x 23cm (5¾"x9").
Tapestry needle.
Matching needle and thread.
Large snap fastener.
Tapestry frame.

☐ Prepare the canvas by folding under the raw edges for 1.5cm (½") and machine stitching. Mark the center of the canvas in both directions with basting. Mount the canvas into the frame.

☐ Starting from the center work each square over 24 threads of the canvas in each direction, following the chart next page for the placement of each stitch. Use four strands of yarn in the needle, with five strands for Florentine stitch.

☐ When all the squares are complete, work a border around them in one row of cross stitch, one row padded satin stitch, two rows of rice stitch, one row of padded satin stitch and a final row of cross stitch.

Finishing. Press the finished needlepoint on the wrong side. Trim the unworked canvas to 1.5cm (½") of the stitching. Fold the turnings onto the wrong side, mitering the corners, and herringbone onto the back of the needlepoint (see Needlepoint chapter 2, page 65).

☐ Press all the creases from the cream linen and place the interfacing onto the wrong side at one end so that there is a 1.5cm (½") margin of linen at the

Basic stitches

The dots on the diagrams indicate the best starting place for each stitch.

Double cross stitch (fig.1). Work a straight cross stitch and then a diagonal cross over it. If you prefer, the diagonal cross can be worked first.

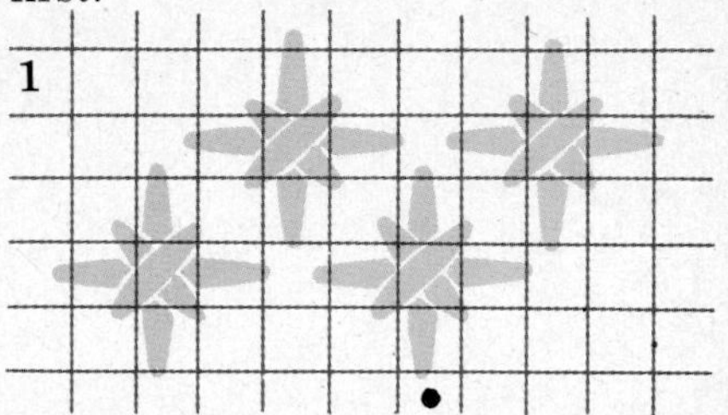

Rice stitch or crossed corners (fig.2). Work a large cross stitch over four threads of canvas. Then work a small diagonal stitch over two threads to cross the corners of each point.

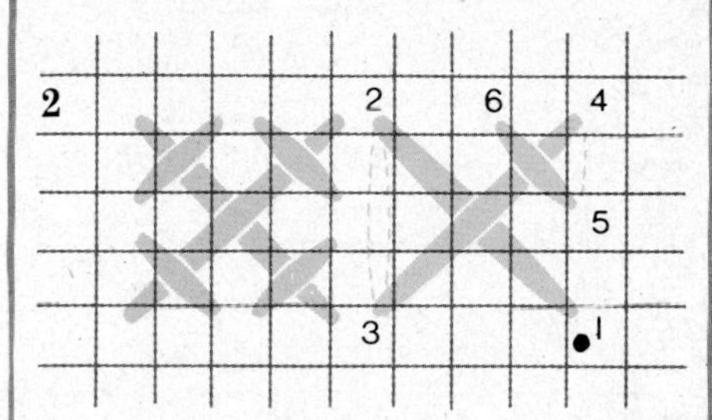

Knitting stitch (fig.3). This is worked as you would a long tent stitch (see Needlepoint chapter 6, page 850), but with the rows slanting in opposite directions.

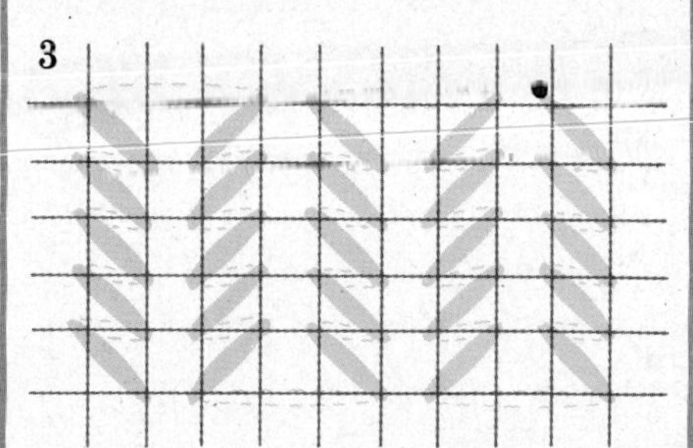

Padded satin stitch (fig.4). Work as for regular satin stitch, but lay a thread over the canvas from right to left and then work the satin stitch over the thread from left to right.

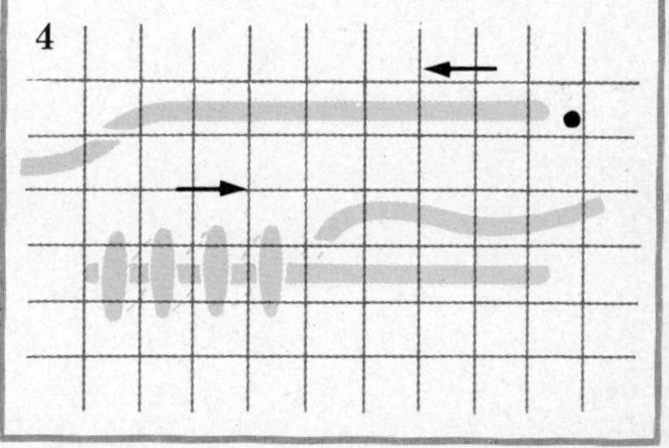

Paul Williams

Rice A3 B2	Knitting B1 B2	Rice A3 B2	Knitting A1 A3	Rice A3 B2	Knitting B1 B2
Padded Satin B1	Florentine A1 B1	Padded Satin A2	Florentine A1 B1	Padded Satin B1	Florentine A1 B1
Double Cross A2 B2	Cross B1 B2	Double Cross A2 B2	Cross A1 A3	Double Cross A2 B2	Cross B1 B2
Cross A1 A3	Double Cross A2 B2	Cross B1 A2	Double Cross A2 B2	Cross A1 A3	Double Cross A2 B2
Florentine A1 B1	Padded Satin A2	Florentine A1 B1	Padded Satin B1	Florentine A1 B1	Padded Satin
Knitting A1 A3	Rice A3 B2	Knitting B1 B2	Rice A3 B2	Knitting A1 A3	Rice A3 B2

Cross A3
Padded Satin B2
2 rows Rice A1 A2
Padded satin B2
Cross A3

Paul Williams

The working chart for the pillow with the shaded area showing the section for the clutch bag.
Color code for pillow only:
A1: lightest shade of main color:
A2: mid-shade of main color.
A3: darkest shade of main color.
B1: lightest shade of contrast color.
B2: darkest shade of contrast color.

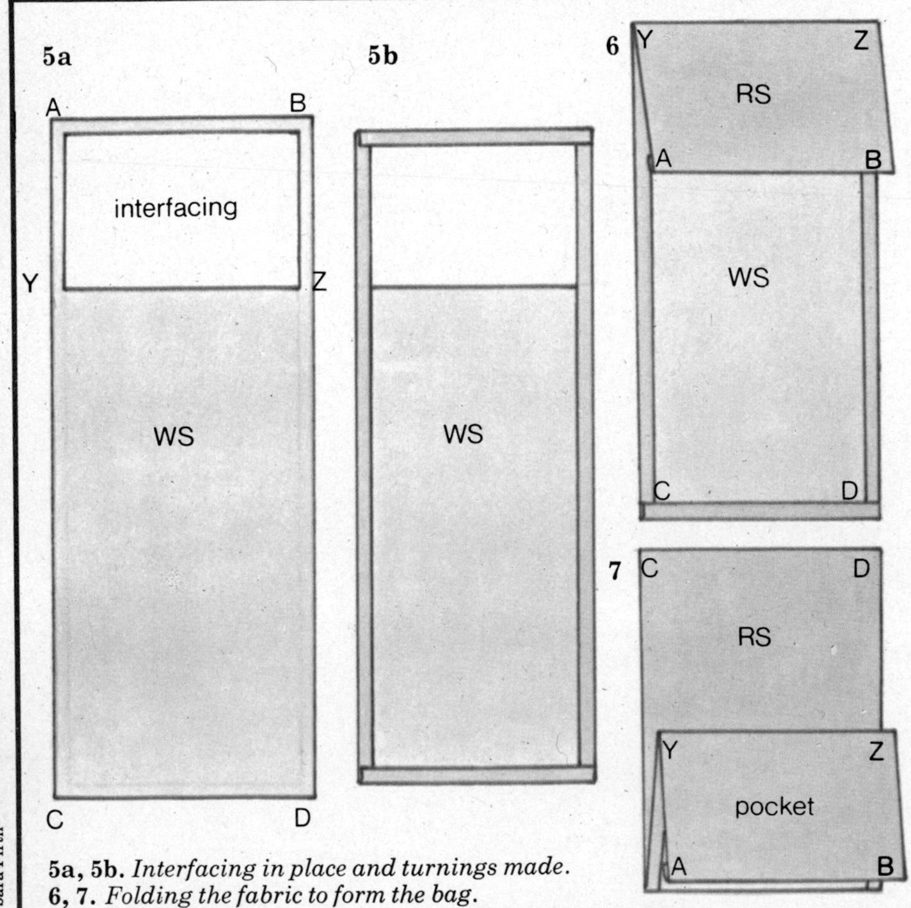

5a, 5b. *Interfacing in place and turnings made.*
6, 7. *Folding the fabric to form the bag.*

Barbara Firth

top and on each side (fig.5a). Iron in place. Turn the edges of the linen onto the wrong side for 1.5cm (½″). Baste and press (fig.5b).

☐ Starting at the interfaced end, fold over the linen, wrong sides facing, level with the lower edge of the interfacing Y-Z; baste (fig.6).

☐ Fold again, accordion-like, level with A-B to form the pocket for the bag and baste from Y-A-B-Z through all thicknesses (fig.7). Overcast firmly.

☐ Place the needlepoint onto the wrong side of the linen on part of bag that will form the back and flap. Pin and hem neatly all around and through all thicknesses.

☐ Finish the bag by stitching the snap fastener to the center of the flap and on the bag to correspond.

Patchwork stitch pillow

Completed size: 32cm (12¾″) square.

You will need:

Single canvas, 14 threads per 2.5cm (1″), 45cm (18″) square.
Yarn, crewel wool with 25gm (1oz) each in three shades of one color and 25gm (1oz) each in two shades of a contrasting color.
Fabric, such as velvet, for backing the pillow, 35cm (13¾″) square.
Pillow form, 32cm (12¾″) square.
Tapestry needle.
Matching thread and needle.
Tapestry frame.

☐ Prepare the canvas as described for the cream bag.

☐ Starting from the central cross, work each square over 24 threads in both directions, following the chart for the placement and coloring.

☐ Work the border as on the chart.

Finishing. Remove the canvas from the frame and press on the wrong side. Trim the unworked canvas to within 1.5cm (½″) of the stitching.

☐ Place the velvet onto the canvas with right sides together and stitch around on three sides taking 1.5cm (½″) turnings. Trim the turnings diagonally at the corners.

☐ Turn right side out and lightly press again on the side of the needlepoint. Insert the pillow form, fold under the turnings along the opening and slip stitch together.

Contrasting colors are used to define the textures of the different stitches in this patchwork stitch pillow.

Machine quilting with batting

The quilting illustrated here is probably the best known type of quilting and can be worked using either hand or machine stitches. This chapter covers fabrics and fillings and gives instructions for a set of bags machine quilted in a simple diamond design.

Quilting with batting

The decorative stitching on this quilting is worked through three layers of fabric—a top and a backing fabric enclosing a soft filling.

The resulting cloth has a variety of uses which will determine the choice of stitching worked. Fabrics and fillings are also dictated by the eventual purpose of the quilting.

Fabrics. The top fabric should be smooth and closely woven to show up the quilting effectively. Fine and medium weight cottons, silk, linen and fine wool are all suitable. The quilted pattern is more apparent on light-colored fabrics.

The backing should be the same as the top fabric if it is to show when the article is completed. If the article is to be lined the backing can be of muslin or organdie.

Fillings. As the filling affects the finished look of the quilting, it is essential to choose the most suitable of the natural and synthetic fillings available. Some of the earliest quilting was padded with clean, carded sheep's wool laid evenly between the layers of fabric. The early settlers in America used or re-used any clean fabric: flannel, flannelette, even old blankets, to fill their elaborately stitched quilts. Domette, a wool and cotton mixture is often used in quilting. This is available with either a flat or fluffy texture, the latter more suitable for quilting. It gives a slight padding and adds warmth without weight to clothes and small household articles. This material is usually not guaranteed for washing and should therefore be dry-cleaned.

Today, synthetic fillings are taking over from the natural ones as they are more readily available and often cheaper. They have the added advantage of being washable and quick drying.

Many modern synthetic materials such as polyester are used quite frequently as fillings, the most popular weights of which are 55gm (2oz), 110gm (4oz) and 230gm (8oz). The lighter and thinner the batting, the flatter and less distinctive the raised areas of the quilted pattern will be. The lightest weight is usually used for decorative purposes—on bags and pillows and on plain garments to create interesting textures and to add weight at hems and cuffs.

The slightly heavier weight fillings produce a more padded look and are used where warmth, as well as decoration is needed—for bed covers and on

Quilted bags made up in Brother Sun fabrics. From left to right: sewing pochette; handbag; drawstring bag.

Chris Lewis

bedheads; and for crib covers and linings. The bulky, heavy-weight fillings are ideal for bed covers.
The different weights of batting can be bought in varying widths; the lighter ones range from 45cm-140cm (18″-54″) while the heaviest fillings are available in 205cm (80″) and 215cm (84″) widths.

bottom (fig.1). On small items start by working from the center to each of the four sides, then working outward from these central lines, work lines parallel to them to form a grid.
Alternatively, the lines on small items can radiate from the center outward. When working machine quilting it is

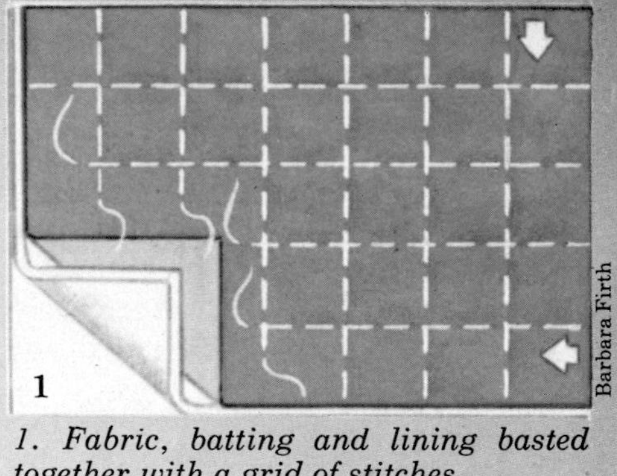

1. Fabric, batting and lining basted together with a grid of stitches.

Simple machine quilting

When beginning machine quilting it is best to start by quilting a diamond or square pattern or simply to stitch in straight parallel lines. First baste the three layers—fabric, batting and lining—together with lines of basting stitches. For large items work a grid from side to side and from top to necessary to adjust the thread tension and reduce the pressure on the presser foot so that the fabric passes under it without fullness being pushed in front of it. It is always best to work a test sample.
A quilting attachment (gauge) is a useful and relatively inexpensive accessory. This is a guide which is used to quilt in straight, evenly-spaced lines.

Quilted bags

These bags are all quilted by machine in a simple, but effective, diamond pattern.

Drawstring bag

The finished bag is approximately 20cm (8") high and has a diameter of 14.5cm ($5\frac{3}{4}$").

You will need:

50cm ($\frac{1}{2}$yd) of 90cm (36") printed cotton fabric.
30cm ($\frac{1}{4}$yd) of 90cm (36") muslin.
30cm ($\frac{1}{4}$yd) of 90cm (36") plain cotton lining.
30cm ($\frac{1}{4}$yd) of 90cm (36"), 55gm (2oz) synthetic batting.
50cm ($\frac{1}{2}$yd) of 6.5cm ($2\frac{1}{2}$") braid.

Note: seam allowance of 1.5cm ($\frac{5}{8}$") included on all pieces unless otherwise stated.

□ In printed cotton fabric cut pieces as follows:
Bag body, 1 piece 45.5cm x 28cm (18"x 11").
Bag base, 1 circle, 16.5cm ($6\frac{1}{2}$") in diameter.
Drawstrings, 2 pieces 61cm x 4cm (24"x $1\frac{1}{2}$").

□ In lining fabric, cut pieces as follows:
Body, 1 piece 45.5cm x 16.5cm (18"x $6\frac{1}{2}$").
Base, 1 circle, 16.5cm ($6\frac{1}{2}$") in diameter.

□ Cut batting and muslin as lining.

□ Cut one piece of braid 45.5cm (18") long.

□ Lay printed fabric for bag body flat and work a line of straight stitching 11.5cm ($4\frac{1}{2}$") from one long edge (the top).

□ Baste batting and muslin to the wrong side of the bag body between the line of stitching and the lower edge and with bottom edges level. Quilt the three layers in a pattern of diamonds with 8.5cm ($3\frac{1}{4}$") sides, using the quilting attachment.

□ On the right side, baste the braid 3.5cm ($1\frac{3}{8}$") up from the lower edge of bag. Stitch in place with four rows of stitching.

□ With right sides facing baste and stitch the side seam (fig.2). Press seam lightly open so as not to flatten the quilting.

□ With right sides facing baste and stitch the side seam on the body lining piece. Press seam open and turn through to right side.

□ Turn in 6mm ($\frac{1}{4}$") at top edge of lining.

□ Baste bag and lining lower edges together, matching side seams and with wrong sides facing.

□ Fold 6.5cm ($2\frac{1}{2}$") at the top of bag to the wrong side and work two rows of stitching, the first on original line of stitching and the second 1.5cm ($\frac{5}{8}$") above the first (this makes the casing for the drawstrings). Slip stitch lining over raw edge of bag top just below lower row of casing stitching (fig.3).

□ Baste base fabric, batting and muslin together and quilt. Baste base lining to base, wrong sides facing.

□ With right sides facing, baste and stitch base to bag, stitching through all thicknesses (fig.4). Smooth turnings together and turn bag to right side.

□ Make four slits in the bag in top layer of fabric only, between rows of casing stitching, 2.5cm (1") from each side of the seam and at corresponding points on the other side of bag, to insert the drawstrings.

□ Blanket stitch the raw edges of slits.

□ Fold one drawstring in half lengthwise, with wrong sides facing, and turn in 6mm ($\frac{1}{4}$") on all edges. Topstitch through all thicknesses close to the edge. Repeat with the other drawstring.

□ Thread one drawstring through the casing from one side seam slit to the other. Thread the other drawstring through the casing using the other two slits. Knot ends of each pair of strings together.

2

3

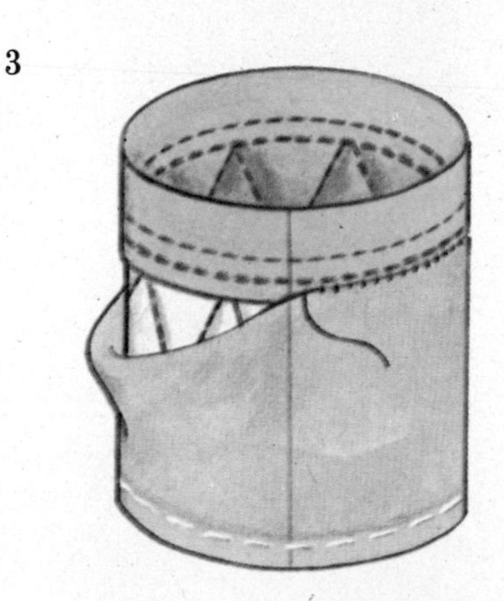

4

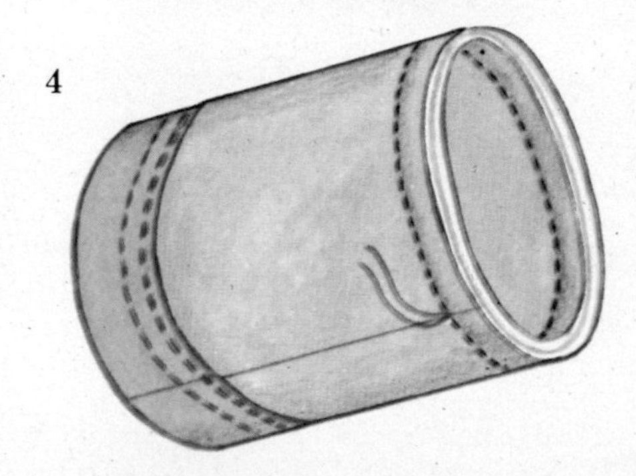

Sewing pochette

The finished bag is 37.5cm x 15.5cm ($14\frac{3}{4}$"x6") when opened out flat.

You will need:

50cm ($\frac{1}{2}$yd) of 90cm (36") printed cotton fabric.
50cm ($\frac{1}{2}$yd) of 90cm (36") plain cotton lining.
30cm ($\frac{1}{4}$yd) of 90cm (36"), 55gm (2oz) synthetic batting.
13cm (5") of 6mm ($\frac{1}{4}$") elastic thread.
Scrap of felt.
30cm ($\frac{1}{4}$yd) of 6.5cm ($2\frac{1}{2}$") braid.

Note: seam allowance of 1.5cm ($\frac{5}{8}$") included on all pieces unless otherwise stated.

In printed cotton fabric cut pieces as follows:
Bag body, 1 piece 40.5cm x 18.5cm (16"x $7\frac{1}{4}$").
Center pocket, 1 piece 18.5cm x 11cm ($7\frac{1}{4}$"x$4\frac{1}{4}$").
Lower pocket, 1 piece 21.5cm x 11cm ($8\frac{1}{2}$"x$4\frac{1}{4}$").
Ties, 2 pieces 23.5cm x 2.5cm ($9\frac{1}{4}$"x1").

□ In lining fabric, cut body and pocket pieces as printed fabric.

□ In batting, cut 1 piece 40.5cm x 18.5cm (16"x$7\frac{1}{4}$").

□ Cut a piece of braid 18.5cm ($7\frac{1}{4}$") long.

□ Baste braid to right side at one end of printed fabric body piece.

□ Treating braid and printed fabric as one, trim the braided, short end of printed fabric body piece and one short end of lining to form top point as shown (fig.5).

□ Trim batting to 2cm ($\frac{3}{4}$") smaller all around than the fabric.

□ Turn seam allowance on printed body piece and lining to wrong side and press.

□ Unfold seam allowance on top fabric, place batting onto wrong side and turn seam allowances over edges of batting (fig.6).

□ With wrong sides together place lining and top fabric together to enclose batting completely.

□ Fold one tie in half lengthwise, with wrong sides facing, and turn in 6mm ($\frac{1}{4}$") on all edges. Topstitch through all thicknesses close to the edge. Repeat with the other tie.

□ Insert one tie between the layers of pochette at the point. Baste the layers together. Quilt through all thicknesses using the quilting attachment and work three straight lines across braided section and a diamond design over the rest of the work, with the sides of the diamond 3cm ($1\frac{1}{4}$") long.

□ Place center pocket and lining with right sides facing and baste and stitch along the long edges (fig.7a). Turn through to right side, turn in the seam allowance on the remaining two edges and baste (fig.7b).

□ Repeat with the lower pocket.

□ Work two rows of stitching 1cm ($\frac{3}{8}$")

apart on the the lower pocket, the first 1.3cm ($\frac{1}{2}$") from one long edge (the top). Thread elastic thread through this casing and secure the ends.

☐ Run a gathering thread along the other long edge of the lower pocket.

☐ Baste both pockets in position as shown (fig.8), pulling up the gathering thread on the lower one to fit. Work a line of machine stitching all around bag 1cm ($\frac{3}{8}$") from the edge.

☐ Slip stitch the lower edge of the center pocket to bag lining. Cut a scrap of felt with pinking shears 7.5cm x 6.5cm (3"x2$\frac{1}{2}$") to make a needle holder and stitch this to lining along its top edge.

☐ Stitch remaining tie to center of right side of bag (fig.9).

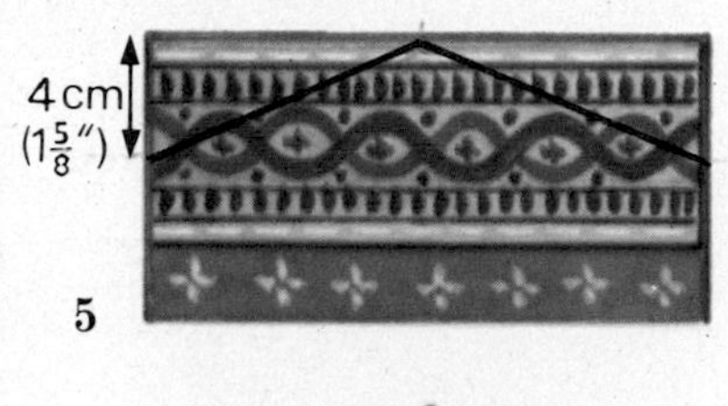

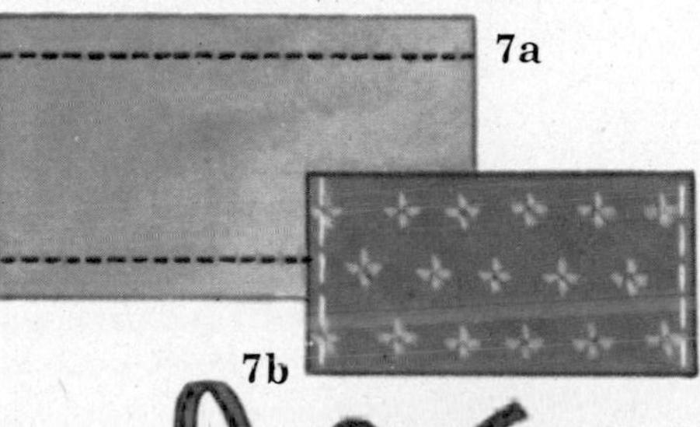

Handbag

The finished bag is approximately 20.5cm (8") high, 25cm (10") wide and 12cm (5") deep.

You will need:

70cm ($\frac{3}{4}$yd) of 90cm (36") printed cotton fabric.

70cm ($\frac{3}{4}$yd) of 90cm (36") plain cotton lining.

70cm ($\frac{3}{4}$yd) of 90cm (36"), 55gm (2oz) synthetic batting.

70cm ($\frac{3}{4}$yd) of 90cm (36") muslin.

90cm (1yd) of 7.5cm (3") braid.

Piece of cardboard, 24cm x 12.5cm (9$\frac{1}{2}$"x5").

2 x 2.5cm (1") button molds (such as Trims).

Note: seam allowance of 1.5cm ($\frac{5}{8}$") included on all pieces unless otherwise stated.

☐ In printed cotton fabric, cut pieces as follows:

Bag body, 1 piece 67cm x 28cm (26$\frac{1}{4}$"x 11").

Side panels, 2 pieces 27.5cm x 15cm (10$\frac{3}{4}$"x6").

Handles, 2 pieces 48.5cm x 7cm (19"x 2$\frac{3}{4}$").

☐ In lining fabric, cut pieces as follows:

Body, 1 piece 62cm x 28cm (24$\frac{1}{4}$"x11").

Side panels, 2 pieces 27.5cm x 15cm (10$\frac{3}{4}$"x6").

Tab, 1 piece 16cm x 7.5cm (6$\frac{1}{4}$"x3").

☐ In batting, cut pieces as follows:

Body, 1 piece 67cm x 28cm (26$\frac{1}{4}$"x11").

Side panels, 2 pieces 27.5cm x 15cm (10$\frac{3}{4}$"x6").

Tab, 1 piece 14cm x 5.5cm (5$\frac{1}{2}$"x2$\frac{1}{4}$").

Handles, 2 pieces 48.5cm x 2cm (19"x $\frac{3}{4}$").

☐ In muslin cut pieces as for batting.

☐ Cut two pieces of braid 28cm (11") long and a piece 16cm (6$\frac{1}{4}$") long for tab.

☐ Round the corners of each tab piece.

☐ On body and side pieces baste batting and muslin to wrong side of fabric.

☐ Using the quilting attachment, quilt a diamond design, with the sides of the diamonds 8.5cm (3$\frac{1}{4}$") long.

☐ Baste a piece of braid 5cm (2") from each short edge on the right side of the body piece. Stitch into place with four rows of top stitching.

☐ With right sides together stitch the side panels to the bag body, enclosing the ends of the braid (fig.10).

☐ Turn 3.8cm (1$\frac{1}{2}$") along top edge to the inside. Press lightly to avoid flattening the quilting.

☐ Baste tab batting and muslin centrally to wrong side of braid tab.

☐ Make a 3.2cm (1$\frac{1}{4}$") bound buttonhole at one end.

☐ Baste tab and tab lining together with wrong sides facing.

☐ Fold in a 1cm ($\frac{3}{8}$") seam allowance on lining and tab, baste and topstitch all around close to the edge.

☐ Work two lengthwise rows of basting through all thicknesses.

☐ Make a slit in the lining to correspond with the buttonhole, turn in the edges and slip stitch to muslin (fig.11).

☐ With right sides facing, baste and stitch lining side panels to lining body. Press and turn right side out.

☐ Turn under 1.3cm ($\frac{1}{2}$") at top of lining and press. Push cardboard into base of lining.

Note: if you prefer, make a cover for the cardboard from spare fabric and slip stitch covered cardboard into lining. The stitches can be easily removed when the bag is washed.

☐ Take one handle strip, turn under seam allowance along each long edge and fold the strip in half lengthwise, wrong sides together.

☐ Cut a piece of batting the length of the handle by the finished width. Place it inside the folded handle piece and baste the layers together. Work four parallel lines of machine stitching along the handle.

Repeat with the other handle strip.

☐ Stitch handles firmly to bag. Place bag inside lining, wrong sides facing, and slip stitch folded edge of lining to top of bag, enclosing the ends of the handles (fig.12).

☐ Cover button molds with braid. Attach plain end of the tab to the outside of the bag, and stitch a button to this end.

☐ Attach the other button to the other sice of the bag and fasten tab.

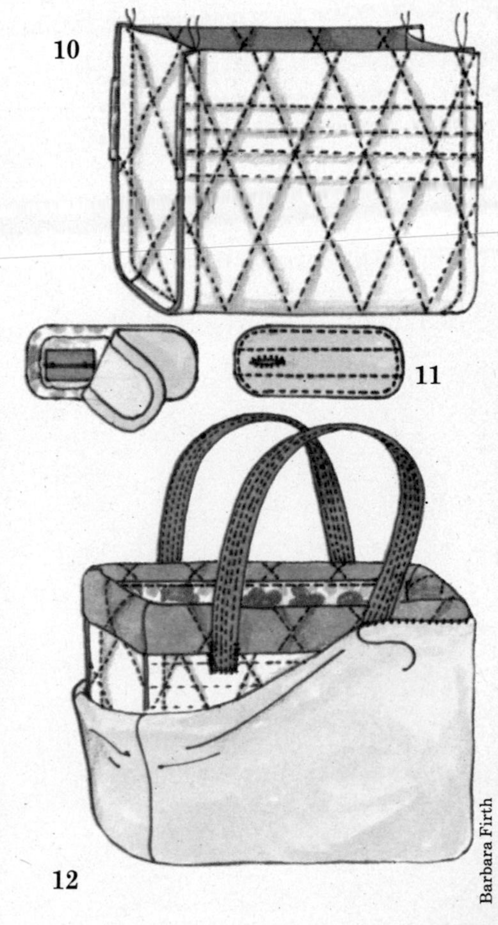

Barbara Firth

Several colors, one linoleum block

Linoleum cuts can be successfully printed in more than one color but you must either re-cut your block for each different color or you must cut a series of separate blocks. This chapter deals with re-cutting the same block—using several blocks is covered in the next chapter.

Multi-colored printing is not as laborious or as complicated as it sounds but you must think out your color scheme beforehand. When using one block, more and more areas become recessed at each stage, leaving only the areas which still require coloring. Also, when using only one block, you must make at the beginning as many prints as you will require since your block will become permanently altered after each step.

Peter Heinz

The house and garden print

The picture of the house and garden is printed from one piece of linoleum cut away in three stages for three successive colors. By cutting the design in stages from the tracing pattern you will begin to get a sense of multi-color printing in linoleum.

Use either oil or water based printing inks and apply and print them using the methods described in Printing chapter 9, page 828.

You will need:

Gouges—a small and a medium V-shaped cutter and a small and fairly large U-shaped one.

Black India ink.

Craft knife such as a Stanley knife.

Printing roller and slab.

Printing paper (eg construction paper).

Printing inks in blue, green, red and brown. (Turpentine if they are oil-based.)

Palette knife or old dinner knife for mixing.

Printing press or burnishing tool such as a spoon.

Linoleum block at least 21cm x 15.5cm (8¼″x6″).

Carbon paper and hard pencil for tracing.

Preparing the design. Cut a rectangle of linoleum to size, 21cm x 15.5cm (8¼″x 6″) and trace the pattern (fig. 1) onto it using a sheet of carbon paper and a hard pencil. Bear in mind that the tracing pattern is the reverse of the printed design since it is a mirror image of the block. This is an important point to remember if you have any lettering to do.

When you have traced the design go over all the lines with waterproof black India ink. This makes the design clearer and, more important, it will not be washed off when you clean up the block after each printing.

Cutting for the first color. Start cutting by removing all the areas which will remain white throughout.

The clouds are outlined with a V-shaped tool and then removed with the larger U-shaped gouge.

The roof ridge is worked with the small U gouge. The raindrops, the lines of brickwork and facing stones and the fencing are all cut away with the two V cutters while the daisies are made by removing small V-shaped nicks. The pebbles on the path are cut with the small U gouge.

Printing first color. When you have finished cutting the block, cut out all the paper you will need, making it a

Colored print on left was made by re-cutting the linoleum after each printing.

1. *Tracing pattern for linoleum: circles near fence indicate cuts for daisies. Path is pebbled by making short gouges.*

Janet Allen

2

3

4

5

Janet Allen

bit larger than the block so you will have a border. You should make as many prints of this stage as you require plus a few others to cover any mistakes. This stage is printed in blue ink as shown in fig.2.

Cutting for second color. While the blue prints are drying proceed with stage two of the cutting after cleaning the surface of the linoleum.

This stage will be printed in green and the further cuts you have to make are shown in fig.3. All the sky except the rainbow must be removed with a large U gouge. The window panes must also be completely gouged out and a cross cut in the doorway to make a panel. The roof tiles are outlined with a small U gouge and the pebbles have been enlarged with the same tool.

To print second color. First make a print of the green stage on its own so you can check your work and also provide yourself with a masking device.

Masking large areas. When you have a large area of open cutting such as the sky on a block, the roller tends to dip down into it and deposit a little ink. To avoid accidentally printing the area you need to mask it. In this case you can do it by cutting out the white area of the sky from your green proof (just roughly around the house and trees, leaving a hole for the rainbow).

Then place a blue print face up on the table and fit the cut-out sky over the same area on this print to protect it from possible damage. Ink in the block in green again and gently lower it on to the blue print starting at one edge as though you were closing a book. It is quite easy to line up the edges of the block with the edges of the blue print. If you are using a press proceed as described in Printing chapter 9, page 828 and, if you are burnishing, carefully turn the block and paper over so you can rub it.

Cutting for third color. The third and final stage of cutting is shown in fig.4. Not very much is left. Further U-shaped gouging with the small gouge has been done on the path and the tree has suddenly produced apples by the same means.

Printing the third color. The red used to print this is mixed with a little brown by blending the two colors together with a palette knife on the side of the inking slab and then spreading the mixture out to be rolled. Never try to mix the colors with a roller.

When the final stage is printed (fig.5) you will have a 'limited edition' of hand-cut prints.

2-4. *Prints showing raised areas of linoleum left at each stage of printing.*
5. *is the finished print in full color.*

Right: linoleum print by Janet Allen.

Peter Heinz

Making jewelry with resin

Once you have a little experience in using polyester resin you will be able to make beautiful jewelry in all kinds of intricate shapes. The resin flows into a mold made by a metal strip and glass, sequins, wire, glitter and small beads can be embedded in it. When cured the resin can be finished in a number of different ways to give you jewelry which is both attractive and durable.

To make jewelry

The materials given below are sufficient to make all the pendants shown here. Since the quantities are so small you should stock up on the full amount even though you may only want to make one pendant. It you do this you will have enough materials to allow for any mistakes or to make several pieces of jewelry.

You will need:
220gm ($\frac{1}{2}$lb) clear embedding resin.
Small bottle of catalyst. (This usually comes in a 56gm (2oz) size and you will need less than half of this quantity.)
Resin pigments in red, blue and green. You will only need a very small quantity depending on the depth of color required.
Aluminum, brass or copper strip about 8mm ($\frac{5}{16}$") wide and 90cm (3') long. This is a very thin, flexible strip used to make a mold for the resin.
Silver-plated, brass or copper wire about 0.6mm (22-23 gauge) thick. You will only need 30cm (1') for making the pendants, more if you intend to suspend the pendants from the wire.
Thin jewelry chains for suspending the pendants if you are not using wire for this purpose.
Epoxy adhesive.
Thin polyester sheet, preferably transparent, or thickish cellophane paper, 90cm x 90cm (3'x3').
Calibrated disposable cups for measuring.
Small cans for mixing resin.
Tin snips or heavy duty scissors.
Smooth stick or spatula for mixing resin.
Masking tape.
Medium-size needle.
Flat, smooth piece of wood about 15cm x 15cm (6"x6"), or a hardback book.
A commercial resin or metal polish.
Medium sandpaper, medium and fine wet and dry silicon carbide paper (for opaque finish).
Polyurethane varnish (optional).
Hand drill and small bit (optional).

Melvin Grey

Pendants and embedding objects: metal strip, wire, sequins and beads.

To make a pendant. Work in a warm, well-ventilated room and set out all the tools and materials you will need on a drawing board or flat, hard surface.

☐ Using the tin snips or scissors cut a length of metal strip and bend it into the shape of the pendant. The metal is flexible but start by making a simple shape. If you are making a circular pendant form the strip around a coin or piece of wooden dowel of a suitable diameter.

☐ Glue the ends of the strip together with the adhesive and leave to dry.

☐ If you are making different colored sections within the pendant cut out strips of metal to fit tightly inside the pendant to act as resin dividers. There is no need to glue these strips.

☐ Cut the plastic or cellophane sheet in half and place one half on the drawing board or flat surface. Tape the edges of the sheet to the drawing board. Make sure that the sheet is flat and taut.

☐ Put the glued metal strip onto the plastic sheet and tape the strip to the drawing board by stretching the tape across the strip from one side of the board to the other (fig.1).

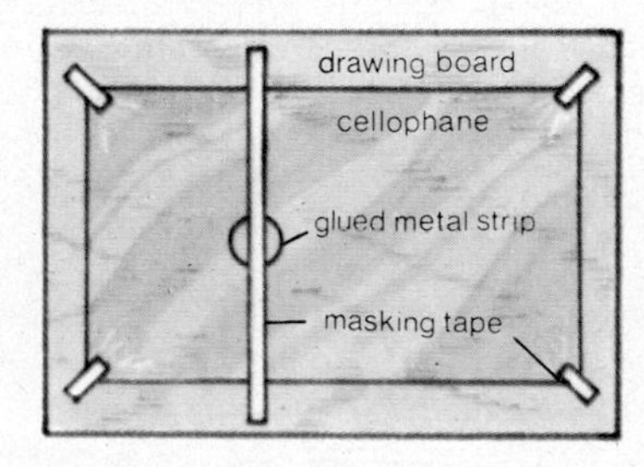

1. *The taped strip remains firmly in place while it is filled with resin.*

☐ If you are making a small pendant the tape may completely cover the metal strip. In this case cut a notch into the tape where it covers the metal strip.

First layer. Mix up 28gm (1oz) resin with eight drops of catalyst and gently pour into the pendant to make the first layer of clear resin. A needle can be used to guide the resin when pouring it. The resin should just cover the bottom surface but should not be more than 3mm ($\frac{1}{8}$") deep. A little resin may seep under the metal strip; this can be removed later.

Second layer. Leave the resin to cure in a warm room for two or three hours until it has gelled. Mix up another 28gm (1oz) resin with catalyst. This second layer of resin contains the colors in the pendant. If you are using three colors, for example, you will need to divide the resin into three cans.

☐ Add a very small quantity of pigment to each can. Add a little more if the color is not deep enough. If part of the pendant is to remain clear throughout then do not add color.

☐ Very gently pour the resin into the sections formed by the metal strips inside the pendant. This is a precise job and needs to be done carefully.

☐ If the pendant is to contain small chips of glass, foil, beads or sequins, add them to the second layer of resin after you have poured it into the various sections.

☐ At this stage do not completely fill the pendant with resin. Leave a small space for 'filling up'. As the resin cures it will naturally shrink very slightly and you will have room for a third layer.

☐ If the first layer of resin has seeped under the bottom edge of the metal strip you can lift it away with the point of the needle. This should be done before it has time to harden.

Third layer. When the second layer has gelled mix up another 28gm (1oz) of resin with catalyst and pour on top of the second layer. This third clear layer finishes the pendant and should be made up to the top of the metal strip.

☐ Place a small piece of plastic sheet across the top of the resin. The sheet should touch the entire surface of the resin. Smooth the sheet with your finger to make sure that no air bubbles are trapped underneath.

☐ Weight the plastic sheet by placing a board or book across the top. This combination of sheet and board will aid the curing process and ensure that the pendant has a flat, smooth surface.

☐ You may find that a little resin dribbles over the top of the mold. This is nothing to worry about.

☐ Let pendant harden overnight.

Finishing off. When the pendant has cured pry away the outside metal strip which will have got a little messy by this time. You can leave the pendant without a band or you can cut another strip, wind it around the edge of the resin and glue as before.

Melvin Grey

Translucent resin butterfly pendant.

To polish. The surface of the resin should be quite smooth and only need a rub with a resin or metal polish to make it shiny.

Frosted finish. Alternatively, you may like to obtain a frosted, opaque finish. In this case, sand down the resin with medium sandpaper, followed by medium and fine wet and dry paper. The sanding will also remove any stickiness left on the surface of the resin.

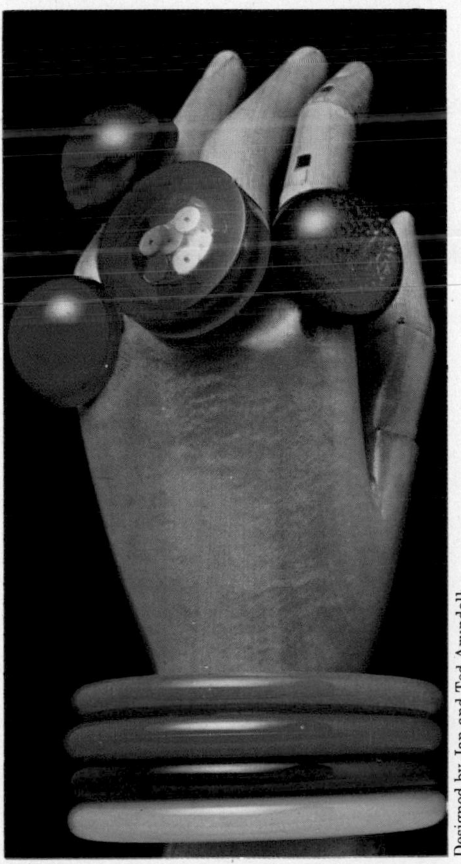

Alasdair Ogilvie

Designed by Jan and Ted Arundell.

Resin rings can be made with a variety of molds, especially plastic lids, and then fitted with a ring mounting.

To varnish. The pendant can also be varnished with a polyurethane varnish which will cover any stickiness and slight unevenness in the resin. The varnish, however, does not give such a good shine as a smoothly polished surface.

☐ If the pendant encloses two or three metal strips (used as resin dividers) the various sections of the pendant can be separated as in fig.2.

Paul Williams

2. *Separate the resin sections to make a completely different pendant.*

You may find that the sections can be rearranged in a number of ways and then held in place by a length of metal wire wrapped around the outside.

To hang the pendant

Method 1. Cut a small piece of wire to make a loop and stick to the top of the pendant with adhesive.

Method 2. Drill a hole in the top of the pendant with a hand drill and small bit. Make a loop with wire to go through the hole.

Method 3. Wind wire around the outside edge (around the metal band if it is there). Twist the two ends of wire around each other at the top to make a loop. This method is only suitable for rounded pendants.

The pendant can be hung on a thin chain, or wire can be used instead.

Pendants also look attractive hung in front of a window or other light source.

Other jewelry such as bracelets, necklaces or rings can be made using the same techniques.

Fringes, tassels and wrapping

The technique of ''wrapping'' is very simple and requires no tools or mechanical aids other than yarn and a pair of scissors, yet its range of application is vast. Single strands of wrapping can be used to create such objects as necklaces and belts; it is a very useful method of adding textural interest or finishing off a hanging; it can even be the method of construction for entire wall hangings.

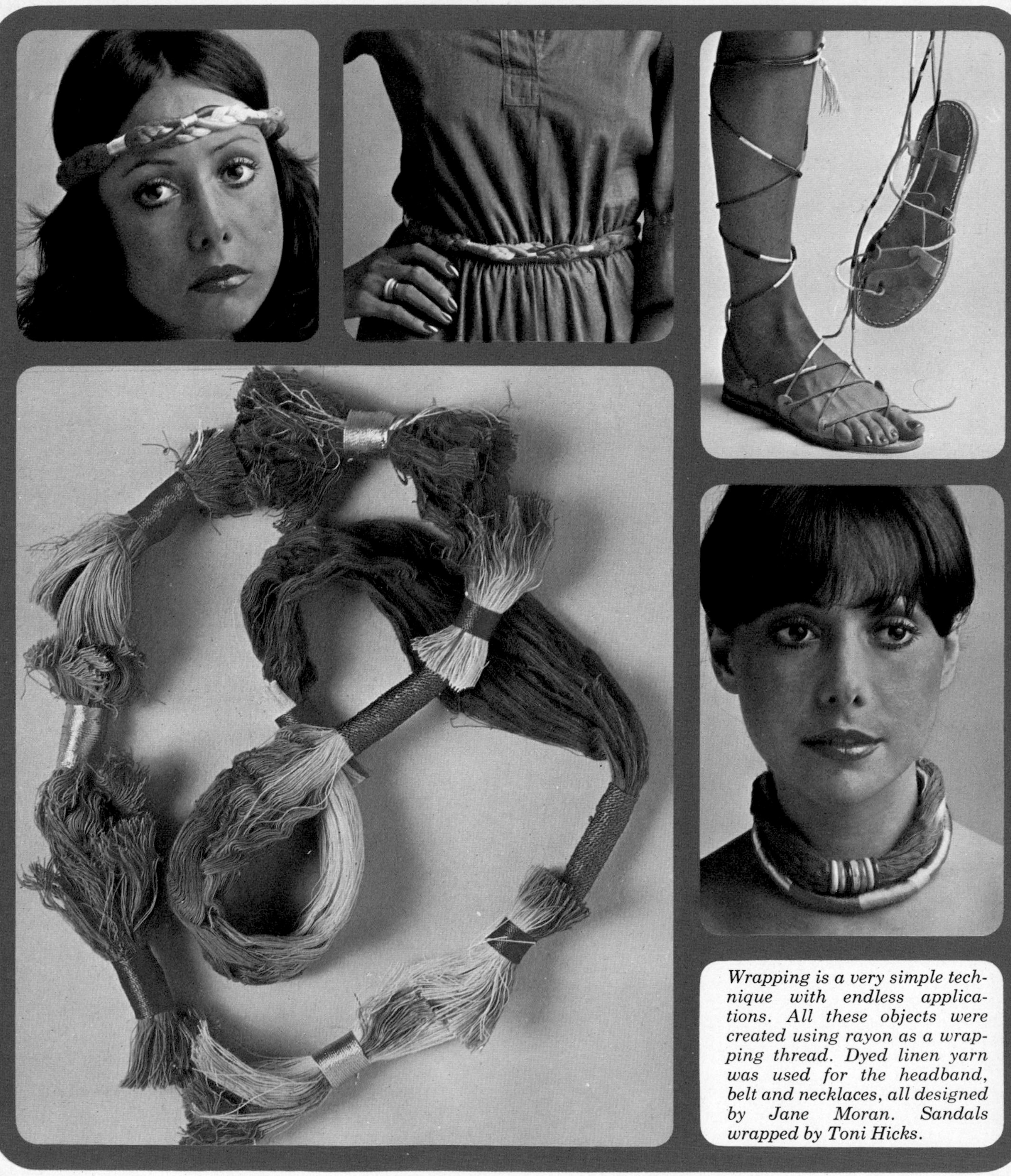

Wrapping is a very simple technique with endless applications. All these objects were created using rayon as a wrapping thread. Dyed linen yarn was used for the headband, belt and necklaces, all designed by Jane Moran. Sandals wrapped by Toni Hicks.

Steve Bicknell

Wrapping is sometimes taught in the boy scouts and girl scouts and may be familiar to some readers as a merely functional form of whipping.
Historically, it was probably used originally for its purely practical benefits—as knife or axe handle surfaces, the hand-grip on bows or for securing rope splices.
Its decorative uses are fairly widespread in the finishing of warp ends and the making of tassels and some ancient Peruvian textiles used wrapping to outline the warp threads in patterns before they were woven with a one-color weft.

Contemporary applications

Today wrapping is used in many different crafts and in widely varying contexts as might be expected of a technique so simple to apply. It is used in conjunction with metal, wood, plastic and leather, although its most common application is with yarn in a weaving context.
Besides its decorative application, wrapping can be used to strengthen a soft or fragile element almost to the point of rigidity if needs be or to disguise and secure a knot or join.
Wrapping on its own. Perhaps its most exciting application is to be seen when wrapping is used on its own. The tough, tubular appearance of a wrapped section of a hanging provides a stark contrast to the full, soft texture of an area left unwrapped, especially if the 'core' material itself is interesting.
Sheila Hicks, one of the most noted exponents of the technique, creates monumental wall hangings using this simple and effective idea. They have an architectural strength and simplicity, and the even rigidity of the wrapping is almost metallic, lending an added impression of softness to the carefully controlled sections where the core appears.

How to wrap

Separate strands of wrapped yarn can be made into handsome necklaces or belts.
For wrapping materials, it is normal to use cotton, linen, string or synthetic yarns as these have more tensile strength than wool which is inclined to break when being pulled through the wraps in the last stage of the operation. In this context, wool provides a very pleasant 'core' rather than a surface.
For the necklaces, use thin linen warp for the core and fine rayon for the silky wraps.

☐ Lay one end of the wrapping element (A in fig.1), along the length of the core element (X).
☐ The other end of the wrapping element (B) is then brought back in a loop to the point where the wrapping is to begin.
☐ Keeping the loop in position, lay end B in tight consecutive wraps for as much of the area as needs to be covered (fig.2).
☐ Thread the end B through the remains of the loop at the bottom of the wrapping.
☐ Pull on end A until end B disappears under the wraps (fig.3).
☐ Trim off end A (fig. 4).

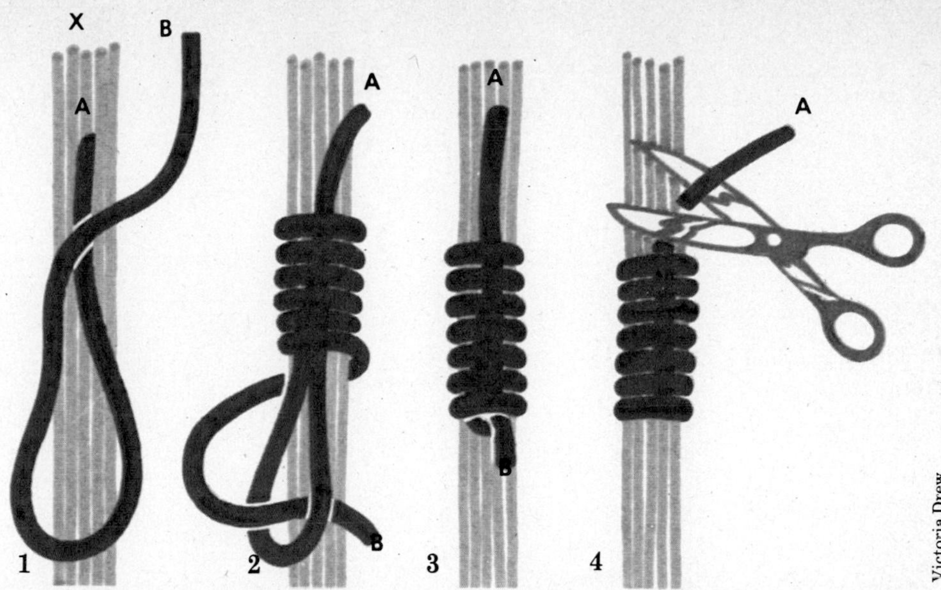

1-4. *To wrap, lay end* **A** *along the area you wish to cover. Wrap around with end* **B.** *Thread* **B** *through the loop and pull end* **A** *until end* **B** *disappears.*

A multitude of wrapped tassels in a hanging designed by Candace Bahouth.

Peter Heinz/Courtesy of the Victoria and Albert Museum, London

Intricate warp wrapping and wrapped tassels in silk. Designed by Sheila Hicks.

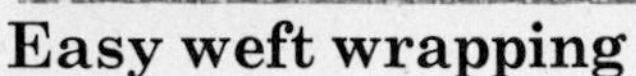

Easy weft wrapping

Interesting effects can be achieved by the controlled wrapping of elements such as braiding which can be woven in like weft with perhaps one end hanging freely on the surface of the weaving.
When used as weft, wrapped elements can be as skinny or as bulky as you like depending on the effect you wish to create.

Warp wrapping

Individual warps or groups of warps can also be wrapped in a tapestry context. This can be used, as in some old Peruvian weaves, as a method of outlining a geometric image (fig.5).
Warp wrapping is useful where a more open effect is wanted in a weave. In this case where adjacent threads are wrapped, wrap the warp threads together in groups to prevent the weave from slipping up and down (fig.6).
If eight to twelve adjacent warp threads of identical lengths are treated this way, and the weft discontinued for that area, then a small window of vertical bars is created in a weave (fig.6).

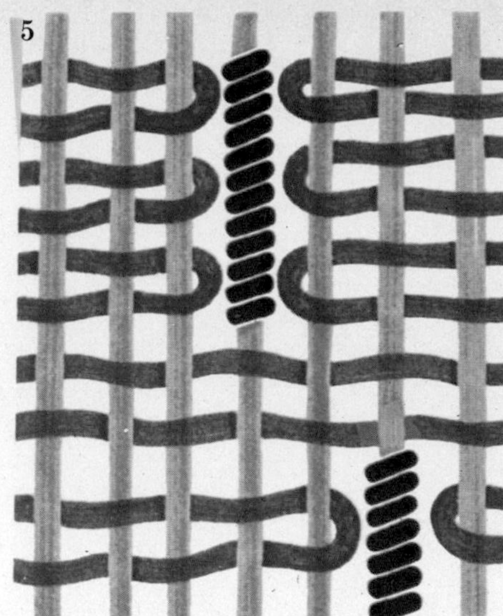

5. *Wrapping individual warp ends.*

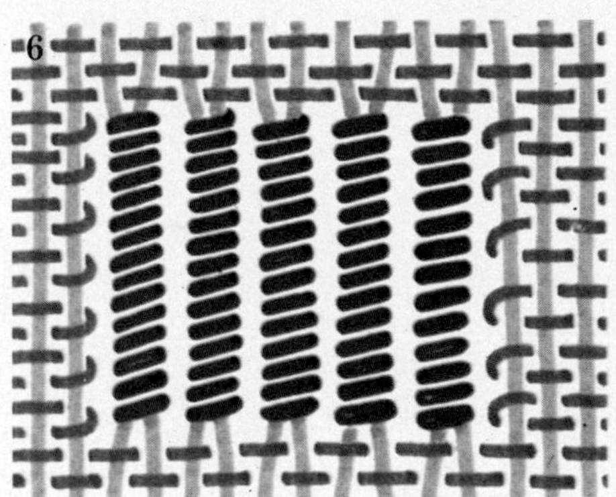

6. *Window of adjacent wrapped warps.*

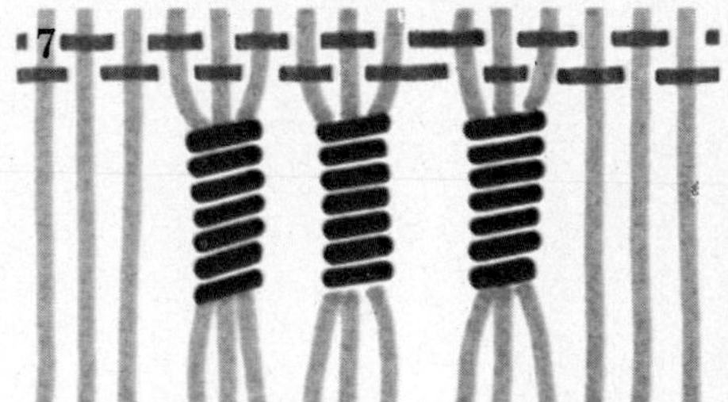

7. *Wrapping to finish off a weaving.*

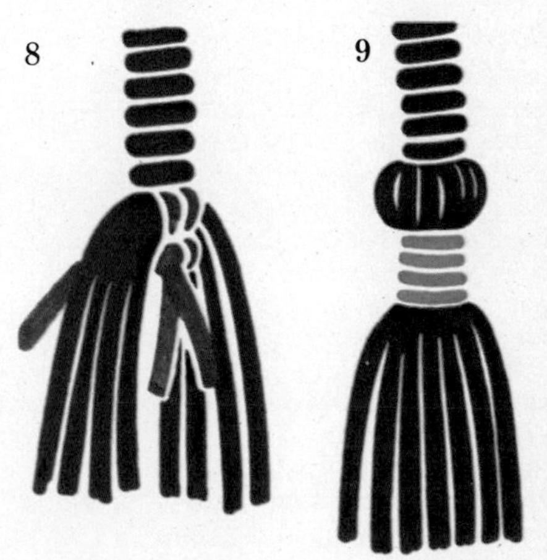

8. and 9. *Wrapped tassels can add an unusual dimension to a weaving.*

Victoria Drew

Melvin Grey

Wool yarn on rope wrapping and tassels as part of an appliqued design. Designed by Jeanette Durrant.

Wrapped fringes

Wrapping the end warp threads can be done where warp fringing would look unsatisfactory, ie a dark toned hanging with a white cotton warp.

Gather the warp threads into groups and wrap from the very edge of the weaving (fig.7).

If a very long, decorative fringe is desired, start your weaving high up on the frame. Then wrap the empty bottom warp threads when the weaving section has been completed. It is much easier to leave the warp threads attached to the frame when wrapping long sections as they are fixed in a stable position. Where long sections are to be wrapped, the loop can be dispensed with until the very end of the wrapping. The first end can be caught and covered by the wraps.

If you have a very large frame then a door curtain could be constructed in this way by weaving a small strip at the top of the frame and wrapping the warp threads in groups.

Including beads

If you want to hang objects such as beads on your wrapped threads, cut the warp threads before wrapping and thread on all the required beads. Retie the warp threads to the frame and wrap the warp threads positioning the beads where you want them. Wrap down to the bead, thread the wrapping element through the hole of the bead and continue wrapping. Make sure that the hole of the bead is big enough for both the warp and wrapping threads.

Wrapped tassels

One of the most obvious applications of wrapping is the wrapped tassel. After reaching proportions of epic grandeur in Victorian times, the tassel suffered a sad decline until more recent years. Now our slowly returning sense of tactile opulence permits the more lavish use of such decorations.

A single tassel can be a lovely object, the cut ends providing an almost furry contrast to the smooth, wrapped stem which can be given added brilliance by wrapping with contrasting colors.

Where a mass of tassels is used together to decorate a surface, the effect is baroque in its richness.

To make tassels

☐ Gather the warp threads into groups. Wrap as in fig.7 and described above.

☐ Take a group of yarns of equal length and double over the middle.

☐ Knot into position with two warp ends (fig.8).

☐ Tuck the extra warps into the center of the tassel.

☐ Wrap tassel to cover knot (fig.9).

Patterns within a pattern

Look at many designs and you will see that they are often made up of several simpler patterns. A box, for example, could be decorated with a combination of marbled paper bordered by stripes or a sweater could be made up of different types of stitches producing a variety of patterns.
Have another look at the component parts of any pattern and the way they are arranged within the overall design. How else could they be rearranged to make another design?
Perhaps you like the patterns in a piece of cloth as in fig.1 and would like to design a tablecloth using the same motifs but rearranged in a different way with a centerpiece and a border (fig.2). There is no need to use every part of the pattern. An effective lampshade (fig.3) can be made with two parts.

1. *One piece of material may be composed of a number of delightful patterns.*

3. *Another design on a lampshade.*

2. *Make a stencil or appliqué the same butterflies, flowers and stripes.*

Experiment

You will need:
Thin white cardboard about 30cm x 30cm (12″x12)″, or larger.
Pencil, scissors, ruler, crayons or other colors.
Look at the designs illustrated here or any other pattern of your choice.
Notice the separate parts of the pattern: circles, stripes, animals, flowers.
On the cardboard draw shapes similar to the ones in the pattern. Keep the shapes fairly small, in proportion to each other and as many as you have room for on the cardboard.
Cut out the shapes.
Now arrange the shapes so they could decorate a child's pinafore or a book jacket; make a border around a mirror or decorate a wooden toy; be embroidered onto a pair of slippers or linoleum printed onto a canvas bag. Which shapes look best together and which ones could be left out? Could some shapes be left small and others made larger? Try out as many ways as you can to make a pleasing design. When you have produced a design, color in the shapes, and use it for your craft work.